D0681283

# REMEMBER

# THE WONDERS

# 1995 GCBA Pastors and Wives' Christmas Party

*STANDING (l/r): Janet and Pat Hail, Barry Hall, Marty and Lenni Nordloh, Sherlyne Hall, Julie and Daryl Bennett, Mary Burke, Loralie Martin. SEATED: Cheryl Ballew, Bill and Naomi Hunke, Gerald Lawton.*

*STANDING (l/r): Top—Steve Martin, Steve and Rebecca (baby) and Jayne May, Dave Cox, Yvonne Davis. Middle—Steve Burke, Jessica and Jason Stoneketter, Carol Cox, Si Davis. SEATED: Alice Lawton, Manny and Angela Martinez. NOT PICTURED: Steve Ballew, Harold Boldins, and Marc Hills.*

# REMEMBER

# THE WONDERS

## A FIFTY-YEAR HISTORY OF
## GRAND CANYON BAPTIST ASSOCIATION

### Naomi Ruth Hunke

PROVIDENCE HOUSE PUBLISHERS
Franklin, Tennessee

Selected Scripture taken from THE AMPLIFIED BIBLE, OLD TESTAMENT. Copyright © 1965 Zondervan Publishing House. Used by permission. Other Scripture taken from the HOLY BIBLE, NEW INTERNATIONAL VERSION. Copyright © 1973, 1978, 1984 International Bible Society. Used by permission of Zondervan Bible Publishers.

Printed in the United States of America

00   99   98   97   96          5   4   3   2   1

Library of Congress Catalog Card Number: 96-69312

ISBN: 1-57736-006-0

*Photographs provided courtesy of Bill and Naomi Hunke*

*Cover design by Ernie Hickman*


PROVIDENCE HOUSE PUBLISHERS
238 Seaboard Lane • Franklin, Tennessee  37067
800-881-5692

# CONTENTS

## Words from the Psalms

I will *recall the years* of the right *hand of the Most High* (Ps. 77:10).

I will [earnestly] recall the deeds of the Lord; yes, I will [earnestly] *REMEMBER THE WONDERS* of old (Ps. 77:11).

Tell to the generation to come the *praiseworthy deeds* of the Lord, and His might, and the *wonderful works* that *He* has *performed* (Ps. 78:4).

*That the generation to come might know* them, that the children still to be born might arise and recount them to their children, that they might set their hope in God, and *forget not the works* of God, but keep His commandments (Ps. 78:6–7).

He *split rocks in the wilderness*, and gave them *drink abundantly* (Ps. 78:15).—Italics by Naomi Ruth Hunke.

# ACKNOWLEDGMENTS

Because this book is the story of churches, missionaries, pastors, and representative summer student missionaries, laypersons, and volunteers who have ministered in Grand Canyon Baptist Association, I have not documented it as a research project. I am deeply indebted to the many sources from which it has been compiled and copied. These include: Grand Canyon Baptist Association (GCBA) and Arizona Southern Baptist Convention (ASBC) annual minutes; Prescott newspapers, *Arizona Miner* and *Daily Courier*; Arizona Historical Archives folders; C. L. Pair's *History of the Arizona Southern Baptist Convention*; Hilton Crow's *Highway in the Desert*; Truman Helm's *Early History of Arizona Southern Baptists*; Ernie Myers' "Summer for the Savior"; Troy Brooks' GCBA notes from 1948 to 1958; M. V. Mears' GCBA notes from 1959 to 1981; Bill Hunke's missionary biographies, research project of seventeen western states' associations, GCBA newsletters from 1987 to 1992, and personal letters; Si Davis' GCBA newsletters from 1993 to 1995; Flagstaff First Southern Baptist Church (FSBC) fifty-year history; and historical notes from Sedona First Baptist Church (FBC) and Greenlaw Baptist Church.

Help also came from personal letters and testimonies by past and present GCBA pastors and their wives, summer missionaries, and Baptist Student Union (BSU) directors; personal interviews with Harold and Opal Dillman, Willard and Katheryn Hardcastle, Marie and Lemuel Littleman, M. K. and Dora Wilder, Garnett and Uma Ridenhour, Ed and Bernice Trotter, Glenn and Corky Young, and Lois Neil. Documents from the Arizona Baptist Historical Society by Marie Cunningham Sutton, Betty Beck, Ralph Bryan, and Paul Barnes contributed. The *Baptist Beacon* and my books, *In This Land* and *God's Warhorse*, furnished some background material.

Bill Hunke collected and took photographs and arranged the picture pages for the history. Gilbert Pogany used his cameras and darkroom to develop many pictures for publication. Those who contributed pictures include Si Davis, Marie Cunningham Sutton, Emily Barker, M. V. Mears, R. A. Guthrie, Glenn Young, Rea-Lynne Gilder, Carolyn Martin, Marc Hill, Ed Trotter, Clarice Maben, and Bill Hunke.

The book cover is the scene from our living room window which was painted by Edna Maxson. Bell Rock, to the left, is the primary vortex and gathering place for New Agers. The painting reminds us that God has promised to split rocks of satanic opposition in the wilderness with the hammer of his Word.

I hope that churches, associations, and individuals will freely use this book in recreating their own histories and heritage appreciation studies. That will make this project worthwhile.

# ABBREVIATIONS

| | |
|---|---|
| AAEO | Annie Armstrong Easter Offering |
| ABC | American Baptist Convention (Northern) |
| ASBC | Arizona Southern Baptist Convention |
| BIA | Bureau of Indian Affairs |
| BSSB | Baptist Sunday School Board |
| BGCA | Baptist General Convention of Arizona (Southern) |
| BSU | Baptist Student Union |
| BYBC | Back Yard Bible Club |
| BYPU | Baptist Young People's Union |
| CSC | Christian Service Corps |
| CSI | Cooperative Services International |
| CSM | Christian Social Ministry |
| CP | Cooperative Program |
| CT | Church Training |
| DMB | Domestic (Home) Mission Board |
| DOEM | Director of Evangelism and Missions |
| ESL | English as Second Language |
| FBC | First Baptist Church |
| FMB | Foreign Mission Board |
| FSBC | First Southern Baptist Church |
| GA | Girls Auxiliary |
| GCBA | Grand Canyon Baptist Association |
| GCC | Grand Canyon College |
| GCU | Grand Canyon University |
| GGBTS | Golden Gate Baptist Theological Seminary |
| HMB | Home Mission Board |
| HMS | Home Mission Society (Northern) |
| ISC | International Service Corps |
| LES | Lay Evangelism School |

| | |
|---|---|
| LMCO | Lottie Moon Christmas Offering |
| MSC | Mission Service Corps |
| NAU | Northern Arizona University |
| NLS | Navajo Language School |
| NOBTS | New Orleans Baptist Theological Seminary |
| RA | Royal Ambassadors |
| SBC | Southern Baptist Convention |
| SEBTS | Southeastern Baptist Theological Seminary |
| SIL | Summer Institute of Linguistics |
| SS | Sunday School |
| SWBTS | Southwestern Baptist Theological Seminary |
| TU | Training Union |
| TWB | Together We Build |
| U.S. | United States |
| VBS | Vacation Bible School |
| WIN | Witness Involvement Now |
| WMC | World Missions Conference |
| WMS | Woman's Missionary Society |
| WMU | Woman's Missionary Union |
| YWA | Young Women's Auxiliary |

# INTRODUCTION

The Grand Canyon is called one of the Seven Wonders of the Modern World. In this most extraordinary environment on earth, people come face to face with the power of the Creator, the vastness of creation, the enormity of time and space, and the fragility of man. The canyon measures nearly a mile deep, eight miles across, and 260 miles long. A place of awesome grandeur with varied colored buttes and minarets fading into countless labyrinths, whose colors constantly change, it contains raging rapids, diaphanous waterfalls, and calm, turquoise pools.

Millions of tourists annually visit Grand Canyon and Oak Creek Canyon where the majesty of wind-sculpted, red-rock cliffs towering into fantastic formations make them among the most photographed spots in the nation. They call to mind Joshua's statement that when our children ask in time to come what these stones mean, we should tell them these split rocks in the wilderness are here so that all the peoples of the earth may know that the hand of the Lord is mighty, in order that they may reverence and fear the Lord our God forever.

In Grand Canyon Baptist Association, remains of eight-hundred-year-old Indian structures perch on limestone cliffs. The Native American religion binds many in its tight grip. Sedona has become the New Age capital of the world because of its metaphysical vortexes, supposedly concentrations of cosmic energy. On a weekend in 1988, around thirty thousand New Agers gathered in the Village of Oak Creek for a "Harmonic Convergence" of psychic energies. Northern Arizona has long been a stronghold of Mormons. Hispanic converts to Christ often refuse to follow through with baptism because of the hold of traditional Roman Catholicism. Jehovah's Witnesses are strong and active.

Thousands of wealthy city dwellers have summer homes in the world's largest Ponderosa pine forest around Flagstaff and Munds Park. Worshippers of creation rather than the Creator, on vacation, not on mission, they often leave Christian commitments behind and refuse to help start new churches. Perhaps in addition to the currently popular concept of finding out where God is working and joining him there, more of us need to accept the challenge of finding a place where God apparently is not working in order to go there and let him work through us.

On August 29, 1946, members from the following churches met at Prescott, Arizona, voted to form a new association, and elected a moderator, treasurer, and clerk: Prescott First Southern Baptist; Wickenburg First Baptist; Kingman First Baptist; and Flagstaff First Southern Baptist. A committee met in Ash Fork on October 3, 1946, to name the association, plan a program, and send letters of invitation to the first annual meeting on October 23, 1946. In response, Roosevelt, Utah, Baptist and Artesia, Colorado, First Baptist joined the above churches as the six organizing members of the Grand Canyon Baptist Association.

# RECALL THE YEARS

## BAPTIST BEGINNINGS IN ARIZONA TO THE ORGANIZATION OF GCBA

When a friend heard that the Grand Canyon Baptist Association was celebrating its fiftieth anniversary in 1996, he commented, "I thought the Southern Baptist Convention had already observed its 150th anniversary. Why did GCBA wait so long to get started?" I told him we had to travel a long, hard road.

When the first Butterfield stage left St. Louis on August 9, 1858, bound for California, the company boasted that it was the longest stagecoach route in the world. It reported later that Arizona was the most dangerous part of the trip because the route traversed Apache territory, and many Butterfield men lost their lives in raids by hostile Indians. Only a few hardy souls braved the desert frontier before the railroads came.

The April 6, 1970, Prescott *Daily Courier* stated that Arizona Territory, unique in the fifty states, had its capital set in a wilderness area and struggled to meet its basic needs in the early years. Supplies had to come long distances, and all activities carried on amid open warfare with the Indians. The territory had a scarcity of Baptists, but plenty of godless people. By 1880 Arizona still had no Baptist churches, only eight Protestant churches, and over five hundred saloons.

### Southern Baptist Convention Unable to Help Arizona

In 1861 the Civil War caused Southern Baptist Convention (SBC) home mission funds to decline until the Baptist Domestic (Home)

Mission Board (DMB) could no longer pay missionary salaries. All SBC missionaries in New Mexico withdrew, and churches closed. Work of the fifteen SBC California missionaries was curtailed, and churches they had established affiliated with the Baptist (Northern) Home Mission Society —HMS. By the 1890s, when the SBC continued to reject pleas to seat messengers from California and the north Pacific coast, they abandoned hope of again relating to the SBC.

The South and the SBC quickly went bankrupt financially because assets were in Confederate money, which became worthless. Their churches lost pastors to the chaplaincy, many of whom were killed, and reported that all able-bodied men had gone to war. Northern Baptists took over SBC churches in the Confederate states when the Union War Department wrote its generals, "You are hereby directed to place at the disposal of the American Baptist HMS all houses of worship belonging to Baptist churches in the South in which a minister does not now officiate." After the HMS forcibly took possession of the church buildings, Southern Baptists had great difficulty recovering their property. When the war ended, Baptist work had been devastated, and the South was destitute.

Also, toward the end of the century, Northern Baptists shifted their major missions emphasis westward. By 1882 their HMS spent as much money in the West as in the rest of the nation combined. After it became apparent that no reunion between the Northern and Southern Baptist Conventions would take place, representatives met September 12, 1894, at Fortress Monroe, Virginia, to work out the comity agreement which assigned the West to Northern Baptists and warned Southern Baptists to a "hands-off" policy. Representatives met in Washington, D.C., April 15, 1909, and agreed that the 1894 policy had transpired and was no longer binding. This ruling was largely ignored by Northern Baptists who continued to maintain for many decades that Southern Baptists had invaded their western territories.

### Northern Baptist Affiliation

When R. A. Windes, an ordained Southern Baptist missionary from Alabama who had worked in the Muscle Shoals mountain missionary program in his state, felt called to do missions work in Arizona in 1879, he appealed to the SBC DMB for support, but was turned down. As a result, he came to Arizona under the Northern Baptist HMS and started the first Baptist church in Arizona. Because the majority of the members in early Arizona Baptist churches had a Southern Baptist background, questions continually arose during the next three decades regarding why the churches affiliated with the Northern Convention. Windes explained repeatedly that early missionaries, pastors, and churches had asked the SBC for help and affiliation. With Arizona so far from the South, the SBC was unable to work out any method of support and cooperation. Only after being turned down by the SBC did they form ties with the Northern Convention.

Another factor that delayed Southern Baptist work in Arizona was the failure of the $75 Million Campaign. After World War I, the SBC adopted with enthusiasm the program to raise seventy-five million dollars in five years. Total subscriptions amounted to almost ninety-three million dollars, but the deterioration of the South's economic situation resulted in collection of just fifty-eight and one-half million dollars. Missions work begun in the West on the basis of having the money pledged had to retrench after heavy indebtedness was incurred. A positive outcome of the period was the development of better methods of raising and disbursing SBC funds, leading to the evolvement of the Cooperative Program (CP).

Even after Arizona Southern Baptists constituted their state convention, travel to the northern part of the state remained difficult, and missions opportunities lay dormant for almost twenty more years. Recalling the struggles and victories of Baptist beginnings in our association's area can lay a foundation of faith on which to continue building for the future.

### Hiram Walter Read: First Baptist Services in Arizona

In 1863 when President Abraham Lincoln appointed Hiram Walter Read as the first postmaster for Arizona Territory, Read accompanied the presidential party to Prescott to establish a post office and assume his new responsibilities. An ordained Baptist preacher, Read held Baptist services in his cabin as long as he lived in Prescott. In addition to being postmaster, he also became chaplain at Fort Whipple, where he remained until 1865.

Read already held the distinction of preaching the first Baptist sermon in Arizona to a group of settlers and military people near Fort Yuma in May 1854; he set the pace for future Baptist development. He had joined a survey team seeking to locate the best railway route from Texas to California in 1852. While his crew was working near Yuma, he preached to them. Born in Connecticut and converted as a teenager in New York City, Read attended college and seminary before entering the ministry in 1844. Feeling called to the West, he received appointment as a missionary

Hiram Read, the first Baptist missionary in Arizona, served as chaplain at Fort Whipple in Prescott, 1863–1864.

President Lincoln appointed Read as first Arizona territorial postmaster. He and the governor traveled together in 1863.

John Fremont, Arizona governor, 1878–1881, lived at Fremont House. Windes came to Prescott in 1879.

The Victorian house William Bashford built at Prescott in 1877 now serves as museum, bookstore, and gift shop.

Old Prescott National Guard Armory is an Arizona historic treasure. It served as first meeting place for GCC in 1949.

R. A. Windes organized the first Baptist church in Arizona at old schoolhouse in Prescott on January 25, 1880.

Lone Star Baptist Church constructed Arizona's first Baptist church building in 1880 at Prescott.

J. C. Bristow preached the first Baptist sermon in Verde Valley on October 3, 1875, under a big cottonwood tree.

Lone Star erected a beautiful sanctuary at Prescott in 1924. The first building was moved to Cortez Street in 1884.

Windes helped Bristow start several SSs in Middle Verde. The Old Rock Baptist Church organized in 1881.

Although Lone Star changed its name to Prescott FBC in 1934, the cornerstone retains the original name of the church.

Sharlot Hall Museum houses artifacts collected from early Arizona pioneers since Prescott's founding in 1864.

by the American Baptist HMS to serve in California.

When Read reached Albuquerque, the military commander there begged him to stay and become chaplain for Fort Marcy. He accepted the assignment with the understanding that he could do missionary work in surrounding areas. During his seven years as chaplain, he preached as far north as Taos and south to El Paso, and organized the first Baptist church in Albuquerque.

During Read's time in Prescott, he became so highly regarded by local residents that he was invited back to assist in organizing Arizona Central Baptist Association (Northern) in August 1882. At that time he was director of the American Baptist Publication Society in El Paso. The *Arizona Miner* reported that Read had preached the first sermon in Prescott and that he was a great pulpiteer. Prescott was in the original GCBA area.

### First Baptist Services in Verde Valley

James Clausent Bristow preached the first Baptist sermon in Verde Valley under a big cottonwood tree near the Verde River on October 3, 1875, with Romans 14:12 as his text. A historical marker on the grounds of the Middle Verde Rock Baptist Church, located four miles west of the junction of Middle Verde Road and I-17, marks the site. Middle Verde's first Baptist service reached a few neighbors, two cowboys, and several soldiers from nearby Fort Verde. For the service, cottonwood logs sawed to use for seats were moved under the shade of the trees to shield listeners from the sun.

Born in Indiana on February 5, 1835, Bristow moved with his family to the Ozark country of Missouri in 1848. He trusted Christ and was baptized at age eighteen. On April 26, 1875, he loaded his wife, six children, and belongings into a prairie schooner drawn by oxen and joined a wagon train for Arizona territory. Four months later they reached Verde Valley and settled in Middle Verde about six miles from Fort Verde army camp.

Because of Bristow's "hard-shell" Baptist background and lack of formal education, he did not at first recognize the need for a Sunday School. When he realized that the Bible should be regularly studied by all age groups, he secured the help of R. A. Windes to lead in organizing Sunday School (SS) classes. After six years the work constituted into a church which grew rapidly. Bristow continued his precedent-setting ministry there until he retired in August 1905.

### Romulus Adolphus Windes

R. A. Windes was the first seminary-trained, ordained Baptist preacher in Arizona Territory from the South. Born in Alabama in 1849, he left home after the Civil War to attend college. When his father died, he moved back to Alabama, where he worked as a missionary. Although successful as a church starter and ordained in the South, he married a Presbyterian woman and returned to Chicago, where he graduated from the University of Chicago and Baptist Union Theological Seminary.

Because Maggie Windes suffered from severe bronchitis, a doctor advised R. A. to take her to a dry climate. Having already felt called to the West to do missions work, he loaded his wife and two small children in a mule-drawn wagon and headed for Arizona. Their only possessions were the mules, a few household items, and $150 in borrowed money. The money was sewed into the hem of Maggie's dress to keep it safe from robbers. When they arrived in Prescott on August 13, 1879, they found the currency in many pieces due to the rigors of the journey. Carefully pasting the pieces together, they were able to salvage the money. In his trunk Windes carried his Bible, a hymn book, and his diplomas.

Windes found Prescott open for the gospel and began preaching in homes or any available building to any group he could get together, including the Methodist church. He taught public school to support his family. J. C. Bristow invited him to come over the mountains to live and help with the Verde Valley work, but he preferred to stay in Prescott, which he stated was "Satan's territory and under his dominion." He continued looking for Baptists, which he said were "as scarce as hen's teeth." By January 1880 Prescott boasted a drug store, meat market, two general merchandise stores, two churches, and eight saloons.

Windes described his problem by saying, "I found a few Baptists who could help materially, but didn't have the moral courage to take hold and try to do something. Others who were willing to help were not financially able. But I moved from the first day and every day thereafter with as much confidence and expectation as if I had a million dollars in the bank. I was blessed with a gift of earnestness which crowded out all discouragements. Though I was not a great preacher and was as poor as Job's turkey, I could be sincere and always mean just what I said." He continued, "Another difficulty we had was the scarcity of water with which to baptize. People used to poke fun at me and tell me that I would have to let my converts down into a well by a rope to baptize them, or else go to the Verde River forty miles away."

**First Baptist Church in Arizona**

With persistence, Windes led in the organization of the Lone Star Baptist Church in Prescott on January 25, 1880. The minutes of that meeting record that "the following brethren and sisters met together for the purpose of organizing themselves into a church: Rev. R. A. Windes, Mrs. Maggie Windes, T. P. Head, Mrs. Mary Joice, Mrs. Eliza Stearns, and Mrs. L. Pemberton. There being no other ordained minister in the territory, the church decided to accept the council of Rev. R. A. Windes, a missionary of the American Baptist HMS, who was at once chosen moderator. After Brother T. P. Head stated that his letter had been accidentally burned and that he had temporarily belonged to the Methodist church, under circumstances which all the body considered excusable, the letters of all the rest were duly examined by the above named missionary, and the church was organized as a regular Baptist church. Adjourned. R. A. Windes, moderator; Maggie Windes, clerk."

The church was named the Lone Star Baptist Church, a name suggested by the Lone Star Mission of India where a great revival had taken place among the Telegus. The organizational meeting took place in the old schoolhouse, one of the first log buildings in the territory, located about a mile west of the center of Prescott. A replica of this first public schoolhouse stands in Prescott's Sharlot Hall Museum Center.

Windes reported that the group only had one Bible and hymn book, those he had brought to Arizona. He wrote, "Nobody could sing, and I had never led a song service in my life, but I sailed right into it with main strength and awkwardness, and we made a noise and an appearance of singing, the audience joining in from memory. We didn't lack anything but the tune." When the church began to grow, converts were baptized in a baptistry the members constructed in Granite Creek.

Lone Star erected the first Baptist church building in Arizona Territory, also GCBA territory, and dedicated it in August 1880. Located on Academy Hill, the building cost twenty-eight hundred dollars. The August 29, 1980, *Courier* stated that the foundation of the church rested on the visible ruins of a prehistoric structure that may have been, thousands of years ago, a heathen temple of worship. In 1884 they moved the building to a site on South Cortez where they met for the next forty-three years under leadership of twenty different pastors. In May 1923 construction started on the picturesque, granite Lone Star Baptist Church at Goodwin and Marina. In 1934 the church became First Baptist.

The August 8, 1888, *Kingman Miner* stated, "Mohave County has a minister shortage problem, and if a minister of the gospel should come to town, he could make a fair living by dealing stud poker on weekdays." The January 1, 1970, *Courier* affirmed the sacrificial spirit, "As far as the Prescott Baptist witness is concerned, there were no 'good old days.' From the beginning to this present, it has been a history of toils, tears, trials, turmoils, and testings. However, with much prayer, patience, perspiration, perseverance, and persistence, many victories have been won for the glory of God."

Lone Star operated like a Southern Baptist church with SS, Baptist Young People's Union (BYPU), Woman's Missionary Society (WMS), and Brotherhood organizations. The members never resorted to bazaars, food sales, or other fund-raising ventures to raise money. In 1918 the work closed for three months due to the severe flu epidemic. In 1925, when a Prescott bank failed, the church suffered the loss of its building fund money. Because of growing tendencies toward doctrinal modernism (liberalism) in the American Baptist Convention (ABC) in the 1940s, the church was one of many Baptist churches in the state and nation which withdrew from the ABC in 1950 to affiliate with the Conservative Baptist Association of America. It has supported its missionary outreach through the Foreign and Home Mission Societies ever since.

Excerpts from the Lone Star minutes reveal that in December 1880, the treasurer reported only twenty-two cents left in the treasury. In 1881 the church sponsored a mission in Verde Valley. On June 15, 1881, a motion passed to send sympathy to the Upper Verde SS, organized June 12, 1881. A motion also passed that the church take a vacation until the pastor returned from a missionary trip to the Verde Valley. In March 1887, a motion was made, seconded, and defeated to have three deacons. A new motion was made, seconded, and carried to have two deacons. In 1896 the church was first illuminated by electric lights. In 1918 "a count of noses" revealed 123 members.

For the next twenty-one years, Windes organized Baptist churches and started Sunday Schools as a missionary of the Northern Baptist HMS. Other churches he started include: Phoenix FBC, organized in March 1883 with seven charter members; a Baptist church in Globe, organized in June 1883 with thirteen charter members, which ceased to exist in 1887; Jerome Baptist Church organized in 1894 with eight charter members, but soon disbanded; and Verde Baptist Church in Cottonwood, organized in 1890. Between 1889 and 1893, Windes also started Sunday Schools at Oak Creek, Cherry Creek, Beaver Creek, Lower Verde, and Peck's Lake on the Upper Verde, feats which we have been unable to duplicate during GCBA history, although these locales have been in our area.

Although Windes doctrinally was a Southern Baptist, prevailing public opinion favored having community churches which accepted into membership all who claimed to be Christian. He finally yielded to pressure to accept baptism by any denomination. Both Northern and Southern Baptists regarded him with suspicion, the Northerners because he had grown up in the South, married an Alabamian, and served as assistant missionary in Muscle Shoals. Southern Baptists distrusted him because he had his education from the North and was employed by the Northern Baptist HMS.

### Pioneer Southern Baptist Preachers and Problems

Pastors like John A. Helm, who served as an evangelist in west Texas and New Mexico before moving to Arizona in 1911, after a revival in Safford in 1908, laid a strong, biblical foundation for Southern Baptist work. His son, A. Truman Helm, told in *Early History of Arizona Baptists* of moving to Glendale, Arizona, and uniting with the Baptist church which met in a small, frame building on the west side of town. He wrote, "The pastor at the time was really a Presbyterian who worked as a clerk in the Santa Fe depot. He would bring a twelve-to-fifteen-minute sermonette on Sunday morning. Later he became the executive secretary to Governor G. W. P. Hunt, first elected governor after statehood, February 14, 1912."

In the following months various questions arose in the Glendale church regarding church polity and practices, especially about baptism, the Lord's Supper, election of deacons without ordination, and comity agreements with other denominations. John Helm, although retired, did some preaching and Bible teaching, and by taking a stand against some of the practices in the Glendale church and state convention, aroused considerable opposition from leaders.

On one occasion the executive secretary of the Northern Baptist Convention supplied the pulpit and spent the time defending the practice of agreeing to keep out of certain territories if they were already occupied by Presbyterians, Methodists, or other groups. This practice of comity made it impossible to begin missions if work had already been started, regardless of what doctrines were being proclaimed. In the course of the sermon, the speaker paused and pointed to John Helm and asked, "Brother Helm, what would you do in a case like that?"

Without hesitation, Helm replied, "I would do as the Lord commanded and 'Go into all the world and preach the gospel.'" Later, a pastor came from California who was weak in Baptist doctrines and practices. When the pastor planned a revival, John Helm recommended T. T. Martin from Blue Mountain, Mississippi, as the evangelist. During the revival the pastor became dissatisfied with his baptism. After Martin returned home, the song leader, Woodie W. Smith from Texas, was asked to continue the meeting. Church members discovered that Smith had secretly baptized the pastor one afternoon at the church. When they requested the pastor to acknowledge his baptism before the church, he refused and soon left the pastorate.

In 1920 at a session of the ABC in Globe, a motion was made to withdraw from the Northern Convention. It was defeated by a substitute motion to withdraw from the Inter-Church World Movement. This motion carried.

J. O. Willett came from Missouri in 1918 upon doctor's orders and opened a trading post on the Pima Reservation at Four Mile Post. He became another pioneer, along with John and Truman Helm, in molding Southern Baptists together in doctrine, programs, and fellowship. He carried on much correspondence with Northern Baptist leaders, trying to explain Southern Baptist faith and practice.

Growing differences caused Southern Baptist leaders in New Mexico, Texas, and the Baptist Sunday School Board (BSSB) to encourage the constitution of the Baptist General Convention of Arizona (Southern). On March 28, 1928, Willett wrote B. D. Gray, Home Mission Board (HMB) executive secretary in Atlanta, that much propaganda being reported was untrue and that Southern Baptists in Arizona would do nothing to embarrass the HMB or the HMS of the Northern Convention. Some churches became discouraged and disbanded before the coming of the Baptist General Convention of Arizona (Southern)—BGCA.

The first attempt to start a Southern Baptist church in the area which became GCBA came in 1923 when Prescott First Southern Baptist Church began as a mission from Glendale Calvary (later FSBC) with layman L. V. Fletcher as mission pastor. It was constituted as a church with thirteen charter members in 1924. The church then ordained Fletcher and called him as pastor.

In 1928 the HMB and Baptist Convention of New Mexico provided a pastoral subsidy to Thomas B. Hart and W. A. King for the Prescott church. It was one of the ten churches whose messengers organized the BGCA on September 20, 1928. W. A. King and the L. V. Fletchers were Prescott FSBC messengers at that meeting. A BGCA December meeting that year listed King and the S. C. Fishers as messengers. When King resigned as pastor in 1929, the church was so beset with financial problems that it was unable to secure another pastor and was forced to disband. The present Prescott FSBC organized in 1945 and became one of the original churches in GCBA.

Another early pioneer in Arizona was G. H. Woodward, who arrived in the early 1920s and united with Phoenix Calvary Baptist (ABC). He was among the seventy-two members who withdrew in 1921 to form the Phoenix FSBC. Woodward was sent to Flagstaff in 1924 by the Phoenix church to establish a mission but was unable to find interested Southern Baptists. In 1925 he pastored the Buckeye FBC which had been started by six women and met in the city jail.

### Baptist General Convention of Arizona Organized

Because Phoenix FSBC had an earnest desire to be a part of the SBC, they sent representatives to the May 1921 convention in Memphis, Tennessee, requesting recognition. They were seated as messengers. In August 1921 the church sent their pastor, C. M. Rock, to the annual meeting of the Southwestern Baptist Association of New Mexico with a statement of beliefs and a petition for admission, which was granted.

On October 11, 1925, the ten Southern Baptist churches in Arizona sent representatives to a meeting at Phoenix FSBC to consider organizing an association that would affiliate with the New Mexico Baptist Convention. John H. Helm moved that the association be organized and recommended that the churches send three messengers each to Phoenix FSBC on October 29, 1925, to complete the organization. At that time Gambrell Memorial Baptist Association constituted and functioned until its fourth annual meeting at Globe on September 20, 1928.

At the Globe meeting C. M. Rock moved that Gambrell Memorial Association cease to exist and that henceforth the organized body become the BGCA. S. E. Stevenson was employed as a field-worker, devoting time to SS, BYPU, and evangelistic meetings. The BSSB helped BGCA with his twenty-five-hundred-dollar salary because of its love for the West. Stevenson's wife wrote that in September 1930 they led a tent revival in Tolleson which initiated the FBC there and did the same in Tucson in 1931 to start FBC in that city. Stevenson served for a year until Truman Helm was elected to succeed him. Helm was bivocational and worked at night to perform his duties.

### Sanford S. Bussell: First State Assemblies Meet in GCBA Area

S. S. Bussell was elected to the office of corresponding secretary in 1931 when the BSSB agreed to provide a salary for him, provided he would devote his time primarily to promoting SS and TU work. While he was New Mexico SS secretary, he had taught SS and WMU training courses in Arizona and later led in all areas of missionary education.

Bussell was largely responsible for the first summer assembly held at Groom Creek, south of Prescott in GCBA territory, in June 1926. Homer Grice of Nashville, the great Vacation Bible School (VBS) promoter, served as camp pastor for the sixty-five who remembered attending those "blessed days." In 1927 Bussell led the camp to convene at the same place. These camps were the forerunners of our Gambrell Memorial and Paradise Valley Baptist Ranch annual state assemblies which always met in the Prescott area.

S. S. Bussell had no office or equipment, except a secondhand type-writer and mimeograph with which he published the first *Baptist Beacon*, a mimeographed sheet. Recognized as a consecrated, cultured, yet humble Christian, he poured a spirit of love and sacrifice into the work of Arizona. After leading the convention from 1931 to 1938, he served as state religious education secretary from 1944 to 1947.

Bussell passed away on Friday, October 3, 1947, after preaching at the GCBA annual meeting at Prescott. Before leaving the meeting, he had gathered friends around the car to pray for their traveling safety. He collapsed and died while his car was being serviced in Wickenburg.

### Henry A. Zimmerman

In 1939 Albuquerque FBC pastor Henry A. Zimmerman accepted the call to be BGCA corresponding secretary. A former Foreign Mission Board (FMB) missionary to Brazil, he had been unable to return because of lack of funds during the depression. Like the other early leaders, he actually served as a missionary for the entire state, holding revivals and directing training events in most of the churches each year and encouraging the pastors and members. At that time the BGCA executive was elected annually, usually by an unanimous, standing vote. After Zimmerman's first year, the 1940 convention highly praised his entire family for their charismatic personalities, musical talents, and spiritual fervor in leading the work.

### State Secretary Zimmerman Preaches at Fredonia

The Mormon town of Fredonia lies north of the Colorado River in Arizona near the southwestern border of Utah. A small group of Christians of different denominations living in this Latter Day Saints stronghold invited corresponding secretary Zimmerman to preach a

S. S. Bussell was BGCA corresponding secretary, 1931–1938. He died after attending a GCBA meeting in 1947.

Cunninghams moved from Texas to Arizona in September 1947. Milton served as BGCA state evangelist.

Willis J. Ray (center) celebrated his ninetieth birthday in 1986 in a tent on GCC campus. Here Ray is pictured with two 1950s pastors who served former GCBA churches: (left) Bill Hunke, Vernal, UT, FBC; and (right) Darwin E. Welsh, Artesia, CO, FBC.

When Milton E. Cunningham served in GCBA, 1944–1947, he organized the Kingman FBC and Flagstaff FSBC.

Marie Tatum Cunningham served as assistant to Willis J. Ray, Baptist Beacon editor, and as WMU secretary.

*Before he died in 1951, Cunningham started 59 churches and missions and helped 16 churches buy property.*

*Kingman FBC organized September 24, 1944, with twenty-six charter members and called T. T. Reynolds as pastor.*

*Wickenburg FBC, oldest of six founding GCBA churches, organized September 14, 1943, following a VBS and revival led by Rev. Ellis and student missionary Leslie Saunders. William A. "Uncle Billy" Barclay pastored the church, 1943–1946.*

*The present Prescott FSBC organized on March 18, 1945. The first Prescott FSBC had disbanded in 1929.*

*Flagstaff FSBC organized on July 19, 1945, after Cunningham and student missionaries held a VBS and revival.*

five-day revival for them in September 1941. These believers had conducted a SS for several months before issuing the invitation. An
eleven-year-old boy was converted.

H. A. Zimmerman served the state until 1944 and afterwards became
a HMB missionary in Washington and pastored in North Pole, Alaska.
We in Arizona should remember with pride that as our leader he made
an eloquent plea to messengers at the SBC in Oklahoma City in May 1941
to seat the California messengers. He was working as missionary in his
native Arkansas when he drowned in a flooded stream while on his way
to lead someone to the Lord.

At first, GCBA territory extended all the way across northern Arizona
and included Winslow, Holbrook, and Burton. Burton mission began in
the schoolhouse at Linden, Arizona, in 1924 when V. A. Vanderhoof orga-
nized a SS. In the spring of 1925, the SS moved to the schoolhouse at
Burton, where the congregation voted to organize into a church on
August 21, 1927. The seventeen charter members called L. H.
Shuttlesworth as pastor. Lakeside FBC began in 1946 as a Southern
Baptist church under the leadership of William Barclay and was invited
to become a founding member of GCBA. It chose to join the Little
Colorado Baptist Association, which organized a few months later.

Probably Southern Baptists' highest tide of spiritual fellowship and
fervor came each summer at the Gambrell Memorial Assemblies.
Speakers from all over the SBC led conferences with attendance running
around 250 even during the war years. A report in the 1943 state convention annual stated: "In spite of tire and gasoline rationing, the number
attending our summer assembly at Prescott was the largest we have ever
had. This meeting in the mile high city is indeed a highlight in our lives."

A part of every report in those years related to BGCA pastors in the
armed services. During 1942–1943, pastors James Carroll, George Wilson,
Jack Maben, and Thomas Hart entered the chaplaincy. Arizona also
claimed chaplains Arlie McDaniel and Homer Reynolds because of their
labors of love in the state.

### Willis J. Ray

In June 1944 the BGCA called Willis J. Ray, who served as executive
secretary until 1956. He had worked as an editor and pastor in Texas
before becoming a district missionary and superintendent of evangelism
and assistant executive secretary for the Texas Baptist Convention.
Regarding his coming to Arizona, Ray wrote Bill Hunke: "I was happy in
Texas and declined the invitation to visit Phoenix for sixty days. When I

consented to visit, they called a special convention. I told them that if I considered coming, I would not be responsible for SS, TU, BSU, or Brotherhood, so they elected S. S. Bussell to those activities. I prayed for some time until God laid Arizona on my heart. The HMB could not help until the SBC met in May 1945."

Arriving four days later than planned, on a 117-degree, high-humidity day in August, after a car breakdown which necessitated a trade and wartime shortages that led to constant delays and discomforts, Ida Ray asked her husband, "Do you reckon we landed in the wrong place?" As soon as he got to the state, Ray led a conference for pastors and laymen at Gambrell Memorial Assembly and conducted a planning meeting called to discuss organizing new churches. Kingman, in GCBA territory at that time, was the first place he targeted for starting a church.

Ray always saw his primary tasks as winning souls and starting churches, and did both in innovative ways. Shortly after coming to Arizona, he established a Trust and Memorial Fund to acquire new church sites and construct buildings. Before the HMB began its pastoral aid program, he led Texas Woman's Missionary Union (WMU) to supplement Arizona pastors' salaries. During Ray's time as executive secretary, Southern Baptist work related to the original GCBA territory extended to encompass nine other states, stretching up to Canada, including Utah, Colorado, Idaho, Montana, Nebraska, Nevada, North and South Dakota, and Wyoming. The number of churches grew from twenty-five to more than two hundred. A man of great faith, Ray always thanked God for providing the answer when he prayed. He headed the campaign to start Grand Canyon College in Prescott and served as its first president when it opened in 1949. He sold his car and gave the one thousand dollars he received to the Grand Canyon College (GCC) fund-raising drive.

Words of wisdom from Ray that present pastors of GCBA might do well to heed include:

> I never pastored a church but what I asked that the church give 20 percent to missions and pay that check before we issued any others. Christ died for the world, not just for the local field. Every place I've been, I've asked the church to see the whole world.

> In my work as a pastor, I was in my office every morning promptly at eight o'clock studying and praying, unless called otherwise. From eleven to twelve I got the mail and answered my

letters. From twelve to two o'clock I was at home having lunch with my family. From two until five o'clock, I was out visiting prospects. Almost every evening we had meetings which required my attendance.

My philosophy was that if you want to build a big church, build it where you are, but too many preachers are always looking at other fields. As long as they're looking at another field, they will never build their own.

I'm so limited in my personality. I'm not handsome like lots of men. I'm not an orator. I've had to let the Lord use what I am. I just want to be remembered as an humble servant of the Lord.

Ray stated in his second convention report, "We come with many reasons for rejoicing. The war has closed; peace again reigns in that men have laid down their arms. We now have the opportunity of giving to the world a permanent peace, as given to us by the Prince of Peace. We rejoice because loved ones are returning home. Millions of lives have been spared, and through it all the Kingdom of God has continued to grow."

He also shared that Arizona was asking the HMB for a missionary to the Mormons "in the vast east central portion of our state which is practically untouched by Protestant churches and without Baptist work. Many of the towns and cities in that section have only Mormon churches although many non-Mormons live there." No missionary was appointed in response to this request. In 1956 Ray became the first executive secretary of the new Baptist General Convention of Colorado, an area that had been served by GCBA and the BGCA. He held that job until he retired in 1962 and returned to Arizona, where he lived until his death at age ninety-six on December 6, 1992.

### Beginnings of Original GCBA Churches: Prescott FSBC
After the Prescott FSBC disbanded in 1929, it remained closed until the state executive board meeting in December 1943 made plans to start the work again. On March 18, 1945, Prescott FSBC was reorganized.

### Wickenburg FBC
During the summer of 1943, a Rev. Ellis from Phoenix and Leslie Saunders, a summer worker from the HMB, conducted a VBS in Wickenburg in the mornings and took a census of the town in the

afternoons. Following the VBS, Ellis preached a revival meeting with George Kendall leading singing. When Ellis became ill, E. K. Dougherty, pastor in Glendale, replaced him. The Wickenburg FBC constituted on September 14, 1943, with William A. Barclay serving as pastor from 1943 to 1946.

"Uncle Billy" and "Muzzy" Barclay were well beloved by Arizona Southern Baptists. He was born May 11, 1881, near Austin, Texas, saved at age thirty-two, and felt led to western mission work when he was thirty-eight. He wrote, "Shortly after my conversion, I felt called to preach. After attending San Marcos Baptist Academy and Southwestern Baptist Theological Seminary (SWBTS), I traveled to the West to fulfil my ministry in North Dakota, New Mexico, and Arizona." After his Wickenburg pastorate, he became field-worker for the Arizona convention from 1946 to 1949. In those years he started work in Show Low, Pinetop, Lakeside, and Springerville. He served as pastor for churches at Hillside, Winslow, and Globe. He died at Phoenix on September 23, 1973, at ninety-two years of age.

### Roosevelt, Utah, Baptist Church: Harold and Opal Beaird Dillman

In 1918 during World War I, Nixon E. Beaird, a Baptist who was city marshall of Lamesa, Texas, read in the paper that it was possible to stake a claim in the Red Wash area of Craig, Colorado. When he moved there with that in mind, he saw the soil was full of alkali and not good for farming. He then moved on to an area near Vernal, Utah. Because the Beaird children, Opal and Nolan, grew up with Mormons, made friends with them, and understood their doctrines, they were uniquely fitted to minister to them.

The children at first attended school and services at the Congregational church, but soon started to school in town and started a Bible study in their home led by Dan Mennick, a ninety-year-old man who rode there on a bicycle. In the eighth grade Opal met Harold Dillman, from Roosevelt, Utah, who was the son of an atheist father and a Mormon mother. She began attending Mutual, the Mormon youth organization, with him. They dated for four years before becoming engaged. In 1928 Opal's father sold the farm and moved the family back to Texas.

Harold was born in his family's mortuary building and grew up with the understanding that he would take over the business. After training in California to be an embalmer, he was told by his grandfather and uncle that because he was engaged to a Baptist girl, he would not be allowed to have any part in the family funeral business. They asserted, "You can never make a living in Roosevelt or any other place in Utah." In 1930 he drove to Abilene in a Model T Ford. There he became involved in Baptist church activities and accepted Christ. Opal and Harold were married September 4, 1930. Not long afterwards, they met Robert and Cora Johnson, and both couples worked together in church programs at the Carrizo Springs Baptist Church. Harold became SS superintendent and was ordained a deacon. He and Opal felt called to missions when a woman from the BSSB taught a study course at their church.

Concerned that people in Utah should have the same opportunity to hear about Christ as those in Texas, they began praying about going back to tell them. While living in Texas, Harold had made annual fall hunting trips into Colorado with a group of friends, driving an empty refrigerated truck. In 1942 he agreed to drive for them on the fifteen-hundred-mile trip only if the group would permit him to load his furniture on the empty truck going north to help him move back to Roosevelt, Utah. "We moved to Utah at the cost of $2.47," he recalled.

Because the family mortuary had gone out of business, as soon as he arrived back in Roosevelt, Harold opened and operated a new funeral home. He testified, "The Lord blessed us so that Opal and I ran around seventy-seven funerals a year, all that we could handle in addition to the ambulance business that went along with it."

Harold felt a burning desire to begin a Baptist church in Utah and begin preaching the gospel to his people. Two years later, they were joined by Robert and Cora Johnson. In 1944 they invited Carrizo Springs pastor W. C. Bennett to come to Roosevelt for a revival held in a vacant Episcopal church building. As a result, they organized a church with eight members on July 2, 1944. The Texas church received them as members, then lettered them out to become the Roosevelt Baptist Church, the first Southern Baptist church in Utah. The group, representing five families, met in the Episcopal building until 1945, when they were driven out.

Their second regular meeting place for six months was the Dillman home. In March 1946 the Dillmans gave a fifty-by-seventy-five-foot lot for the construction of a cinder-block church building. They again rented the Episcopal facility until their church basement was ready for use. It was finished in time for their third annual revival which began on June 16, 1946. Harold remembered that "the building cost us a little over three thousand dollars. The Arizona Convention loaned us five hundred dollars and sent another five hundred dollars to help us finish it up, but we didn't need that, so we sent it back." Because Willis J. Ray and other BGCA leaders had encouraged the church, on April 7, 1946, the Roosevelt Baptist Church petitioned Central Association in Phoenix for admission and was received into the association over eight hundred miles away on April 22, 1946. It affiliated with GCBA when it organized that fall.

"The Roosevelt church getting started was a like miracle," Opal said. "An interdenominational preacher in town had fought us and was trying to destroy all our efforts to win people. I remember praying one day that if the Lord wanted that kind of work here, to help us know it. If not, to take that man out of our way. I picked up the newspaper later that week and read that he had left town. That same day Bob Cure and his family came to town wanting to help us. He had read about our work in the *California Southern Baptist.*"

On August 11, 1946, Robert Eldon Cure from San Lorenzo, California, accepted the call to come as the first pastor of the fifteen members. In September 1946 the church began a mission at Clearfield, Utah. Although Clearfield was not an organizing church of GCBA, it was a part of the association through the mother church at Roosevelt. On December 27, 1946, the first baptism in a Southern Baptist church baptistry in Utah took place when James Butcher was immersed in the uncomfortably cold, unfinished Roosevelt Baptist building. The service was a high hour in the early life of the church. Before this time, baptismal services had taken place at Lake Borham, about twenty miles west of Roosevelt.

Roosevelt Baptist organized their Training Union (TU) and WMS in April 1947. That summer field workers came with T. T. Reynolds to help with VBSs in Roosevelt, Gusher, and Myton. As a result a SS started in Myton with Harold Dillman as superintendent. In September Charles Ray accepted the Roosevelt pastorate. When the first workers' conference in Utah was held at Roosevelt on July 22, 1948, Olen Perryman was ordained as a deacon at the meeting. Mission services at Whiterocks and Fort Duchesne were conducted for the Indians during 1948. Although prayers were offered for several years to start a mission at Gusher, not until 1951 did the work there start permanently.

### Artesia, Colorado, FBC

On March 27, 1946, the Roosevelt church began meetings in Artesia, Colorado. Hundreds of oil workers from Texas and Oklahoma were moving into the area as oil fields opened up. The Artesia church started after a revival preached by A. C. "Shorty" Maxwell in the school near

Wiley's Resort. During the services when Mrs. Tom Elliott called a meeting to discuss the need for a Baptist church, Maxwell led in organizing FBC. On April 4 the meeting place was changed to the Kiva Theater. Evening services began May 29 in the schoolhouse.

John L. Alexander, who was called as the first pastor on September 15, 1946, taught school to supplement his income. During the time the Artesia FBC remained in GCBA, R. H. Miller, Marvin Elam, R. E. Cure, A. K. Peveto, and Nolan Beaird served as pastors, with Charles Ray, Harold Dillman, and field workers T. T. Reynolds and Fred DeBerry holding services between pastors. On September 29, 1947, the church purchased two lots with houses on them, one for a pastorium and the other to be remodeled for the church services. The first VBS was held in 1947 with summer workers Lewis Martin and Dan White coming from the HMB to lead.

On May 29, 1946, the Artesia FBC voted to join Central Baptist Association of the BGCA; it affiliated with GCBA when it was organized. Beginning in January 1947, Roosevelt, Vernal, and Artesia, with the help of the HMB, maintained a radio broadcast three times a week. Because of the surrounding mountains and weak radio signals in those days, people had no choice but to listen to the gospel broadcasts if they turned their radios on.

In 1946 Roosevelt Baptist Church bought a lot in Vernal, Utah, for a church. On November 10, 1946, they began a revival on the lot under a large army mess tent which had been purchased for this purpose. Bob Cure preached with Harold Dillman leading the singing. "Robert Johnson loaned us his oil burner for heat in the tent," Harold reported. "It snowed four inches one night while we were having services. The revival led to the organization of Vernal FBC under the tent on November 22, 1946, with seventeen charter members."

Vernal constituted a month too late to be a founding church of the GCBA, but joined in the association's activities from the beginning. Cure accepted the call as half-time pastor on December 1, 1946, with Opal and Harold Dillman responsible for services on the other Sundays. The new church rented the Episcopal building in Vernal, and later the Imperial Hall, for their services. The Beaird family's petitions for a church in their town had been answered more than twenty years after they began praying.

In 1948 the Vernal FBC borrowed twenty-five hundred dollars from the Trust and Memorial Fund to construct a basement on which an auditorium would later be erected. In September 1951 an interested couple paid off the loan on the finished basement so that a ten-thousand-dollar loan could be obtained to complete the building. During a slump that came from 1948 to 1950 when oil workers left, Harold Dillman conducted services in the absence of a pastor. "Sometimes just Harold and one woman who came to start up the fire came for services," Opal stated. When a new group of oil workers arrived in 1950 and revitalized the work, the church called Nolan Beaird as half-time pastor. Within a year he became full-time. Services were held in the basement as soon as it was completed in September 1951. When Bill Hunke came as pastor in 1953, the church had recently begun meeting in the unfinished, upstairs audi-torium. During the following year, Hunke and builder Charlie Tague worked long hours to complete the Tudor-style building, which was one of the most attractive in town.

### Missionary Milton Emery Cunningham

As soon as Willis J. Ray came on the field as executive secretary in Arizona, he called Milton Cunningham to come out to help in the work. Milton accepted his invitation, arriving in September 1944. He was jointly employed by the BGCA and HMB to serve as a field-worker (missionary) at large. On December 1, 1944, the HMB assumed responsibility for Cunningham, who became director of evangelism for Arizona.

Cunningham was born in Lexington, Texas, April 27, 1894. He was saved at age nine and surrendered to God's call to preach at age fourteen. The Taylor, Texas, FBC licensed him to preach when he was seventeen, and the Copeland, Texas, Baptist Church ordained him. He married Bertha Smith, who died in 1928, and they had a son, Milton Emery Jr. He married Marie Tatum on August 22, 1939. He pastored a number of Texas churches before serving in the armed forces during World War I. He pas-tored in Kentucky and Indiana while going to Southern Seminary, then accepted the Hillcrest Baptist Church in Austin.

During the two years when Cunningham preached as an independent evangelist in the Rio Grande Valley, he learned to appreciate Willis J. Ray who had become the director of rural evangelism for the Texas conven-tion. After directing the Arizona evangelism program for three years, Cunningham became a field-worker for California Southern Baptists on October 1, 1947. During his ministry in the West, he had a part in begin-ning twenty-four missions and thirty-five churches. He assisted sixteen churches in raising funds to purchase sites or construct buildings. He served as interim mission pastor of fifteen churches, strengthening them until they could employ a pastor.

## Kingman FSBC (Formerly FBC)

When a call from Southern Baptists came from Kingman to help them start a church, Willis J. Ray sent Cunningham to respond. The city had a population of seventy-five hundred, a large lumber industry, an army camp nearby, and the largest gold mining operation in Arizona. It also had seven churches, none of which was Baptist. Cunningham arrived in Kingman early on Saturday, September 16, 1944. He immediately visited all the interested Baptists and located a meeting place in the American Legion Hall. He began revival services the next morning, which continued each night that week, accompanied by extensive visitation and distribution of fliers advertising the revival and announcing the organization of a Baptist church at 4:00 P.M. on September 24.

Willis J. Ray came to lead in the church constitution, assisted by Cunningham, J. B. Rounds, who preached a challenging message, and W. G. McArthur, contact man for the military camp. After the church adopted the articles of faith in Pendleton's *Church Manual*, they called Cunningham as pastor. Twelve members representing seven families were received at the organizational meeting, one of whom came upon profession of faith requesting baptism. In spite of pressures to hinder the new work, the Kingman FBC enjoyed the blessing of additions every week; when charter membership closed at the end of October, they reported twenty-six members.

Because the American Legion Hall was well outside the city and hard to find, after three weeks the group secured the Odd Fellows Lodge hall free for a month with rent charged thereafter. Members of the lodge and friends gave eighteen dollars to help with expenses, with some leading citizens also expressing concern and offering financial help. Milton Cunningham remained as pastor through January 15, 1945, when he went to Globe and started Trinity Baptist Church in a city of twenty thousand where two existing Baptist churches already had a membership of over six hundred. Trinity ran 125 in SS by the time it was two months old. His next assignment from the Lord was Mesa, a city of ten thousand completely dominated by Mormons where Baptists had previously been unable to secure a meeting place. On June 21, 1945, fifty-six people came for the organization of the Mesa FSBC. Cunningham acted as pastor for a few weeks until the work was firmly in place, and another urgent call for help had been received at the convention office.

Meanwhile, Kingman FBC carried on for almost a year before securing T. T. Reynolds as pastor. They purchased the John H. Ware residence, a three-story building with twelve-inch stone walls, hardwood floors, a complete basement, and furnace. The upper story had six rooms which were used for the pastor's home and SS. Located at the corner of Oak and Sixth Streets, the church had a 145-foot frontage and a garage and two room quarters in the rear. The 40 members assumed $7,000 of the $12,000 cost of the property, with $5,000 raised for down payment.

At the church's fiftieth anniversary on the weekend of October 24–25, 1994, Ruby Harris from Winslow, whose father was an early pastor at Kingman, shared memories of living in the church. She remembered children arriving early on Sundays and coming to their living quarters to help her father get ready. "It seemed as if the children were always so thirsty that by the time services were over, every glass in the house had been used," she shared.

After the church appealed to the BGCA for help, the convention found four men to underwrite the loan until HMB assistance through the Annie Armstrong Easter Offering (AAEO) could be secured. The laymen included: John D. Davis, a groceryman and deacon from Glendale Calvary; Barry Casey, owner of the Barry Seed Company and deacon at Phoenix Central; Harold Hensley, paint contractor and deacon at Phoenix FSBC; and F. S. Hawkins, teacher, contractor, and deacon, also at Phoenix FSBC. The nearest Baptist church to Kingman was at Needles, California, fifty miles away.

T. T. Reynolds, who succeeded Milton Cunningham as pastor of the Kingman FBC in December 1944, was born September 8, 1897, at Franklin, Texas. Because his father died when he was three, he grew up helping his mother and sister with farm work. He was saved at age fourteen and surrendered to preach at twenty-seven. He married, had two children, and pastored Texas churches for eighteen years before coming to the West. He gained a reputation as a gentle, unassuming, consecrated man of God.

While at Kingman, Reynolds led VBSs in Chloride, Kingman Heights, and Bullhead City to start Southern Baptist work. He had to return to Texas for one year to hospitalize his sick wife, but returned as BGCA general missionary for northern Arizona. He helped extend the work into Utah and served as interim pastor for a number of churches. In December 1950 he returned to Texas to pastor the Splendora FBC and later served as missionary for Neches River Association.

### Flagstaff FSBC

When interested Southern Baptists in Flagstaff expressed the desire for a church, Willis J. Ray again called on Milton Cunningham to take student summer missionaries up to take a census. To the surprise of almost everyone, they found hundreds of prospects. Flagstaff, lying at the foot of San Francisco Peaks and at the head of Oak Creek Canyon, with the Navajo reservation nearby, was a city of seventy-five hundred with a state teachers' college (now Northern Arizona University—NAU), lumber camps, and extensive ranching interests. Although thousands of tourists and summer visitors came to the city, fewer than one thousand attended services in the various churches on a given Sunday.

Cunningham began a revival and VBS in the only available building, a forsaken tourist court where some Pentecostals had previously held services. After they hung a lantern on a post in order to have services outside, it started raining, and everyone had to go inside or stand on the porch. The Willis J. Rays, Marie Cunningham, Elmer Holt, and L. D. White drove to Flagstaff to assist in the organization of the new church on July 19, 1945. That night nine members joined by letter or statement and four by baptism, with three more coming by baptism as the revival continued, bringing the total members to sixteen by the next Sunday.

The new church began meeting in a vacant garage but was forced out of the building thirty days after its organization. The A. C. Everetts invited the church family to meet in their home on Second Street until a building was rented on Santa Fe Avenue. They moved again to Third Street before land was purchased in 1947 and a building begun at 508 West Cherry Avenue, where it now serves as an apartment complex. The church met in the basement until the church facility was completed in 1951. The coming of H. R. Spraker to Flagstaff to be interim pastor of FSBC released Cunningham to serve other fields. The California Convention called him and Marie to begin field work in the Los Angeles area on October 1, 1947, where they served until his death.

Milton Cunningham died on November 8, 1951, near Paragould, Arkansas, while he and Marie were participating in the Greene County school of missions. He had spoken at the Center Hill Baptist Church the evening before in spite of feeling cold and having to lie down after lunch that day. Marie wrote that when he spoke before the group of twenty-one missionaries, he outdid them all. The last gesture she saw him make from the pulpit came when he described the comity agreement with a upraised, closed fist, then proclaimed, "But my Lord said to go into all the world," and swung his arm around in a circle.

He had been quite interested in the messages brought by Lee Aufill of New Mexico and Luke Johnson of Arizona about work among the Indians, and had expressed his approval many times by a loud "amen." He had also enjoyed talking and joking with Mrs. Carl Hunker, a missionary from China (Carl has been on our mailing list to receive the *China Diary* for several years). When the doctor was called about midnight, Marie also received a call at New Hope where she was staying. "We drove like mad to get to him," she reported. "When we got there, I was told to sit down on the divan. The doctor sat down next to me and told me that my husband had expired just fifteen minutes earlier. He had only reached the home ten minutes before I did, so we were both too late. I cannot express to you my feelings of shock!" He was buried at Memorial Park cemetery in Austin, Texas.

Marie Tatum Cunningham was born December 4, 1907, at Converse, Louisiana, and was converted and baptized in a creek near Converse during a revival in 1919. She graduated from two colleges and SWBTS before beginning her school-teaching career. While serving with her husband as field workers in Arizona, she was Willis J. Ray's assistant, edited the *Baptist Beacon*, and became the first paid state WMU director. She directed the first Girls Auxiliary (GA) coronation held at Tucson FSBC and the largest GA and Royal Ambassadors (RA) youth camps held up to that time. She has been elementary principal of the Hawaiian Baptist Academy and director of housing and training students for mission projects at Dallas Baptist University. She married Roy F. Sutton, retired ASBC director, following the death of his second wife, and still retains a keen interest in ASBC work.

### Missionary Herbert Ross Spraker

In 1945 H. R. Spraker was encouraged by Willis J. Ray to move to Arizona and serve as general field-worker for northern Arizona. Spraker was born June 3, 1891, in Texas, where he was saved, baptized in Cobles Creek, and ordained by the Cobles Creek Baptist Church. He had pastored a number of Texas churches and served as chaplain for state prisons in Brazoria and Fort Bend Counties where he met Ray. During the two years he served in the GCBA area, H. R. and his wife Hattie helped the Wickenburg church and also lived in Kingman, Flagstaff, and Prescott. In 1947 he succeeded Milton Cunningham as state evangelist and moved to Chandler.

Spraker led BGCA in its first simultaneous statewide evangelistic campaigns. When the Sprakers returned to a pastorate in Texas in 1950, all the churches in Arizona had felt the impact of his influence and were looking forward to the great simultaneous revivals to be conducted in all SBC churches west of the Mississippi that year. Spraker died May 30, 1953, and was buried at Huntsville, Texas.

# Hand of the Most High

## GCBA'S FIRST FIVE YEARS

The great goodness of God is evident in his guidance of the early GCBA pastors and leaders to bring about the organization of an association that would be called a "Mother of Associations." Grand Canyon witnessed the following other associations organized with churches formerly affiliated with GCBA: Utah, Lake Mead, Mohave (River Valley), Estrella, Hassayampa (Troy Brooks, Yavapai), and Four Corners. In the ensuing decades, churches from nine states joined with conventions formed in areas opened by GCBA's willingness to sponsor and fellowship with groups in neighboring states. God's mighty hand is both lifted in power to defend his people and extended in tenderness to sustain them.

### Organization of GCBA

On August 29, 1946, members from Southern Baptist churches in Wickenburg, Flagstaff, Kingman, and Prescott, Arizona, met at the Prescott FSBC "to formulate plans and organize a Baptist association in the northern part of Arizona." A motion was carried that the new association be formed. The new entity was defined as "an organization of Southern Baptist churches banded together to further the work of God in the boundaries of this association and working with the General Convention of Arizona of the Southern Baptist Churches." Those present included: T. T. Reynolds, Kingman; J. L. Alexander, Flagstaff; W. E. Bush, Wickenburg; H. G. Behrman, Lester O. Probst, George Oller, and C. B. Myers, Prescott; and J. N. Phillips, city missionary for Phoenix and Tucson.

J. N. Phillips had been appointed by the HMB and began serving Arizona on October 1, 1944. While serving as field secretary for San Marcos Academy in Texas, he had led in raising three hundred thousand dollars for endowment. Willis J. Ray announced his addition to the state staff by saying, "He is a distinguished preacher of the gospel and a clear, constructive, analytical thinker. He is a good business man and a builder. He is far visioned, has convictions, and the courage to back them up." Although Phillips was handicapped by illness for many months after arriving in Phoenix, he worked to start more missions all over the state. He served as interim pastor at both Prescott FSBC and Flagstaff FSBC, holding together the work already started in those cities.

At the organizational meeting, those present elected the following officers: moderator, Lester O. Probst, Prescott; treasurer, George Oller, Prescott; and clerk, J. L. Alexander, Flagstaff. They also appointed a committee to meet in Ash Fork on October 3, 1946, to arrange a program for the first annual meeting of the association to be held in Flagstaff on October 23, 1946, and to select the name for the association.

They instructed the clerk to send letters to the following churches inviting them to become members of the association: Artesia, Colorado, FBC; Wickenburg FBC; Roosevelt, Utah, Roosevelt Baptist; Kingman FBC; Prescott FSBC; Flagstaff FSBC; and Lakeside FBC. Each church was entitled to three messengers, and one additional messenger for every fifty members, or major portion thereof above one hundred members, providing that no church should be entitled to more than twelve messengers. All the churches except Lakeside responded to the invitation. Because San Carlos Baptist Association constituted shortly thereafter, the Lakeside church elected to be a part of that organization.

The Utah and Colorado church invitations were extended because on December 11, 1945, the BGCA executive board had discussed for the first time the possibility of accepting churches located in other states into the convention's fellowship. Willis J. Ray reported that when a congregation in any western state sought help from the HMB, the board would refer the church to the BGCA. John D. Davis moved "that the BGCA look with favor upon receiving churches of like faith and order from neighboring states." The motion was adopted unanimously.

### 1946 GCBA Annual Meeting at Flagstaff FSBC

The Grand Canyon Association of Southern Baptists (as recorded in the minutes, but later voted to be named Grand Canyon Baptist Association) held its first annual meeting at the Flagstaff FSBC on Wednesday, October 23, 1946, at 2:00 P.M. Messengers present included:

the T. T. Reynolds, Artesia FBC; Mrs. Young Yeazey and the J. W. Barksdales, Flagstaff FSBC; John J. Johnston, Kingman FBC; C. B. Myers, J. A. Teague, and Mrs. Lester Probst, Prescott FSBC; Harold and Opal Dillman, Roosevelt Baptist; Mrs. H. P. Davidson, Mrs. H. E. Dunkin, and Bernard Fugatt, Wickenburg FBC. After moderator Lester Probst called the meeting to order, W. H. Henry made a motion, which was carried, that the organization of the association as set up at Prescott on August 29 be made permanent.

The afternoon program consisted of a SS report by Harold Dillman from Roosevelt; TU report by J. L. Alexander from Flagstaff; bookstore report by Mrs. Farris from Phoenix; and missions reports by R. E. Cure from Roosevelt, W. E. Bush from Wickenburg, and S. S. Bussell from the state office in Phoenix. The reports emphasized that the greatest missions progress in the history of Arizona Southern Baptists had come during 1946 with thirteen new churches coming into the convention. Messengers thanked God that although they were in the aftermath of a bloody war and living in troublesome days due to strikes, rising prices, and family adjustments, God had given victories, and his work moved on. The foreign missions report indicated that at the close of the first one hundred years of the SBC, five and a half million of us were represented by 550 missionaries working in twenty nations. The session closed with a Brotherhood report by W. E. Bush.

The Wednesday 9:00 A.M. session opened with a digest of church letters by clerk J. L. Alexander. The churches reported the following number of baptisms and members during the year: Artesia, 9 baptisms and 30 members; Flagstaff FSBC, 18 baptisms and 44 members; Kingman FBC, 7 baptisms and 62 members; Prescott FSBC, 22 baptisms and 75 members; Roosevelt Baptist, 3 baptisms and 21 members; Vernal FBC, 5 baptisms and 35 members; and Wickenburg FBC, 10 baptisms and 63 members.

State field-worker H. R. Spraker brought a report on education and benevolence, followed by a report on civic righteousness by Mrs. J. N. Phillips from Phoenix. J. N. Phillips preached the annual sermon. After R. E. Cure was elected vice moderator, W. H. Henry of Wickenburg moved that the moderator, vice moderator, and clerk serve as the program committee for the 1947 annual meeting. The time and place for the second annual meeting were set for October 1-2, 1947, at Prescott FSBC. Before adjournment the messengers gave an offering of $24.66.

By the time of the next annual meeting, a constitution had been set in place. Some noteworthy articles in this first document included:

Number 2. The object of this association shall be the extension of Christ's kingdom, the cultivation of a missionary spirit, the promotion of piety in the churches, and the spread of the knowledge of salvation through Christ.

Number 5. The officers of this association shall be a moderator, a vice moderator, a clerk, a treasurer, and a historian. . . . (Records do not reveal the names of historians who may have served, and annual minutes do not contain their reports except that a table appeared each year with names of the moderator, clerk, treasurer, and preacher of the annual sermon.)

Number 6. Standing committees of three shall be appointed at each annual meeting of the association to report at the next annual meeting on: Christian Education, Orphanage, Foreign Missions, Home Missions, Sunday Schools, Training Unions, Denominational Literature, Social and Public Welfare, Hospitals, Relief and Annuity Board, Baptist Brotherhood, Woman's Missionary Union, and Obituaries.

In addition, ten bylaws were accepted. Number two stated, "'Mell's Manual of Parliamentary Practice' shall be the rules of order followed in this association."

Unique aspects of GCBA at its beginning were the enormous territory it encompassed and the distances early messengers were willing to travel to attend its meetings. Until Little Colorado Association was constituted, the eastern border was the New Mexico state line. On the west GCBA extended to southern Nevada and California, and from Wickenburg on the south to Artesia, Colorado, on the north. Burton Baptist and Winslow FBC still affiliated with the ABC, although Uncle Billy Barclay and other early field workers and missionaries often supplied for those churches as well as for Holbrook Baptist after it organized in 1947.

**Prescott Partnership Conference**

On May 26–30, 1947, a historic group of 125 denominational leaders, missionaries, and pastors met in GCBA at the Prescott assembly for a joint conference on the partnership concept of missions whereby state conventions could extend an arm to churches in neighboring states who requested affiliation. Pastors, missionaries, and state workers stood to their feet in a pledge of support to Willis J. Ray, the BGCA, and the HMB. The gathering was the forerunner of an assembly in the West like Ridgecrest.

Incidents which led to the conference included: approval by the Arizona state board on December 11, 1945, to sponsor work in other states; affiliation of Roosevelt, Utah, Baptist Church with BGCA on April 27, 1946; affiliation of Artesia (Dinosaur) Colorado, FBC with BGCA on May 29, 1946; affiliation of Sweet Home, Oregon, FBC with the California Convention; disbanding of Interstate Baptist Mission to form Northwest Baptist Association with two Washington and five Oregon churches; concern for Alaska Southern Baptist work; an invitation from J. B. Lawrence, HMB director, to Alaska to attend the 1947 SBC in St. Louis; election of H. A. Zimmerman, former BGCA director, to serve as missionary in Washington and Oregon; affiliation of Hawthorne, Nevada, FSBC with California; and establishment of Southern Baptist churches in southern Colorado by the New Mexico Convention. HMB involvement in partnership missions was hammered out in this landmark meeting in the GCBA.

The first associational meeting of BGCA churches outside the state occurred when GCBA convened a workers' conference at the Roosevelt Baptist Church on July 22, 1947, with five of the six churches in the association represented. Before the second annual meeting of GCBA, Milton and Marie Cunningham had resigned as field workers and moved to California. Until the middle of 1948, no missionary was assigned to serve GCBA. At various times, Willis J. Ray assigned different state field workers to assist in strengthening the churches and expanding the work.

Among those who worked the area was Allen B. Barnes, a graduate of New Orleans Baptist Theological Seminary (NOBTS) and pastor of the New Orleans Metaire Baptist Church for eight years, who arrived in Phoenix in 1943 looking for a climate which would improve his wife Laura's health. Barnes served as associate pastor to Vaughan Rock until he was employed as a general missionary for Gila Valley Association. During the next two years, he organized nine churches, traveled two hundred thousand miles, led hundreds to Christ, and pioneered Southern Baptist work in Utah, in addition to his Gila Valley duties.

### 1947 GCBA Annual Meeting at Prescott FSBC

The historic atmosphere of Prescott has long been a drawing card for visitors who like to review old times at the Sharlot Hall Museum Complex or see the building that housed Arizona's territorial government before statehood. The program for the second annual meeting at Prescott FSBC on October 1–2, 1947, centered on the theme, "Christ Our

Foundation." In addition to Willis J. Ray, state leaders who took part on the program included: S. S. Bussell, leader of the SS Department; Paul Davis from the TU and Brotherhood Departments; Barry Garrett, editor of the *Baptist Beacon*; Margaret Maxwell, WMU Department; Ruth Ely, manager of the book store; and T. T. Reynolds and H. R. Spraker, field-workers. Bussell closed the program with a sermon on "Building on the Foundation." After this session, he died of a heart attack on his way back to Phoenix.

The first afternoon session began with the WMU meeting in the audi-torium and the men in a SS room. At the joint meeting, reports were given on WMU by Mrs. Short from Arkansas; state missions and the CP by Dr. Ray; and foreign missions by Margaret Maxwell. After appointing com-mittees, messengers gave a $10.50 offering for printing the minutes, with those for 1946 to be included with 1947.

With the SS, TU, WMU, and Brotherhood reports came full slates of associational departmental officers to serve during 1947–1948. The TU officers included: M. B. Stump, Wickenburg, director; Boyd Dismukes, Flagstaff, assistant director; Mrs. Lester Probst, Prescott, secretary; Mrs. Charles Nichols, Kingman, adult leader; Lester Probst, Prescott, young people leader; Mrs. W. H. Henry, Wickenburg, intermediate leader; Mrs. W. A. Hodges, Prescott, junior leader; Lena Maddox, Kingman, story hour leader; and A. K. Peveto, Flagstaff, pastor advisor.

The SS officers were: J. J. Johnston, Kingman, superintendent; H. K. Stringer, Prescott, enlistment; T. T. Reynolds, Artesia, VBS; Charles Ray, Roosevelt, training; T. T. Reynolds, Artesia, evangelism; Mrs. W. A. Hodges, Prescott, secretary; Mrs. Ray Temple, Prescott, cradle roll; Mrs. R. C. Johnston, Roosevelt, nursery; Mozelle English, Wickenburg, begin-ners; Mrs. Ernest Carleton, Prescott, primary; Mrs. Bessie Morse, Artesia, juniors; Mrs. A. K. Peveto, Flagstaff, intermediates; John Lynch, Wickenburg, adults; Harold Dillman, Roosevelt, extension; and I. P. Simmons, Artesia, group superintendent.

WMU enlisted Mrs. T. T. Reynolds, Artesia, president; Mrs. W. A. Hodges, Prescott, secretary; Mrs. J. J. Johnston, Kingman, young people; and Mrs. Lester Probst, Prescott, pianist. Brotherhood officers were C. B. Myers, Prescott, president, and Norman Beckman, Prescott, secretary-treasurer. In addition to the workers' conference at Roosevelt, conferences met at Wickenburg and Kingman for leadership training and fellowship.

Resolutions passed included appreciation to the host church; a request for every church to write its history and send it to the clerk; the goal for SS and TU study courses in every church; and efforts to have at least three standard Sunday Schools in the association. The 1948 annual meeting was set for October 6–7, at Flagstaff FSBC, with John J. Johnston of Kingman to bring the annual sermon.

The first church membership table for GCBA appeared in the 1947 minutes and revealed that Artesia FBC had 9 baptisms and 22 by letter for a total of 53 members. Flagstaff FSBC received 13 by letter and had 55 members. Kingman FBC had 8 baptisms and 36 by letter for a total of 90 members. Prescott FSBC baptized 31 and received 53 by letter for a total of 138 members. Roosevelt Baptist had 19 baptisms and 20 by letter for a total of 37 members (having lost several by letter). Wickenburg FBC had 12 by baptism and 21 by letter for a total of 87 members. All churches reported revival meetings, with Flagstaff and Roosevelt having 3 during the year. Every church had at least one active WMU organization and had given generously to the CP.

### Vernal, Utah, FBC

Vernal FBC, the second Southern Baptist church in Utah, had constituted on November 22, 1946, and petitioned for membership in GCBA at its second annual meeting. Although no messengers from Vernal attended in 1947, and the request was deferred, the state convention annual for that year lists Vernal as a GCBA church, with A. C. McAlister as pastor. The church reported eleven baptisms and a membership of fifty-five.

During 1947 several pastors moved, a pattern that prevailed during the next few years. J. L. Alexander went from Flagstaff FSBC to Artesia, with A. K. Peveto coming to Flagstaff. After R. E. Cure resigned at Roosevelt, Charles Ray had been called. W. E. Bush had gone from Wickenburg, with M. B. Stump succeeding him. John J. Johnston had come to Kingman. The only pastor still in place from 1946 was Lester Probst at Prescott FSBC.

The first encampment of GCBA outside the state was the Uintah Baptist assembly which met at Big Park in Uintah Canyon, Utah, July 13–17, 1948. Fred McCaulley, HMB western field-worker from Fresno, California, led morning worship, and Solomon F. Dowis, HMB cooperative missions secretary from Atlanta, led evening services. Californians George J. Burnett and Bonnie and Royal Beaird also assisted in providing leadership for this first Southern Baptist camp in Utah.

### Provo, Utah, FBC

In the spring of 1948, a group of workers from Roosevelt drove to Provo, Utah, at different times to take a religious census of the city. When an ad was placed in the Provo newspaper asking for persons who might be interested in forming a Southern Baptist church, three people responded and became a nucleus around which the church was formed. That summer HMB field-worker Allen Barnes and two student summer missionaries held a VBS and revival, at the end of which the church organized with eighteen charter members. Provo FBC became the third Utah church to unite with GCBA.

Fred M. and Leona DeBerry from Martha, Oklahoma, also served as Arizona general missionaries from 1948 to 1950 with their primary assignment being Central Association. During the two years they helped lay foundations for churches in Utah before leaving the state to serve associations in California. They are best remembered for their leadership at WMU youth camps, the state assembly at Prescott, and BSU retreats.

The second annual GCBA camp in Utah met July 11–19, 1949, at Little Park in Uintah Canyon. Fred DeBerry together with Courts Redford, Fred McCaulley, and Wiley Henton of the HMB staff were speakers for the assembly. Reports indicate that 71 registered; 19 made professions of faith; 45 rededicated their lives; 3 surrendered for special service; and 48 qualified for awards. Attendance doubled that of the previous year. Participating churches included Artesia FBC, Roosevelt Baptist, Vernal FBC, and Provo FBC. Heavy rains during the first three days threatened early closure but let up after prayers were offered.

The first missionary assigned to GCBA was Vester E. Wolber, who came with his wife Carolyn in March 1948. Originally from Arkansas, Wolber had pastored in California and knew the challenges of new areas. The Mohave and Little Colorado Associations were later formed in the areas he worked. After only two months, he accepted the position of Texas Tech Chair of Bible and moved to Abilene, Texas.

### Missionary Troy Brooks

Troy E. Brooks was born March 19, 1892, at Bangs, Texas, and was saved at age eight and baptized in a pond by Bangs Baptist Church. He was ordained in 1923 after graduating from Muleshoe High School, Howard Payne College, and NOBTS.

He married Katherine Stapp and served as pastor of twelve churches and many missions, associational missionary, and United States (U.S.) army chaplain. He served in the states before being stationed on Okinawa, on mid-Pacific islands, and in Japan in 1943–1946. He received a citation of merit for his work with the armed forces. Troy and Katherine planned to go to Brazil as SBC foreign missionaries, but health problems following the birth of their child and failure of the SBC $75 Million Campaign prevented that dream's fulfillment.

After completing two years of graduate work at the University of Arkansas, the Brooks became interested in pioneer mission work in the West. After correspondence with Fred McCaulley, HMB western representative, and Willis J. Ray, they were invited to meet with Ray and other Arizona leaders at the SBC meeting in Memphis in May 1948. Becoming increasingly interested, they visited Arizona to view the field. When they met with the state executive committee in June, they were offered the position of general field-worker, or area missionary, for GCBA with their home to be located in Prescott. After a tour of Prescott, Ash Fork, Seligman, Kingman, Bullhead City, and Flagstaff, they decided to accept the position and rented an apartment in Prescott.

Katherine Brooks wrote to Clarice Maben about Troy's response upon gazing at the vast territory his work would encompass. He prayed, "Lord, give us these mountains, giants and all." God answered that prayer many times over during the next decade as he started missions and assisted churches across northern Arizona, southern Nevada, and Utah.

They attended their son's wedding in El Paso, resigned their church in Arkansas, bought a sixteen-foot trailer house and started out heavily loaded. They reached Flagstaff on July 1, 1948, where they spent the night with the Pevetos, and arrived in Prescott ready to go to work the next day. Their first workers' conference was at Roosevelt, Utah, over six hundred miles from Prescott.

**Bullhead City FBC**

The Bullhead City FBC was the first church the Brooks assisted in organizing in Arizona. It had been a mission of Kingman FBC and was pastored by Troy Young, an engineer who was working on the construction of Davis Dam on the Colorado River. The church constituted in the summer of 1948.

**Chloride FBC**

The Chloride FBC had been loosely affiliated with the ABC until 1948 when the Kingman FBC began conducting services for them. Edwin White, Earl Thompson, Charles Nichols, and others had led these at various times. In the fall of 1948 the Chloride congregation inaugurated a movement to affiliate with Southern Baptists. Under the leadership of Kingman FBC pastor John J. Johnston, and assisted by Willis J. Ray, they transferred title of the building to the BGCA after some outstanding debts were paid. This small church played a vital part in the development of Southern Baptist work in the western part of GCBA.

## Williams FBC

Williams FBC was chartered on November 23, 1941, with Mary Murray of the ABC the key leader in its formation. Because many of their members were Southern Baptists who began to look to SBC churches for fellowship and assistance, missionary Troy Brooks was invited to preach for them several times in the fall of 1948. When their pastor, Walter Pratt, asked for one of our student summer missionaries to assist them in a VBS, Brooks arranged for Doris Ellis to help them in a school to begin June 13, 1949.

The church voted to enter into a dual fellowship, continuing their ties with the ABC, but also asking for fellowship in GCBA, dividing their missions gifts equally between two conventions (ABC and SBC). They operated on this basis for a time, but when trouble arose, those who opposed the dual relationship withdrew and organized the Calvary Baptist Church to be affiliated wholly with ABC. Williams FBC then became solely Southern Baptist.

## 1948 GCBA Annual Meeting at Kingman FBC

At the third GCBA annual meeting at Kingman FBC on October 6–7, 1948, Troy Brooks reported that since coming as missionary on July 1, he had traveled 6,150 miles, visited 16 churches, held a revival meeting, taught 2 study courses, and preached 41 sermons. At the meeting petitionary letters were received from the Bullhead City FBC, Provo FBC, and Williams FBC. The churches were accepted into the association and their messengers seated. Also seated as a messenger by special vote, Edwin White of Oatman led one of the song services, brought a devotional, and chaired the obituary committee.

For many years the state language work was under the HMB direct missions program and reported directly to the board, instead of becoming an integral part of the associational work. Although their churches were not included in GCBA reports, the Indian and Spanish work was of great interest and presented a continuing challenge to leaders in the association. Missionary H. E. Baer of the Flagstaff Baptist Indian Center attended the 1948 annual meeting.

Among the resolutions passed at the 1948 annual meeting were an expression of thanks to the *Mohave County Miner* for the publicity given

*Troy E. Brooks, a former army chaplain, served GCBA as missionary from 1948 until an auto accident in 1958.*

*Williams FBC organized on November 23, 1941, affiliated with GCBA in 1948, and renovated their building in 1995.*

*Kingman FBC helped initiate three new associations in Arizona: GCBA, Mohave, and River Valley. During the 1950s, Kingman's seventy-five hundred people worked in lumber, gold mining, tourism, and a military base which brought in Southern Baptists.*

*Vernal, UT, FBC organized on November 22, 1946, after a tent revival. Heavy snow did not stop sixteen charter members.*

*After VBS and revival, Prescott Miller Valley Baptist Church organized with a student pastor on January 15, 1950.*

*Ash Fork mission started after VBS in a Nazarene building in July 1949. Ash Fork FSBC organized June 1, 1952.*

*Prescott FSBC pastor D. C. Martin led several GCBA committees in 1950. He also served as GCC Bible professor.*

*BGCA missionaries at Glorieta: GCBA pioneers pictured above include Gracie Marks, Charles Ray, Bob Jenkins, Ophelia and M. V. Mears, Harold Dillman, M. K. and Dora Wilder. BGCA staff: Dawson, Childress, McKay, Hunke, and F. Sutton.*

*Mt. Elden Baptist Church organized July 22, 1956, with Calvin Sandlin as pastor. Name changes: Calvary and Greenlaw.*

*GCBA leaders pictured: Opal Dillman (second woman from left), W. B. Minor (white shirt), and Ira I. Marks (dark suit).*

to the meeting; deep appreciation for those who entertained messengers in their homes; thanks to the state workers for their presence, messages, and contributions to the program; thanks to Walter Bishop of Las Vegas, Nevada, for his attendance and heart-stirring sermon; and goals of conducting a school of missions in each church and promoting at least two regional youth camps in the association in 1949.

### Ash Fork Mission

As Troy Brooks drove through Ash Fork on his way to engagements, he was aware that it had no Southern Baptist work. After visiting some families, he located the Methodist Community Church SS superintendent and suggested that volunteers would conduct a VBS in Ash Fork in July 1949 if the Methodists would permit them to use their building. Although the superintendent was enthusiastic about the possibility, he was unable to get permission for use of the facility and told Brooks to try to secure the little Nazarene building. The Nazarenes had a small SS of a few children and three teachers, one a Nazarene, another a Methodist, and the third a Christ of Christ member.

With the teachers happy to cooperate, the date of July 13 was set to begin the VBS. On Sunday morning the missionary left summer workers Doris Ellis and Jerri Eli off in Ash Fork and suggested that one attend the Nazarene SS and the other go to the Methodist SS and make necessary announcements and arrangements for the children to meet that afternoon for the preparation session. Brooks went on to Seligman to preach for the community church there. When he returned to Ash Fork, the workers met him at the car and informed him they could not have the VBS as planned, and that he was to meet with the official board of the Methodist church at 2:30 P.M.

After eating the lunch they had brought, Brooks bought a Sunday newspaper and settled back to read it with no plans to attend the meeting, much to the dismay of the summer workers who had promised he would be there. Instead, he went to the home of the superintendent, who was just leaving for the meeting, and informed him that he would not be coming. Brooks asked him to announce that the VBS would begin at 8:30 the next morning as planned. The Methodist board decided to begin a VBS in their own church the next day. They gave it up after a few days, and most of the children came over to the Nazarene church for the Southern Baptist school, which was a good one.

As a result, Brooks was invited to maintain a preaching service and supervise the SS in the Nazarene church. Later that summer, when he was asked to assume all responsibility for the work, Dr. Ray negotiated with Dr. Mann, head of Nazarene work in Arizona, for the transfer of all their property in Ash Fork to Southern Baptists. After GCC began in Prescott in September, different ministerial students conducted regular services, resulting in a steady growth of the mission. Brooks reported that more than twenty people were baptized during the first year of work in Ash Fork, including the Nazarene SS teacher and three of her daughters and the Methodist SS teacher. The Williams FBC began sponsoring the mission from its beginning in July 1949.

**Prescott Miller Valley Baptist Church**
Prescott FSBC began the Miller Valley mission in the summer of 1949. After Allen Barnes and other volunteers conducted a successful VBS in a tent near the present site of Miller Valley Baptist Church, a SS and later a preaching service resulted. GCC ministerial student H. K. Stringer was called as pastor. The congregation met in a large residence until they began their building program. The church constituted on January 15, 1950.

Women of the Miller Valley church formed a club for fellowship which was dubbed the "Recreation Club," and had some riproaring good times together before the club was disbanded because "everybody had to go to work," according to Minnie Ainsworth, one of the original members. "Some of these women dated back to the early days of Prescott," Mary Stephenson remembered. "They met once a month and contributed to many early day charitable needs."

**Parker FBC**
Soon after the opening of GCC, the Prescott Miller Valley Church made a series of surveys in Parker, Arizona, followed by a visitation program. In January 1950, Ewell Allison, a ministerial student at the college, began services in Parker homes because no suitable building was available. The first SS classes started on February 19, 1950, with twenty-five present. When summer missionary Eva Burnett arrived to conduct a VBS that year, she gathered a group of children who helped her clear weeds under a large cottonwood tree near the Colorado River. With women of the community helping, she taught ninety-one children under the tree. The Parker FBC organized in September 1950 with thirty charter members and Fred Barnes serving as pastor.

Sixty people from Southern Baptist churches in Roosevelt, Vernal, and Provo, Utah, met at the Roosevelt Baptist Church for fellowship during simultaneous revivals. Speakers included Leroy Smith of GCBA and

H. A. Zimmerman of Richland, Washington. After the host church provided lunch in the church basement, Provo FBC baptized three new
members in the baptistry. This meeting looked forward to the Utah
churches having their own association.

### 1949 GCBA Annual Meeting at Provo, Utah

The 1949 GCBA annual meeting convened with the Provo FBC on
October 4–5 with fifty persons present for the first session in the Odd
Fellows Lodge hall. The challenging message brought by Willis J. Ray
about GCC was enthusiastically received. After Ray's evening message
about the CP and state missions, two persons made public professions of
faith, and five rededicated their lives. Messengers were stirred again
when Charles Ray presented the report on the youth camp at Little Park
in Uintah Canyon. Katherine Brooks gave a report on GCBA's youth
camp at Prescott.

### Yarnell FBC

Southern Baptist work in Yarnell began in November 1949 under the
leadership of Glen Murphy, a GCC ministerial student. First services
were held in the community school house. Missionary Troy Brooks
remembered one Sunday after 11:00 P.M. when Glen knocked on his door
and said, "I just had to wake you up and tell you that we won John Reed
to the Lord today." Brooks responded that he could be awakened anytime
day or night to hear about that kind of experience.

### Little Colorado Baptist Association Organized

Four churches in northeastern Arizona organized the Little Colorado
association on March 9, 1950, at Holbrook. Although these churches
never actively affiliated with GCBA, during the early years their members met with GCBA in workers' conferences and annual meetings, and
GCBA pastors and missionaries ministered to their area. S. S. Bussell
envisioned the rapid expansion of the associational territory and growth
of churches when he preached his last sermon just a few hours before his
death. The early pastors who accepted his challenge helped build a
program of missions which extended into five states and up to the
Canadian border in just three years.

### 1950 GCBA Annual Meeting at Flagstaff FSBC

When GCBA met at Flagstaff FSBC on October 3–4, 1950, the first
order of business was a petition from the churches of Utah and Colorado

for letters in order to organize a new association in Utah. Letters were granted to Provo FBC, Roosevelt FBC, Vernal FBC, and Artesia FBC. After plans for organization were drafted at this fifth GCBA annual meeting, Utah Baptist Association organized at Roosevelt Baptist Church on November 18, 1950. The Saturday meeting attracted seventy-five Southern Baptists from five churches, with Provo messengers unable to attend because snow made roads impassable. Charles Ray, Roosevelt pastor, was elected moderator. The 4 churches had 27 baptisms in 1950 and a total membership of 265.

**Missionary Ira Marks**

Arizona field-worker for Utah, Ira Marks, had helped constitute Carbon Baptist Church of Dragerton, Utah, in August 1950 and a mission in Salt Lake City which started in his home and organized as Rose Park Baptist Church (FSBC) on November 12, 1950. These churches awaited the organization of Utah Baptist Association instead of coming into GCBA. Marks had begun working other fields like Denver, where Temple Baptist would be organized in a few months, and Casper, where the first Southern Baptist church in Wyoming would come into being on July 15, 1951. Likewise, on March 26, 1951, Marks led in organizing the Idaho Falls Calvary Baptist Church, the first Southern Baptist church in Idaho to join the BGCA. These churches affiliated with Utah association until their own states developed associations.

Ira Marks gave the 1950 associational missions report which included an account of his service in Louisiana. His work in the Atchafalaya area attracted nationwide attention when he bought a ferry on which he built the "Little Brown Church" to float to the isolated French-speaking villages along the Atchafalaya River. He built and staffed a hospital and schools at Hog Island, Grand River Flats, Bayou Boutte, Little Pass, and Myette Point, and employed twenty-four missionaries to work with him.

When he left Louisiana to be employed by the BGCA for the Utah position, Marks gave the Louisiana state convention title to one hundred thousand dollars worth of property and equipment. He and his wife Gracie led in starting sixty-two churches, including the first work in Salt Lake City, Denver, Wyoming, eastern Nevada, and eastern Idaho.

Harold Baer impressed the GCBA messengers with his HMB report when he spoke of the many Indian tribes in the state with no SBC witness in spite of the fact that they had asked for the gospel. Following his report, Baer displayed thumb prints (signatures) of a number of Navajos at Window Rock asking Southern Baptists to come into their reservation.

A song service led by Baer and a group from Baptist Indian Center featured songs by Native Americans in their own language. When Helen Sebery sang "I Will Never Cease to Love Him" in Navajo later in the program, the entire congregation was greatly moved.

After Roland Beck presented the GCC report, missionary Troy Brooks introduced GCC student mission pastors Ewell McKinnie from Chino Valley, Norman Kelly from Santan, and Gene Hamlin from Jerome (sponsored by the Post, Texas, FBC). More than one hundred people attended sessions of the fifth annual meeting.

Resolutions in 1950 included: to have a VBS, and at least one mission VBS, in every church; to promote the total stewardship program in every church; to have an active Brotherhood in every church; to contribute vigorous support to youth camps and assemblies; and to pledge full support to GCC and the new president Leroy Smith. The 1950 annual minutes list twenty-five pastors and preachers in GCBA, in addition to thirty-two ministerial students attending GCC. The Prescott FSBC reported 11 baptisms and 137 new members coming by letter, and Miller Valley reported 22 baptisms and 102 by letter.

When the GCBA executive board met on December 12, 1950, at Ash Fork, they elected the following steering committee for the proposed simultaneous crusades in 1951: chairman, D. C. Martin; director, H. K. Stringer; organizer, Troy Brooks; finance, C. B. Myers; publicity and radio, John J. Johnston; fellowship, D. C. Martin; rallies, Gene Hamlin. Quarterly associational meeting dates were set, and the petition of the Chloride FBC was accepted subject to approval at the next annual meeting.

Toward the middle of 1951, the *Beacon* published an article by Troy Brooks telling of the missions activities in which he and Katherine were involved. The Parker FBC had been organized as had a church at Boulder City, Nevada. Kingman FBC was sponsoring missions at Yucca, Hackberry, Oatman, and Hualapai. A SS had begun at Wikieup. Wickenburg FBC was sponsoring a mission at Yarnell. Prescott Miller Valley sponsored one at Salome, and Prescott FSBC had missions at Mayer and Chino Valley. Flagstaff FSBC held preaching services at Happy Jack and planned to renew services at Fredonia. Williams FBC sponsored Ash Fork, and a church at Post, Texas, agreed to sponsor the Jerome mission after sending their pastor, T. M. Gillham, and his wife, Lillie, to hold a revival in Jerome to initiate the work. The Gillhams later returned to Arizona. Thirteen VBSs were held that summer, including those at Parks, Seligman, Peach Springs, Wikieup, Whitney, and Vista Salona.

## 1951 GCBA Annual Meeting at Prescott Miller Valley: Mohave Baptist Association Organized

With the sixth annual meeting of GCBA on October 2–3, 1951, came the following letter about forming a new association: "To the GCBA: Whereas, the churches of Mohave Zone have expressed their desire in their zone meeting to form a new association in their section because of the long distances and other difficulties in cooperating with GCBA as they would like to; and Whereas, so few of their messengers are able to attend the meetings of the association; and Whereas, a new association formed by these said churches will aid in overcoming these difficulties; Be it resolved the GCBA grant letters of dismissal to these churches, to be effective upon the action of the individual churches. Signed, John J. Johnston, James McFatridge, Troy E. Brooks."

In addition to the Kingman FBC, Bullhead City FBC, and Chloride FBC, a new church that Troy Brooks had helped to start at Boulder City, Nevada, helped organize the new association, with another new church at Needles, California, joining soon thereafter. An African-American church in Las Vegas, Nevada, that was never officially a part of GCBA, had also joined its activities for fellowship. Named the Mohave Baptist Association, the new organization met at Kingman FBC on October 28, 1951, to elect their first officers and appoint a committee to write their constitution. Lake Mead Association took the Nevada churches when it was organized in 1955, leaving Mohave with two churches which helped constitute River Valley Association in 1964. For years the same missionary served GCBA, Mohave, and Little Colorado Associations.

D. C. Martin, Bible professor at GCC and chair of GCBA committee on program and calendar of activities, made a lengthy report at the Miller Valley meeting. Recommendations included an all-day quarterly meeting on the Thursday following the first Sunday of each quarter with sessions starting at 10:00 A.M. The WMU and executive boards would meet at 1:00 P.M., followed by a business meeting and inspirational message. Martin announced plans for the 1952 simultaneous revivals, youth camps, and simultaneous schools of missions with four missionaries to visit one night in each church.

### Davis Carney Martin

Born February 6, 1923, at Elizabeth City, North Carolina, D. C. Martin was pastor of Prescott FSBC when GCC began in 1949. Many of the early faculty and students joined his church. Martin devoted almost forty years of his life to the college and taught Bible and Christian doctrine to thousands of students. He died December 18, 1995.

While pastoring the Rustin, Louisiana, Temple Baptist Church, Martin led M. K. Wilder to accept God's call to preach. When Boulder City, Nevada, called Wilder as pastor, the Rustin church gave the Wilders a car. When they came to Page to start FSBC, Temple provided the Wilders a trailer to live in.

Chris Potts wrote in the *Baptist Beacon* about D. C. Martin: "He became a legend. Students found in him a man of remarkable, studied dignity, and a most unpredictable giddiness. A man cagey and candid, nutty and knowing; a man able to chase a storied rabbit 'til the hounds collapse, a-heaving,' and then—just when you think the point has eluded him forever—pause and pierce a ripe illusion with one pithy stiletto of a sentence. . . . They knew he was the professor who can dance a jig in chapel, and look them dead straight in the eye an hour later, outstretched thumb converging on closed fist, and say: 'You must believe in Jesus. Believing on him is not enough.'"

### Estrella Baptist Association Organized

At the annual meeting of the Central association at Phoenix Calvary Baptist Church on October 15–16, 1951, eight churches west of Phoenix organized Estrella Baptist Association. Two of those were Wickenburg FBC and Parker FBC from the GCBA. Estrella organized with thirty-one messengers on October 16. The only churches remaining in GCBA were Flagstaff FSBC, James R. McFatridge, pastor; Prescott FSBC, D. C. Martin, pastor; Prescott Miller Valley, Irl W. Atwood, pastor; and Williams FBC, Joseph B. Greer, pastor.

# PRAISEWORTHY DEEDS

## GOD WORKING IN GCBA THROUGH 1958

The psalmist told us to remember the deeds of past leaders and to imitate their faith. Good leaders have preached Christ and drawn people to him, not to themselves. They have shown Christ in their walk and work, demonstrated a limitless loyalty to him, and left us an example and inspiration. Ancient orators advised men to keep turning over in their minds illustrious deeds and virtuous persons of old. Men empowered by God have built up the churches in the past and given him all praise for deeds that were done. He is still as powerful as ever to conquer evil and love sinners. He is ever seeking those who will bring men to him and him to men.

### Willard and Katheryn Hardcastle

When bleeding ulcers caused Willard Hardcastle to collapse during a revival in 1953 while he was pastor of Flagstaff FSBC, he and Katheryn moved to Sedona, expecting him to die. In 1996 they will celebrate their seventy-second wedding anniversary.

While working in a mission sponsored by Pampa, Texas, FBC during the depression, Willard felt God's call to preach. He and Katheryn sold their home and business and moved to Plainview to attend Wayland Baptist College. On weekends they served on a volunteer missions team working with small churches. He led music, sang solos, and preached; she played the piano and taught Bible studies.

While at Baylor University in Waco, Texas, Willard pastored several half-time churches. Challenged by the spiritual needs of the West, he accepted churches along the Mexican border, then at Lovington, New Mexico, FBC, where the building was just a tar-paper covered basement. Wherever he served, he left behind new auditoriums, educational buildings, or parsonages. Always active in associational and state work, Willard also led singing, with Katheryn as accompanist, for revivals with George W. Truett, J. B. Tidwell, and other renowned preachers.

After helping Willis J. Ray in revivals, Willard became interested in Arizona and followed the Lord's leading to pastor Flagstaff FSBC in January 1952, where he served until May 1953. The Zell Flowers opened their home to provide room and board for the Hardcastles until their furniture arrived, and they could move into the partially finished parsonage next door to the church. They remember that snowdrifts got so high that winter that they could step over the clothesline in the backyard.

They spent most of their time looking for and visiting prospects. As SS attendance doubled and they could no longer provide space in the auditorium with divider curtains, they had to finish out the full basement which was being used for storage. Volunteer work by the members resulted in new classrooms and a fellowship area. Katheryn led the women of the church into WMU mission action projects which helped meet the needs of the Indians at the Baptist Indian Center where blankets, bedding, and personal hygiene kits were in demand.

During the summer of 1952, the church held VBSs at Fredonia and Happy Jack. Three Mormon mothers helped in the first school, and other women provided refreshments for the sixty-five children enrolled. When Katheryn decided that her six year olds would wear graduation hats, they spent much time designing mortar boards out of poster paper and fitting them snugly to each child. On commencement night, however, most of the little boys had gotten new haircuts, and instead of the bushy, curly hair they had been measured for, they had closely cropped hair which caused the mortar boards to move about loosely on their heads. Katheryn remembers that they managed to keep them on until the end of the program, but when they bowed their heads for prayer, the loose crowns thumped to the floor one at a time. At the Happy Jack logging camp, they used a primitive storage building for the school and reached about fifty children. The added space at FSBC enabled them to provide for a large number of children from the community in addition to those already attending church.

In the spring of 1953 Willard began experiencing health problems, which were diagnosed as bleeding ulcers. Although Katheryn continued her daily visitation to prospects and members, the doctor told Willard that he could no longer handle the stress of pastoring and urged him to do physical labor to work off tension. They had bought a lot in Sedona, thinking it would be a beautiful place to retire someday, and then decided to move into the partly finished cottage on the property. Katheryn began selling cosmetics to help financially, but Willard insisted on returning to FSBC to lead music for a revival which had already been scheduled. That was the time when he collapsed. Instead of going to the hospital, he came home to the Sedona cottage.

Willard lived on goat's milk and stayed in bed for many weeks because that was the accepted remedy for ulcers in those days. He and Katheryn managed a Hi-Jolly fruit stand to make a living during the long days of his recovery. When he got stronger, he built a home and rooms to rent, which became the Vue Motel on Highway 89, the main street in town.

Katheryn wrote, "When we moved to Sedona in 1953, it was indeed a very small community, so small that when the community had a social gathering, everyone was invited with invitations placed in every box in the local post office. People stood in line to use the only telephone in town. It had only three churches, the Wayside Church, Assembly of God, and First Christian, which was meeting in the pastor's home."

Katheryn did volunteer work at the Sedona library when it comprised one wall in the chamber of commerce building. She had started libraries in all churches where they served and did the same for the Sedona church. Becoming interested in antiques, she opened a shop in the office of their motel—the first antique shop in Sedona. Willard built a retirement home on Redwing Lane, where they lived for the next forty years until they moved into the Baptist retirement community at Sun City.

When Sedona FBC completed its fellowship building in 1987, they named it Hardcastle Hall in appreciation of the couple's long years of faithful service. Their daughter Fayly Cothern and her husband Gaylon are well known to Arizona Southern Baptists for their work with missions, conferences, historical preservation activities, and writing a *Baptist Beacon* column for many years. During the 1950s, the Cotherns drove to Sedona from Phoenix every weekend to help in the FBC ministries. Gaylon served as SS superintendent and TU director, and Fayly taught intermediates in SS and TU.

After a trip to the Holy Land in 1980, Katheryn painted *The Shepherd's Field*, which was appraised at twenty-five hundred dollars before framing. She donated the original to GCC. A framed print hangs in the vestibule of Sedona FBC. Numbered, autographed, and framed prints go

to people who make a gift of five hundred dollars or more to the
Hardcastle Family Scholarship at the school. The fund assists students
training for church-related ministries. To celebrate their sixty-fourth
anniversary on May 1, 1988, the Hardcastles were honored guests at the
annual GCBA senior adult meeting at Sedona FBC. Willard brought
special music. Their special cake and decorations highlighted the fellowship hour.

### Sedona FBC

When population growth accelerated in Verde Valley, Troy and
Katherine Brooks decided it would be the best place for the GCBA missionary to live, and the convention bought them a home in Clarkdale. As
soon as the Brooks' furniture was set in place, they began efforts to get a
church started in the Sedona area. The nearest church was twenty-eight
miles up the twisting, dirt road which ascended three thousand feet along
Oak Creek Canyon.

After visiting with Willard and Katheryn Hardcastle, Brooks rented
the Sally Black Red Rock Building for fifty dollars a month. Many hours
of hard work were required to make the building usable. It had been a
cafe and gift shop in Grasshopper Flat, located two miles west of Sedona,
and later became the property of St. John Vianny Church. The Brooks and
Hardcastles conducted the first service there on April 3, 1955, with
Willard leading singing, Katheryn at the portable pump organ, Katherine
teaching the Bible study, and Troy bringing the message. Eighteen people
came to the next service. On May 15, 1955, James Gore, a student at GCC,
was invited to preach and was called as pastor.

On May 17, 1955, an organizational meeting for the Sedona mission
was held at the James H. Hickey home. Flagstaff FSBC sponsored the
work. Those attending, in addition to the Brooks, Hickeys, and
Hardcastles, included Frank Sutton, the J. A. Teagues, and the Ray A.
Allens. The first contributions to the new work came from friends in
Texas and New Mexico and were designated to purchase hymn books,
chairs, a piano, and other equipment. That month $3.50 was given to start
a building fund, and seventeen dollars went to GCC. After the
Hardcastles opened their home to the mission, their carport and large
breezeway were used for meetings. Beginning June 8, 1955, they conducted their first VBS with twenty-six enrolled.

Sedona's first week of prayer for the Lottie Moon Christmas Offering
(LMCO) was an exciting time for women of the GCBA. Mrs. P. E. Cockrell
of Flagstaff, who had joined the mission, bought an unfurnished house in

Sedona and invited all the women of the association to come together there for the program. The speaker was O. M. Andrews, a nephew of Lottie Moon, who inspired and challenged the packed house as he told the life story of his Aunt Lottie. The Sedona church later had as guest speakers Aiko Tairo from Hawaii in 1956, Josephine Pile from Nashville in 1958, Aletha Fuller, missionary nurse from Joinkrama, West Africa, in 1962, and Ross Hanna, missionary to the Indians at Sells, also in 1962.

When Sunday morning worship attendance began to overflow the Hardcastles' carport, breezeway, and garage, the group purchased two lots at the corner of Apple Lane and Jordan Road from George Jordan. At the November 13, 1955, business meeting, Ray Allen moved that the mission recommend to the Trust and Memorial Fund committee that a frame structure be erected on the lots to be used as a chapel and living quarters for the pastor. At the July 1956 business meeting, the members unanimously accepted a loan from the Trust and Memorial Fund on which they would pay twenty-five dollars a month on the principal, plus the interest. On July 26, 1956, they held groundbreaking services.

Willard Hardcastle remembers a hot afternoon that summer when the men had been working at leveling the lot to erect the building. As he approached the Hardcastles' antique shop after work, he noticed two men sitting on the steps while their wives browsed in the shop. Coming closer, he was surprised to recognize one of the men as W. A. Criswell, pastor of Dallas, Texas, FBC. Willard invited the men to visit the church site. A few days later the Sedona mission received a check for three hundred dollars from Dallas FBC for their building fund.

After the ground was leveled, forms set, and the foundation laid, the mission set a special Saturday workday to frame up the building. Gaylon and Fayly Cothern brought a crew of workers from Phoenix FSBC, which included state Brotherhood president S. F. Hawkins and many Brotherhood members. As part of the crew, S. F. brought his sister, Floy Hawkins, who had just returned from China, where she had served as a missionary for twelve years. She joined a large group of women who not only prepared a chuck wagon dinner but also helped hold large beams while the men nailed them together.

On September 30, 1956, the mission invited Gaylon Cothern, who lived in Phoenix, to serve as educational director, a job he held, spending every weekend in Sedona, until July 1960 when the Cotherns resigned to begin a new mission in Phoenix. During their four years of service, Gaylon organized the educational program and led out in taking a census and visiting prospects. Fayly taught the children and youth groups.

Gaylon often filled the pulpit and spent many hours working on the building. The Cotherns' gifts to the church more than doubled the ten-dollar-per-week salary he was paid.

In November 1956 the Sedona members began a fellowship gathering at the Bob Roberts' home, which was designated the "Sheep Shed." Their many happy times together formed a precious link within the group. Saturday, February 9, 1957, was another special workday at the partially completed building. Classrooms were made ready for use for the first time the following day. The mission bought used opera seats from Phoenix FSBC for the auditorium. M. V. Mears preached a revival, and on March 31, 1957, the first service was held in the new auditorium with twenty-eight attending.

After James Gore resigned as pastor in May 1957, a frustrating time began for the group in their efforts to provide money to secure a pastor. They asked Willard Hardcastle to supply for Sunday morning worship, Gaylon Cothern on Sunday evenings, and Bob Roberts to take Wednesday prayer services. Several men who desired to serve as pastor were unable to find supplementary jobs in the small village of Sedona. In March 1958 the group was honored to have Josephine Pile, an editor of the SS Department in Nashville, as speaker for morning worship.

Not until November 30, 1958, was a pastor called who actually came. In order to serve as pastor, B. A. Dickenson and his family moved their house trailer on the church grounds and had access to the church bath-room facilities. On Sunday afternoon, April 5, 1959, Dickenson moderated as the mission constituted into Sedona FBC. Charter member-ship was extended to December 31, 1959. *Baptist Beacon* editor J. Kelly Simmons preached the organizational sermon; M. V. Mears, pastor of the sponsoring church, prayed the dedicatory prayer; and Jack Maben, area missionary, led the benediction. The new church voted to affiliate with the GCBA and the BGCA. That evening the church voted to purchase a lot on which to build a parsonage.

At the next business meeting, the church elected Willard Hardcastle and Robert Beckendorf as chairmen of the building committee with all men of the church to serve on the committee. Work on the parsonage started the following week with all members involved in the work. When Dickenson resigned in July 1959, the church asked Hardcastle to be interim until a new pastor could be secured.

Bill Hunke, state director of missions, had been bringing all the area missionaries to Sedona for their annual retreat and planning sessions which were held at FBC. He had witnessed the church's struggles to secure a pastor because of limited financial resources and job opportunities. At the 1959 fall SBC Executive Committee meeting in Nashville, Hunke had several conversations with A. C. Miller, director of the SBC Christian Life Commission, about what he planned to do in retirement.

Upon learning that Miller had made no commitments, Hunke began to tell him about the beauty of Sedona and the need of the newly organized church for mature leadership. Miller became very interested and promised to pray about the possibility of coming to Arizona. When Hunke submitted Miller's name to the pulpit committee, the church extended a call, and the Millers moved on the field in January 1960.

In September 1961 the Millers took a leave of absence in order to vacation with their children in Germany. The Roy McCullochs from Nashville served FBC during this time, readily winning the hearts of the members and leading them into a most cooperative work with their pastor. Because their main objective was to win souls, a memorable highlight in the life of the church came when a family of seven were baptized into their fellowship. Under the Millers' leadership, the church became a well-established and fruitful organization.

### 1952 GCBA Annual Meeting at Prescott FSBC

The Ash Fork FBC was constituted on June 1, 1952. At the GCBA 1952 annual meeting on October 14–15, 1952, their petitionary letter was accepted. B. O. Herring, new GCC president, brought the Christian education report. After Bill and Naomi Hunke were married in 1946, they spent their honeymoon at Herring's home in Berkeley, California, where he had recently moved to be president of Golden Gate Baptist Theological Seminary (GGBTS). His son Jack was Bill's best childhood friend, and Bill, Jack, and Fayly Hardcastle Cothern attended junior high school together in Waco, Texas.

Before his evangelistic message, Willis J. Ray gave an exciting report on state evangelism director Leroy Smith's trip to Alaska to help in simultaneous revivals. Just a few months earlier, the Alaska Convention, after a long struggle, had been accepted as an SBC affiliate. Many messengers had trouble visualizing a state twice the size of Texas, one-fifth the size of the U.S., with five thousand glaciers and ice fields, more than all the rest of the inhabited world put together. It has almost thirty-four thousand miles of coastline, more than the rest of the U.S., but in 1952 Southern Baptists had only a few churches and no work among the native people groups. The hearts of Arizonans were touched to pray for the great state, and in years to come, leaders from the state would go to direct the Alaska work, pastor churches, take building crews, and preach revivals.

At the 1952 meeting Juanita Holland, SS and TU field-worker from the state office, brought the SS report and addressed the report. Because the slogan "A Million More in '54" had been adopted across the SBC, her challenge was to win people to Christ by beginning new SSs and enrolling prospects. Juanita had come to Arizona from Littlefield, Texas, FBC. She is Daryl Bennett's mother. (In March 1954, a few days after the birth of Jim Hunke, Juanita came to our church in Vernal, Utah, to promote the "Million More" campaign. With our children Dixie, age five, David, not quite two, and Jim, less than a week old, Juanita had to stay in our small apartment and sleep on a pullout couch in the living room. I'm surprised she ever had any children after spending that week with us.)

Also of interest that year was the report that the committee charged with finding a permanent location for the state assembly hoped to be able to present a site known as Foxborough located in the mountains between Sedona and Flagstaff. Other possible locations were at Granite Dells and Groom Creek, all in GCBA. On May 26, 1954, a permanent site for the Gambrell Memorial Baptist Assembly was recommended to the convention executive board and approved. The 79.1 acres known as Paradise Valley Ranch, located on Aspen Creek about five miles from Prescott, was purchased for $12,500. James E. Godsoe, pastor of Clifton-Morenci FBC, led dedication services on the site on August 19, 1954.

When the twentieth session of the assembly met at the location, renamed Paradise Valley Baptist Ranch, with an all-time high of 304 campers registered in 1955, not enough time had elapsed to permit extensive development. The auditorium, dining room, bath houses, and WMU cottage had been built, however, and promotion materials had stressed the "Pioneer Week" theme. The prospect of roughing it did not discourage people from attending because they were thrilled to at last have their own campgrounds. Everyone who registered was given a KEEP SMILING slogan to wear, which encouraged them to endure hardships without complaint, although they were staying in tents and trailers and sleeping bags.

### 1953 GCBA Annual Meeting at Williams FBC

At the 1953 annual meeting, Troy Brooks recognized new pastors H. M. Robison of Ash Fork and W. R. Thompson of Prescott FSBC. He announced that I. B. and Opal Williams of Tucson were transferring to

Williams to begin the first work among the Mexicans in GCBA. In the FMB report, W. R. Thompson explained the board's four-point program: (1) to lead people to personal faith in Christ; (2) to bring them together in churches for worship and service; (3) to teach and train them in stewardship and cooperative giving; and (4) to aid them in developing their own schools and institutions for training pastors and church leaders.

### Baptist General Convention of Colorado Constituted
In 1954 the seventy-one churches in Colorado, Wyoming, Montana, and North and South Dakota that were affiliated with the Arizona Convention asked for letters of dismissal in order to become part of the new Colorado Convention which was organized at Colorado Springs FSBC on November 21, 1955. The churches from Utah and Colorado that helped initiate GCBA in 1946 had extended their influence beyond almost anyone's dreams.

### 1954 GCBA Annual Meeting at Flagstaff FSBC
When state missions superintendent Frank Sutton brought his report at the 1954 annual meeting, he commended the association on its vision and outreach and also expressed relief that his travel time and miles would be greatly reduced now that he no longer served nine states. GCBA annual letters in 1954 show Ash Fork FBC with 3 baptisms and 6 additions by letter, Donald D. Childers, pastor; Flagstaff FSBC with 30 baptisms and 52 by letter, John C. Wiles, pastor; Prescott FSBC with 7 baptisms and 24 by letter, Lloyd Gentry, pastor; Prescott Miller Valley with 39 baptisms and 16 by letter, Irl Atwood, pastor; and Williams FBC with 12 baptisms and 21 by letter, B. B. Adams, pastor.

### Seligman Mission
In 1955 when three families employed by the Santa Fe Railroad in Seligman asked for a SS for their children, Harold Baer began a work there on February 13. O. R. Moore, pastor at Ash Fork, led his church to extend an arm to carry on this mission work. Their meeting place was an abandoned store building next to the railroad.

### Greenlaw Baptist Church (Mt. Elden, Calvary)
Because Calvin Sandlin had a vision for a Southern Baptist church in east Flagstaff, Mt. Elden began in 1955 with Flagstaff FSBC as sponsor and Sandlin as pastor. When he could no longer carry on the work because of extensive surgery, a member of the mission who was not a

*Page began services in a metal school-house in 1957. They had 105 in SS after just four weeks of services.*

*Page FSBC organized December 19, 1957, with M. K. Wilder as pastor. Members came from thirty-three states.*

*Willard Hardcastle pastored Flagstaff FSBC in 1952–1953. Health problems led to his resignation and move to Sedona. Pictured here (l/r): Bonnie, Willard, Katheryn, and Fayly when Hardcastles celebrated their sixty-fourth wedding anniversary in 1988.*

*Sedona entered a new building during a 1957 revival led by M. V. Mears. Sedona FBC organized on April 5, 1959.*

*Seligman FBC organized in 1961. The mission began in 1951 with three Santa Fe Railroad families.*

*TOP (l/r): Paul and Maxine Jakes, Bill Thornton, Harold Dillman. CENTER: Charles Ray, Major V. Mears, Truman Webb. BOTTOM: Lillie Gillham, Dora and M. K. Wilder, Eugene Mockerman, Margaret and George Hook.*

*I. B. Williams (top left corner), Opal Williams (directly in front of I. B.), the Robert Greenes (directly below the Williams), A. A. Moore (to the right of Mrs. Greene), Ruby Moore (in front of A. A.), and Irvin Dawson (lower right corner).*

Southern Baptist assumed leadership. Problems arose between the mission and FSBC after a closed business meeting held by Mt. Elden to determine whether it would remain with the SBC. The church withstood all attempts to change its affiliation. The congregation met at first in a warehouse with homemade pews and later in the Cecil Everetts' garage.

The mission constituted July 22, 1956, with the following charter members: Ralph and Pat Ayers, Ethel and Dorene Byrd, James and Katharine Cecil, Donal and Dorris Childers, Walter and Roxie Claburn, Willie and Barbara Cole, Jimmy and Joyce Dykes, Aulty and Ruth Dunkin, Charles and Enone Gordon, Melba Holsomback, Britt and Bula Jones, Wesley, Mary, and Nancy Jordan, Ted, Ruby, and Carolyn Slayton, Mammie Polish, Young and Zera Veazey, Betty Wester, and Bobbie Dunlap. SS attendance averaged fifty; the weekly budget was $69.86.

They purchased property on Fourth Street that same year and began construction of a small, wooden building. The group was so excited about getting into their own building that the men came early one Sunday morning to put on the roof in order to hold their first service with just a subfloor, exterior walls, and the roof. They used a woodburning stove with the stove pipe sticking out of a window until their furnace was installed.

When Mt. Elden voted to sponsor a mission at Cameron in 1957, Lee Cook drove the 180 miles round trip every week to conduct the services. At first the group met in an abandoned garage, a tin building with the windows broken out.

Under the leadership of George Bruce, Mt. Elden Church changed its name to Calvary Baptist in 1958. When they outgrew the small building, pastor Vernon Grace helped them to obtain a HMB loan in 1958 for a new building. With supervision by pastor Lee Cook, the members began building the cinder-block facility. When Bill May came as the first full-time salaried pastor in 1967, he had eleven in the congregation his first Sunday. May enlisted BSU students to teach and work in the SS. With an annual budget of five thousand dollars, they purchased new church furnishings. A young serviceman visiting the church made a donation of five hundred dollars, and the Tom Harbottle family donated one thousand dollars in memory of their son Jimmy, who was killed in Vietnam. Irene Gregory and Trixie O'Conner donated the organ.

With the establishment of Greenlaw subdivision came a time of transition from residential to business property around the church. They changed the church name to Greenlaw Baptist and found a new location, purchasing the first parcel of the Old Fanning Ranch on Lockett Road and

Fanning Drive in 1974 and the second parcel in 1975. During 1978 the church began a television ministry on KNAZ-TV.

Memorable moments include pastor Bob Batchelder's crashing through the ceiling while working in the attic; a skunk that made its home under the wooden building and produced an aroma that met members at the door and lingered throughout the services; its descendants that remained faithful until the building was torn down; and a mouse that scurried up the aisle to answer the altar call during the invitation.

After the church property on Fourth Street and Sixth Avenue was listed for sale, it went into escrow fourteen times. The site took so long to sell that the "For Sale" sign had to be repainted twice. An NAU student wrote on his visitor's card that he could remember the sign "Future Home of Greenlaw Baptist Church" when he was an elementary student at Thomas School. In 1986 the old property was sold to Russ Lupton Enterprises in exchange for a new building on the Lockett Road site. John Byrd was the elected church representative during construction. Groundbreaking ceremonies were held November 23, 1986. The congregation met for Sunday services in the East Flagstaff Junior High School music room, with prayer meetings and the church office in the Pueblo Plaza Building, until they completed the new facility.

On Wednesday, April 29, 1987, they began moving into their new church, with the first Sunday services on May 3. James Cecil, who brought a dedicatory message, was the first person to surrender for special service at Greenlaw. He served on the FMB staff as director of the overseas partnership evangelism program. Nineteen others have surrendered for special ministries and are actively serving the Lord. In addition to Cameron, Greenlaw sponsored Faith Mission at Parks and Flagstaff Bethel. The following pastors have led the church: Calvin Sandlin, Donal Childers, Thomas E. Barrett, Harold E. Baer, George Bruce, J. A. Myers, Vernon Grace, Lee Cook, Joe Flippen, Carl Johnson, Bill May, Robert Batchelder, J. B. Ryals, and Steve May.

### 1955 GCBA Annual Meeting at Prescott Miller Valley

When GCBA met in 1955, for the first time the minutes listed missions and language work. Although Ash Fork FBC was without a pastor, their report, including the Seligman mission, showed fourteen baptisms and sixteen additions by letter. Flagstaff FSBC, with John Wiles as pastor, reported separately the statistics for Mt. Elden, Sedona, and Baptist Indian Center. Calvin Sandlin, who lived at Tuba City, pastored Mt. Elden, and James Gore of Phoenix pastored Sedona. The Norman Kellys were at the

Indian Center; O. M. Jones had come to Prescott, FSBC; J. A. Myers was interim at Miller Valley, and Homer Ivy was at Williams FBC. A recommended change in the GCBA constitution proposed that pastors of all the missions in fellowship with a local Southern Baptist church in the association be included in the executive board.

### Lake Mead Baptist Association Organized

After missionary Troy Brooks brought a moving report of work in Las Vegas, Nevada, and the difficulties of starting missions there, a motion was made and carried that a letter of commendation be sent to the newly constituted Lake Mead Association. Las Vegas FSBC, Henderson FBC, and Boulder City FBC had withdrawn from Mohave Association on October 3, 1955, to organize. Because those areas had so recently been a part of GCBA, messengers expressed much concern for them. Bill Hunke remembers riding up to a spot overlooking Las Vegas with Troy Brooks and seeing him drop his head down on the steering wheel and sob for the great burden he bore for the city that was bursting forth below.

After the new Colorado Convention extended Willis J. Ray the third call to be its first executive director, he accepted the position. GCBA members joined with many across the state at a farewell reception in Phoenix on March 4, 1956, to honor the Rays for their eleven years of leadership. W. Barry Garrett, editor of the *Beacon*, served as interim in Arizona until Charles L. McKay came in October 1956 to be the new executive director for BGCA. Yarnell FBC constituted on January 8, 1956. That year Troy Brooks began and pastored a mission in Clarkdale which reported thirty in SS and thirty-six in VBS.

### 1956 GCBA Annual Meeting at Williams FBC

At the 1956 annual meeting, Yarnell FBC and Mt. Elden were accepted into full fellowship of GCBA. M. V. Mears recommended that a committee be authorized to study and revise the GCBA constitution. He also brought dates for the school of missions in 1957. Although all reports were given, they were not included in the annual minutes. Flagstaff FSBC's report totals included Sedona mission, Baptist Indian Center, Tuba City mission, and Red Lake mission. Thomas E. Barrett of Holbrook was pastoring the new Mt. Elden Church; John Howerton was pastoring at Yarnell; C. E. Russell of Prescott was pastoring the Clarkdale mission; W. C. Rounds had gone to Prescott FSBC; and Hugh Sawyer was at Prescott Miller Valley.

Late in 1956 Charles McKay wrote in his *Beacon* column that if each of the ten thousand readers would contribute a minimum of one dollar each, they could sponsor a new mission. The idea caught on and contributions came in sporadically. After careful consideration, an advisory committee decided to locate the "Beacon" mission in Page, Arizona, a new town on the Utah-Arizona border that was being built for workers employed in building Glen Canyon Dam. Although gifts never reached ten thousand dollars, enough money came in to provide significant help in getting the work underway. Flagstaff FSBC sponsored the new mission.

On January 1, 1957, a "pastoral missionary program," which had been approved by the HMB and BGCA, became effective for four pastors who would serve in the state convention territory. M. K. Wilder, who would pastor at Page, was one of the four appointed during the year. The others were Harold Dillman at Cedar City, E. J. Jenkins at Nampa, and Bob Wayman at Richfield.

### Page FBC: M. K. and Dora Wilder

When Troy Brooks and M. V. Mears, pastor of Flagstaff FSBC, contacted M. K. Wilder about being pastor of the new mission to be located at Page, Wilder told them he would not think of moving from his church at Boulder City. After the missionary persuaded him to come over to look over the field, Wilder's reaction was, "Man, there's nothing here. It's as blank as a baby's back." Dora Wilder had told her husband she was willing to go anywhere the Lord led as long as they could see some trees, but all he could see was sagebrush and tumbleweeds. I remember hearing Wilder tell a tourist from the South who was complaining about the lack of trees that they had cut them all down in order to see the beautiful view. The Wilders came without hesitation once the Lord assured them that it was his will.

When they held the first service on October 6, 1957, the only building in town was a little, metal schoolhouse. Any group that wanted to meet had to use that building. Because they were the first to request a time, the Baptists had 10:00 A.M. SS and 11:00 A.M. worship times, with other denominations coming at staggered periods all day long. "We started off with 10 the first Sunday, then had 36 and 74 the next two weeks, and by the fourth week, our SS attendance was 105. We were so squeezed in we couldn't even stand up to sing. The only road to Page was a forty-nine-mile dirt road from The Gap which was impossible to navigate in bad weather, so with nothing else to do and nowhere to go, everybody in town came to church," Wilder explained.

The group bought chairs and a portable organ, and every Sunday they had to haul all their equipment in a little trailer purchased for that purpose. Soon they also built a folding partition to provide separate SS space for the children. Wilder said, "Every Saturday night we moved the school desks out, put up the chairs and organ, and set the partition in place. All the other churches asked permission to use our setup. When Catholics started meeting in the afternoon, they even wanted to use our offering plates. As they came out, we filed back in for TU. One time Dora noticed some money in the plates, and thinking that the treasurer had forgotten to take the offering home that morning, she put it her purse. Later, a Catholic member came in, looked around, and asked, 'Who stole the loot?'"

Another time the Jesuits from Tuba City sent up a priest dressed in a brown robe and hood. When the Conservative Baptist pastor saw him, he called out to Wilder, "Look yonder. They dress their man up like Mama; they call him Father; and they won't let him have any children."

After the school built a larger building, the only way the Baptists could have permission to use a bigger room was to prove they had more people in attendance than any other group. Wilder recalls, "Besides us, the Conservative Baptists, Methodists, Catholics, Lutherans, and Assembly of God were all using the school in shifts. We were so isolated up there that we had great fellowship with all of them and rejoiced to have a place to meet. We were 135 miles from the nearest town in Arizona and seventy-four miles from the nearest town in Utah, with the road to it still unfinished. The bridge wasn't built yet over the Colorado River." By December 19, 1957, when the Page church organized, it had become financially stronger than the sponsoring Flagstaff FSBC.

People from thirty-three states made up the membership at Page, all with different ideas about doing things. In addition, the government bureau workers and construction workers came into constant conflict. Wilder called it a real "Mulligan's stew," but added that with all their differences, they developed a closeness from fellowshipping together, often even going ten miles out into the hills for picnics and outings.

One thing that drew the group together was that they had to do all the labor on their building by themselves. They floated a fifty-thousand-dollar Broadway bond issue and voted to sell only enough bonds at a time to pay the bills for what they were currently buying. When the bond coupons came due the first time, they were able to clip one thousand dollars worth of unused coupons. In spite of having a six-month strike hit the town, they still came out six hundred dollars ahead on the bond coupons. They hauled all their own supplies to save freight charges and were able to complete the building, install pews, furniture, and a twenty-five-hundred-dollar organ for fifty-two thousand dollars.

In a letter to his mother on May 7, 1958, Bill Hunke wrote, "I have just been up to Page which is another new town growing up in the Arizona desert. It will have about ten thousand people in the next two years and is the site of the new Glen Canyon Dam on the Colorado River. Where the bridge will be, they have a small walkway made of cables and floored with chicken wire stretching about eight hundred feet above the river from rim to rim. I walked out over the middle of the canyon for the thrill."

When the dam was completed, the government and construction workers moved away, bringing the town's population from sixty-five hundred down to thirteen hundred almost overnight. Wilder believes that if the HMB had not helped at that time, the church would have folded up. He said that the congregation experienced an almost complete turnover about every five years.

Wilder remembers that two of Page's greatest revivals were when Grey Allison and Frank Sutton preached. When Allison came, six ladies in the church had unsaved husbands, and five of them had come with burdened hearts. One said, "If my husband isn't saved now, I don't think I can stand it any longer." Another said that her husband was a nut, and she did not think they could ever get him to a revival service. As Wilder and Allison visited the first five men, they each accepted Christ as if they had been ready and waiting for someone to lead them to him. Glen Hurst told them when they came to the door, he had been watching for them to come. The pianist, Mrs. Quattlebalm, kept on praying for her husband until he finally came to the service. When the evangelist began talking to him afterwards, she told Wilder that she hoped he would not say the wrong thing and make her husband mad. Wilder said, "Let's pray," but he kept his eyes open. When he saw the husband grab Allison around the neck, he told Mrs. Quattlebalm to look. She was amazed to see her husband rejoicing and hugging the preacher for bringing him to Christ.

Wilder said that Frank Sutton taught him a lesson about soul winning. When they visited an unsaved husband, he told them that he was a Christian already. Sutton responded, "Bill, tell us about it; when and where did you become a Christian?" The man said that he had been sprinkled when he was a baby. Sutton explained that he was talking about being born again and told Bill the way of salvation. After about thirty minutes, he accepted Christ. Wilder shared that we always need to ask people to tell us about their salvation experience.

As a young man, Wilder played professional baseball with a Charlotte, North Carolina, team as a pitcher from 1928 to 1930. On one occasion when his team was playing the New York Yankees, he struck out both Babe Ruth and Lou Gehrig in the same inning. By the time he was saved when he was thirty-nine years old, he admits that he had been drunk every weekend for seven years. His mother had nine ladies in his hometown praying regularly for him.

One morning after his usual drunken weekend, Wilder woke up so sick that he thought he was dying. He usually slept off his drunken orgies at the fire station. That day he was sitting at the back of the station leaning over newspapers spread on the floor feeling overcome with nausea. An article about a tent revival caught his eye because it said that the evangelist would be preaching that night on "The Coming of the Beast." He had no idea what it meant but remembered his mother's prayers and knew he was lost and condemned and needed to get right with the Lord. He asked the firemen to help him sober up. After they threw water over him, they were astounded to learn he was going to church. "You had better wear one of our helmets," they joked, "because the roof will fall in when you show up."

"That's all right," Wilder told them. "It's just a tent roof." All the way to the tent, Wilder was telling the Lord, "Here, take me. I'm turning everything over to you." He was so happy that he did not hear anything the preacher said and did not learn what the beast was. He could not wait for the invitation to come so he could publicly acknowledge Christ. When the preacher told the pianist the number for the invitational song, Wilder bounded down to the front before she even got to the piano stool.

Going back to his seat, Wilder heard the Lord speak to him as plain as day, saying, "I want you to preach." That frightened him, but he was moved when a number of the ladies who had been praying for him came by to say how happy they were for him. When he called his mother to announce that he had been saved, she was not surprised, but told him how thrilled she was that her prayers were answered. Then he told her that God had called him to preach, thinking that would really startle her because he knew about as much about preaching as a cat knows about scaling a fish. His mother replied, "If the Lord has called you to preach, you'd better preach!"

At that time Wilder was intending to marry Dora, a widow with several children. "I didn't mind telling Dora that I'd become a Christian," he said, "but I was afraid that if I told her the Lord wanted me to preach, she'd have me committed, so I didn't tell her." Wilder tried to run away to Texas, thinking it was so big that the Lord would not find him out there. "The Lord cut me off in Louisiana. I went back and married Dora and moved the family down there where we joined a Presbyterian church because I remembered hearing one of their preachers say that a layman could serve the Lord as well as a preacher. That may be true, but not if the Lord is calling you to preach."

One night the Wilders heard D. C. Martin, the interim pastor of the Temple Baptist Church in Rustin, Louisiana, preach on TV about what happens when the Lord calls people into special service, and they refuse his call. The next day Wilder made a special trip into Rustin to talk to Martin about how he was running away from the Lord's call and how he was so miserable that he had even contemplated suicide. Martin called Grey Allison to come to pray with them, and Wilder surrendered to the call to preach.

When he told Martin that he wanted to join that Baptist church, he agreed to extend an invitation on Wednesday night. Wilder still had not shared his decision with Dora. That Wednesday they sat with four of the children between them. As the invitation began, Wilder looked over to see her expression as he started down the aisle and was surprised to see her going down ahead of him. When Martin presented them for membership, he asked permission to tell the church about Wilder's surrender to preach. "I figured Dora couldn't hit me in front of all that crowd, so I told him to go ahead. Afterwards I turned to her and told her that I hoped she would go with me into the ministry, but I had to go no matter what. She promised to go with me, and from that moment our lives have been turned around," Wilder asserted.

The church helped Wilder preach at a mission while he went to NOBTS. When the Pleasant Hill Church called him as pastor, they also called for his ordination. At a meeting on Saturday night before the ordination council was to meet, Wilder gave his testimony that he had been baptized at age twelve and saved at age thirty-nine. When the pastor asked if he had been baptized after his salvation, he turned red as a beet and confessed that he had not. The next morning, on his forty-second birthday, he was baptized in the morning and ordained in the afternoon.

Grey Allison introduced the Wilders to Leroy Smith from Arizona, who was in revival at Gulfport, Mississippi. After services one night they talked to Smith in his hotel room until 1:00 A.M. "The stories he told about the West had me so wrapped up that I was ready to quit seminary and leave for Arizona, but Leroy felt I should finish school," M. K. admitted. When Boulder City, Nevada, needed a pastor, at Smith's recommendation, the church extended him an invitation to come in view of a call. Boulder City paid expenses for the trip, and Temple Baptist gave the Wilders a car with the understanding that they would keep the church informed about developments. Wilder reported, "It was pathetic! Boulder had thirty members who met in the American Legion hall. They couldn't afford to pay a pastor or supply a house." After a week the church called Wilder. While driving through Texas on the way home, he felt impelled of the Lord to go as pastor.

When he got back to Temple Church, they asked, "They called you, didn't they? When are you leaving?" Wilder shared that he did not know how he could afford to go, but he was on his way. Pastor Murphy told him, "About the rent—our church has already voted to pay it for a year, so get going." The first thing he did on arrival was to lead Boulder City in a building program. "That was good practice for building the Page church," he laughed. Always missions minded, in 1958 Page FBC reported a mission at Chi-Chi Jima in the South Pacific.

### Forward Program of Church Finance

Coming to Arizona from the BSSB in Nashville, executive director Charles McKay was sold on all the programs and promotional resources of the SBC boards and commissions. Because he was eager to introduce to Arizona the Forward Program of Church Finance, one of his first staff changes was to invite BGCA area missionary Bill Hunke to join the state staff and give full time in 1957 to demonstrating the advantages of the new stewardship materials in as many churches as possible. A survey which revealed that 85 percent of the ten million Southern Baptists did not tithe punctuated the need for the new tithing emphasis.

### 1957 GCBA Annual Meeting at Flagstaff FSBC

Hunke was invited to bring a report on the Forward Program to GCBA messengers at the 1957 annual meeting and make the materials available to the churches of the association. The Arizona Convention later was given special recognition by the SBC for having the largest percentage of churches using the Forward Program, at least in part. The 1957 quarterly meetings at Yarnell, Williams Spanish mission, Seligman, and Flagstaff Baptist Indian Center emphasized the new stewardship program and materials.

### Hassayampa Baptist Association Organized

At the close of the 1957 GCBA annual meeting, the churches in Yavapai County brought petitionary letters for the purpose of forming a new association. The Hassayampa Baptist Association was constituted November 3, 1957, at Prescott by messengers from three churches from GCBA and one church in Estrella Association, together with their missions. These included: Prescott FSBC; Prescott Miller Valley; Yarnell FBC;

and Wickenburg FBC; and missions at Clarkdale, Bagdad, Congress Junction, and Mayer.

New pastors in 1957 were H. E. Baer at Mt. Elden, C. H. Peaden at Prescott Miller Valley, J. N. Swafford at Williams, and H. E. Lair at Yarnell. A resolution taking a stand against use of teenagers in liquor advertising was approved and sent to the *Beacon* for publication. After C. H. Peaden expressed appreciation for the sweet fellowship he experienced in GCBA, other messengers offered similar praise until Troy Brooks concluded the annual meeting with a prayer of thanks for the thoughts of love that had been uttered.

On June 16, 1958, missionary Troy Brooks suffered severe injuries in an accident when his automobile left the road ten miles south of Kingman and plowed into a huge boulder. The two student summer missionaries riding with him were not hurt. After being confined to the Fort Whipple Veterans Hospital at Prescott for more than four months, Brooks decided to retire in October 1958 at age sixty-six after ten years as missionary in northern Arizona. Hassayampa voted to change its name to Troy Brooks Association to honor its former missionary. At Brooks' request the association changed the name to Yavapai in 1974.

After his long recovery period, Troy and Katherine moved to Tucson, where he pastored Corona de Tucson Baptist Church for eight years. They moved to El Paso, Texas, in 1970. She wrote on March 9, 1986, "I am glad to live long enough to have seen what God wrought from 1948 till now. I am eighty-five; I live alone and attend to my own affairs, a very quiet life now. Troy was overcome with Parkinson's disease, and the last five years of life, he was an invalid. God called him home on April 5, 1982. He had preached a Men's Day sermon sitting in his wheel chair at age eighty-five. He was ninety when he died."

### 1958 GCBA Annual Meeting at Flagstaff Mt. Elden

At the 1958 annual meeting, the motion was made and carried to place Troy Brooks' picture in the front of the 1958 minutes. An announcement was made that the men of GCBA would help build a three-room cottage on the state assembly grounds for the Brooks.

Page FSBC was accepted into GCBA, and its pastor, M. K. Wilder, was presented, along with George Bruce at Mt. Elden, Reeves Knowlton at Seligman, and missionary Ross Woodruff at Tuba City. A telegram from Troy Brooks was read. A motion passed that if the GCBA missionary wished to send out a newsletter, the executive board had authority to place the expense for it in the budget.

# WONDERFUL WORKS
# HE PERFORMED
## INDIAN AND SPANISH WORK IN GCBA

Memories make a museum of our minds where we preserve treasured accounts of notable deeds. They make the fleeting past and present last forever and cause words and deeds, scenes and circumstances to appear before us, for they can both retain and reproduce. Because they are a source of pleasure and profit, a foundation of faith, and a basis for confidence, past deeds worthy of praise need to be impressed on the hearts and minds of every succeeding generation.

After B. Frank Belvin became superintendent of Indian work for the HMB in 1951, an old Navajo woman told him of James Milton Shaw who had come as the first Baptist missionary to the Indians in the West in 1851. Her father had become a believer at that time. "You preach just like my father believed. I believe in Jesus, too, for that is how my father taught me," she shared with pride.

"That early missionary went away," she continued sadly, "and no one came to take his place. If other missionaries had come, we would all be Baptists now." Her dim, brown eyes peered out the window where the trackless sand dune, moved intermittently by desert winds, was inching toward her adobe hut. Some day it would engulf her village just as sin had engulfed her world.

As Frank visited the Indians of Arizona, he found blue skies, red sunsets, and, too often, wrenching poverty. The prevalent belief was peyote religion practiced by the Native American Church which was formed in

1918 to prohibit the extinction of usage of the habit-forming drug. Peyote affects the mind, nervous system, and heart, and after prolonged usage, some Indians become violent and beat their families.

### Flagstaff Baptist Indian Center: Harold Baer

The HMB appointed the S. L. Isaacs as missionaries to work with Indians in Flagstaff in 1946, but they served only a short time. Harold Baer, pastor of Holly Wood Baptist near Chatham, Virginia, felt called to work with the Navajos when he realized they were among the most neglected and needy people in the world. His church gave him leave to come to Arizona to survey the field. Upon his return, they raised two thousand dollars and sent it to the HMB designated as salary for Harold. One of the deacons moved the Baers to Arizona in his truck at his own expense.

For six months the Baers lived on the reservation before the HMB officially appointed him; however, for years the Virginia WMU allocated his salary each year through their AAEO. Baer's horse Star also was moved to Arizona, where he became a welcome asset because of lack of roads on the reservation. One day Baer and Frank Belvin rode their horses to the top of a hill in northern Arizona, where they dismounted and sat under a windblown pinon pine tree. Talking about the vastness of the work and the lack of leadership, the missionary arose and waved his arm in a circle, saying, "Look, Dr. Belvin, in any direction for one hundred miles, and you will not find another church doing anything about the salvation of the Navajo people."

"Roan Horse built a new hogan over the hill," Baer continued. "He built the front of it of beautiful native stones. His baby has been sick. Let's go over to see how they're doing."

Galloping over the hill, they could see the frame of a new hogan with bright stones in front. Riding up, they found it deserted and the roof caved in. The end of charred logs pointed upward over the cracked walls like wrecked cannons of a fallen fort, indicating the baby had died, and the family had moved on.

The Baers moved to Flagstaff and first held services in their home, later at Flagstaff FSBC, and finally in the First Colored Baptist Church. The need for an Indian center was imprinted on Baer's heart when a Navajo was arrested and mistreated by a Flagstaff law officer. When Indians came to town from the reservation, they had no place to go and no one to befriend them. The HMB purchased eight lots for five thousand dollars and allocated twenty-five thousand dollars for construction of a missionary home and building to begin on June 6, 1949. The men of FSBC had to wreck an old building and clear the property before an auditorium with several classrooms could be erected. On November 13, 1949, a day of celebration and praise marked the completion of the building. The Snuggs family from Virginia attended the service and brought a truckload of food for the Baers and the Navajos.

Sensing a reluctance on the part of Indians to receive baptism after conversion, the missionary finally learned that they had been told they must be baptized nude. Another story had gone around that the missionary would hold them under the water until they drowned. Having seen only sprinkling, they thought that was why Baptists required them to be immersed. One little boy felt the Lord wanted him to obey him by being baptized although he had never seen a church building or witnessed a baptism. As he started on his way to request immersion, people along the way all warned, "The missionary will drown you." He responded, "I know it, but I'm still willing."

In 1948 Florence Begay, a Navajo who had been won and baptized by the Baers, was valedictorian for Flagstaff High School. The missionaries prayed she could fulfill her dream of entering a Baptist college to prepare herself to serve among her people.

From the beginning of the Baptist Indian Center until God led him to Copper Mine in April 1951, Baer baptized forty Indians. One year two Georgia churches presented him with a new Chevy truck, a large amount of food, one hundred dollars of clothes for himself, and a good offering. At the fifth annual meeting of GCBA, he displayed thumbprint signatures of a number of Navajos at Window Rock, asking Southern Baptists to come to their reservation to begin work.

In the summer of 1951, Bill and Norma Crews came from the pastorate at Sanders to the Baptist Indian Center after being appointed by the HMB to work at Flagstaff. Following a year of consecrated service when it became evident that Norma could no longer live in the high altitude, the HMB made arrangements for them to exchange places with the Norman Kellys at Santan.

### Copper Mine

The Baers had negotiated with the government for a year and a half before they were permitted to open a mission on the Navajo reservation, but in April 1951 the family moved to Copper Mine to get work started. The mission was 110 miles from Flagstaff and 60 miles from a post office. With no school available, the Baers were not only missionaries to the

Indians, but also teacher and doctor to their own children.

The Navajo tribal council made three buildings available: a home for the family, another house for a teacher and interpreter when they could get one, and the third for the mission lunch room and classes and for preaching services in the winter. Summertime meetings were all out-doors.

Jane Grey, whose husband had been translating for Harold on the reservation, agreed to serve as teacher and interpreter. She had graduated from the teachers' college at Flagstaff and was probably the only qualified Navajo teacher anywhere. She and her husband had been won to the Lord and baptized by Harold. Mrs. Baer tried to teach all grades, but found they must send their oldest child to live with the Kellys at Flagstaff to attend school.

During their first year at Copper Mine, the Baers led nineteen Navajos to become believers. When Willis J. Ray took a trip with Harold, they heard the plaintive cry of a lamb that ran toward the truck. Harold remarked that coyotes would devour it that night if they could not find its owner. Ray insisted that they take the lamb up into the truck and search for him. They drove to hogan after hogan until they found a man who said the lamb belonged to him. Willis J. often used the incident as a illustration of the Indians being the helpless prey of Satan and his evil forces unless someone seeks them out and restores them to the Master.

The 1953 GCBA minutes state that Norman Kelly was missionary at Flagstaff Baptist Indian Center; Guy John, an Apache Indian, was also at Flagstaff; and D. A. Dalby had been placed at Copper Mine. It reported that forty-two children had enrolled in the Indian VBS; sixty children had enrolled in the Mexican VBS; and eighty-four had attended an all-Indian Bible institute at Copper Mine.

Copper Mine was not only the first mission established on Navajo land, but also the most remote of the HMB's mission fields in the state. When former BGCA language missions director Irvin Dawson visited the mission, services were conducted in the area chapter house which was leased by the HMB. He wrote, "I remember sitting there in the one room, rock chapter house building on wooden benches without backs. The Navajo ladies who came simply sat on the floor when they tired of sitting on the benches. I remember walking from the meeting place toward the house where the missionaries lived and seeing a sidewinder rattlesnake sliding across the desert floor."

In the early 1950s while D. A. Dalby was serving at Copper Mine, Baptists fell heir to the well there which was 1,230 feet deep and had cost the mining company about fifty thousand dollars to dig. Dalby had done the cleaning and repair work necessary to make the well usable. Some Indians came to help, and after dark one evening, they had it almost ready, but needed light to finish. "Tomorrow we will finish up and make it pump," the missionary promised.

"Oh, no, let's do it tonight," the workers urged. They built a big bonfire and completed the repairs by its light. When fresh water came bubbling out of the pump, they threw their hats in the air and yelled for joy. In that desert country water holes were far apart. One old man made a round trip of seventy-five miles in a wagon to get two barrels of water from the well and was much encouraged to have a water supply.

### James David Back

When J. D. and Virginia Ruth Back were missionaries at Copper Mine from 1956 to 1959, they held campout VBSs, did hogan visitation, and taught classes in the local Indian school. On one occasion the Backs had two summer workers from back East helping with summer mission work. J. D. told Irvin Dawson that he was not going to have any more summer workers because they insisted on taking a shower every day, and that simply could not be done where water was so scarce and depended on a well and pump. Keeping the pump operating proved expensive.

J. D. Back was born September 10, 1931, at Ozark, Missouri. He was saved at age six, baptized in Bull Creek during the summer of 1938 by Victory Baptist Church, and ordained August 27, 1950, by the same rural church. He wrote, "While attending our associational family camp at Baptist Hill, Mt. Vernon, Missouri, I went forward during morning worship and was saved. My second cousin, who was a pastor, and my mother talked to me to help clarify my decision."

J. D. married Virginia Pumphrey August 24, 1952, at Springfield; they have three children. He graduated from Southwest Missouri State and GGBTS and pastored churches at Ozark and Galena. He shared, "My wife Ginny and I served at Flagstaff Indian Center as student summer missionaries in 1955. I was interim pastor for three weeks while Norman Kelly finished GCC and took a vacation. We worked with Harold Baer and Norman in revivals and VBSs on the reservation. When we learned missionary D. A. Dalby was leaving Copper Mine the next summer, we prayed and became aware of God's call to go to Copper Mine."

The Backs also served as language missionaries on White River Indian Reservation and pastored two Alaska native churches at Fort Yukon and Fairbanks. He was missionary to Tustumena Baptist Association and

Alaska state mission director. J. D. and Ginny retired in 1994 and moved to Columbia City, Oregon.

When the Backs were at Copper Mine, the mission met in the old mine company office building, and they lived in the home built for the mine superintendent. One day when J. D. was driving across the reservation with a rifle in a gun rack behind him, he picked up two men walking down the sandy road. Eyeing the rifle, they asked if he was hunting. He replied, "I am looking for a couple of Mormon missionaries," without giving a hint that he knew that was what they were. He reported that they were very quiet all the way in to the trading post.

### Lemuel and Marie Littleman

Marie Littleman's father was a medicine man. When he was dying, he called the children to him and said, "I'm going off this earth now, so there's no one to help you. Hold on to the everlasting person who made this world." He did not know Jesus, but he wanted his family to keep their beliefs.

Marie is a Navajo who was born at Burnt Springs, about thirty miles north of Winslow. Because of her parents' separation, her "real father," a strong Catholic, put her in a Catholic boarding school from ages eight to fifteen. "We had such strict rules that I never had any fun, went to a party, or knew what was going on outside. I didn't know what Jesus was to me, but only about Mary and the saints. I finally told my father I had to get out of there!" she declared. She attended Albuquerque and Phoenix Indian schools, then took a nursing course and worked as a nursing partner during World War II.

Lemuel Littleman was born in 1910 at Potato Canyon on the Navajo reservation. At age ten he went to a government military school where students worked in the mornings and went to classes in the afternoons. He attended the Presbyterian church in Tuba City, the only church in town, where he learned to read the Bible.

In 1946 Lemuel and Marie moved to Flagstaff in order that their children could go to public schools. He began working at NAU and continued for thirty-five years. One day Harold Baer rode into the Greenlaw area on Star, his pinto horse, and asked to take the children to church. Marie still went to the Catholic and Lemuel to the Presbyterian churches. "We were so miserable because we had never been in a church together that I told the kids to go ahead with the man to the Baptist mission," Marie stated.

One day their oldest daughter Sue urged, "Mama, Jesus is coming back again. Why don't you come to church with us and learn how to be ready when he comes?" After Lemuel and Marie started going with their children to the mission, they both accepted Christ and were baptized by Norman Kelly in April 1955.

"We had been going to church a long time when the pastor told us, 'You can't just come and hear me preach. The Lord says to go out into all the other areas and tell people about Jesus. Go to your unsaved people out on the reservation and witness to them,'" Lemuel explained. "That was the first time I ever heard about witnessing. In 1962 we started preaching and Bible studies on the reservation, and we've never stopped. Through the years we've spoken in white churches back East and held services in homes in Page, Dry Lake, and Copper Mine. We've visited and prayed with the sick in hospitals in Phoenix, Gallup, and Albuquerque. We still enjoy all the Lord leads us to do," he continued.

Irvin Dawson wrote, "One Sunday when I was preaching at Tuba City, I remember being approached by Lemuel Littleman about getting some funds so that they could build a hogan-type preaching place on the reservation. I requested five hundred dollars from the HMB and understand that they built a large hogan structure with up to two hundred people coming to services, far more than in any of our nicer mission buildings. I think that Lemuel's ability to speak the language, identify with their culture, and meet in a building like those they were accustomed to made the difference."

For years while the children were in school, Marie worked as a cook. She met with the women's sewing class at the mission to make quilts and sew for needy people. She has woven many Navajo rugs. "I'm the only one in the family who can speak and read Navajo. I'm trying to teach the children to speak it," she affirmed.

The Littlemans have six daughters and a son. Their children teach school, make purses and silversmith articles to sell, cook for hotels, and do oncology nursing. Marie said they have twenty-five grandchildren and twenty great-grandchildren, many of whom have remained faithful members at the Flagstaff Baptist Indian Church through the years. As Bill Hunke took radiation therapy for six weeks at the Flagstaff Oncology Center in 1994, he looked forward to seeing the Littlemans' daughter Cindy almost every day. When the Hunkes hosted a GCBA pastors' family Christmas dinner in 1988, the Littlemans brought four generations of family members.

Marie attested, "We're still serving the Lord. I work all year making quilts to give the old ones in their nineties at Christmas time. I also do crocheting and beadwork. I tell the children, 'Always ask the Lord to lead you by His Holy Spirit in whatever you do.'"

Marie's mother, who lived at Page, celebrated her 105th birthday in 1988 with five generations present for the occasion. She once told Marie about going to a camp meeting where the preacher told that Jesus was coming some day to receive his loved ones. "I'm going to be in that bunch," she testified.

### Tuba City Navajo Trail Baptist Mission

When the HMB appointed Calvin and Wilma Sandlin to begin a work among the Navajos and Hopis at Tuba City, Flagstaff FSBC agreed to sponsor the work, later named the Navajo Trail Baptist Mission. The work began outside Tuba with a VBS at Red Lake (Tonalea). Stella Mae Russell, a teenager from Flagstaff FSBC, helped in the school. The work was later moved to the Big Hogan, a community building in Tuba which was also used by the Catholics and others. Every Sunday morning the priest and missionary went early to sweep beer cans out of the building and prepare it for services after the Saturday night dances.

BGCA leaders quickly made application to lease land on which to build a church at Tuba City. Reservation land could not be sold, but could be leased without charge with council approval. After seven years of praying, Southern Baptists received approval of two acres by the Navajo tribal council. The location chosen was close to the community building and easily accessible from a main highway through the city. The council insisted that the mission provide kindergarten training for the children. They were not interested in religious teachings but wanted children to receive quality education.

The Navajo Trail mission had English services on Sunday mornings with many in attendance who were non-Navajo: Indian school teachers from Oklahoma, public health workers, and other Indian tribal people. For a number of years, Lemuel Littleman led Navajo services on Sunday evenings. Irvin Dawson remembers driving to Tuba City for a building dedication service the Sunday after President Kennedy's assassination. During the service someone reported seeing Lee Harvey Oswald shot and killed on television. Dawson had a report showing the mission had 110 members and a SS enrollment of 84 with 73 average attendance in the early 1960s. It also reported an active WMU with all the youth and children's mission groups.

Norman Kelly, who had been appointed to do field work on the Navajo reservation, started a work at Tonalea which was named Red Lake Baptist Mission. When M. V. Mears, pastor of Flagstaff FSBC, learned that the work had no sponsor, he led the church to sponsor it. Although three missionary pastors had already served at Copper Mine, it likewise had never had a local sponsor. J. D. Back gladly accepted the Flagstaff church's sponsorship of that work as well.

Because Calvin Sandlin, pastor at Tuba City, wished to finish college, he and Ross Woodruff of Phoenix exchanged positions in the summer of 1958. While he was a senior at GCC, Ross had begun working at the Phoenix Indian School as director of student activities. The Tuba City mission was still meeting at the Big Hogan. Ross would later get a doctorate in Navajo studies and teach that program at NAU. He also pastored the Flagstaff Baptist Indian Center from 1983 to 1986 and the Seligman FBC one year. During that time he led Seligman to pay off debts of more than thirty-five hundred dollars that a previous pastor had incurred in the community.

### Arthur Austin Moore

A. A. Moore probably was never larger than 5' 5" and 140 pounds, but he was a spiritual giant. Born May 7, 1915, into a large family on a farm near Madison, South Carolina, he was saved at age twelve and joined the Old Liberty Baptist Church of Madison in 1927. He worked at farming, road construction, sawmilling, carpentry, and as a building contractor. During World War II he worked at the Norfolk Navy Yard, Portsmouth, Virginia, as a joiner and shipwright.

Although he had been active in church work and was ordained a deacon in 1940, he did not feel a definite call to preach until 1945 after World War II. After discussing his call with his pastor, he announced his decision to the church and began to prepare for the ministry. While in school he worked at Burlington Mills, as a carpenter, and as a teacher in veterans administration schools.

After college and seminary, he became pastor of Tallulah Falls Baptist Church in Georgia. While pastoring there, he and his wife were appointed by the HMB as missionaries to the Indians in Arizona. They received word about their appointment when Loyd Corder, HMB director of language missions, called them in early June 1959, saying it was effective June 1, and they were to get on the field at the Copper Mine mission as soon as possible.

Assured they would have electricity, they moved all their electrical appliances, only to find no electricity. Worse, they had no water. The well no longer worked, and they had to haul their water from the Gap, twenty-seven miles away on a torturous, dusty road. They ministered to Navajos who knew little English, although they knew no Navajo.

Their ministries not only included conducting church services, but also transporting people to and from the Tuba City hospital, fifty miles away, chopping and hauling wood, and hauling water for both people and their sheep. They regularly visited every hogan and family in the area. During the school year, they held weekly religious education classes at Kaibito Boarding School, twenty-five miles away. Every Sunday afternoon they invited children to their home for games and fellowship.

After a year they were moved to the Flagstaff Baptist Indian Center, where they spent fourteen years ministering to Navajos, Hopis, and other tribes. At one service they had fourteen tribes represented. The mission building had a kitchen, bedroom, two bathrooms with showers, a room about 12 x 15' with a fireplace and baptistry, and the auditorium. The bedroom and auditorium had gas heaters.

The center, located adjacent to the Santa Fe railroad, was easily accessible from Highways 66 and 89. Families came from all directions and many states for showers and lodging. When a state leader asked why the mission was located next to the railroad, the reply was that it was on the path to an area where Navajos had a campground when they came to town for the annual Indian pow wow, and all the Indians who came to town would know where the mission was. When the leader asked why the chapel had a flat roof which heavy winter snowfalls caused to leak frequently, the response was that the HMB had only allocated so much money, and they had to build within the allowance.

One night a group from the Navajo reservation came for the night and built a fire so big that the flames were leaping out the top of the chimney. When the police saw the fire, they came rushing in with sirens wailing to see what was going on. Because the Moores were getting no funds to operate a Baptist center type of ministry, they decided to change the ministry and name of the work to the Flagstaff Baptist Indian Mission.

Beginning with a small attendance, as they contacted every member, ministered to the local Indians, college students at NAU, and boarding school children, they saw their congregation increasing. Moore wrote, "At one time we were packing thirty-five juniors into that 12 x 15' room. A representative from the state SS staff came by and suggested we put the boys' SS class in the baptistry, which we did. We had converts and baptized both young and old every year."

The Moores also carried on the mission work at Cameron, meeting during the week. At one meeting two Mormon missionaries came in after they had served refreshments. Kool Aid had been brought in a jug and the empty jug placed under a table. During prayer they noticed the Mormons smelling the jug to determine what they had given the group to drink. Another time during VBS at Cameron, the tent they were meeting in blew down while everyone was inside.

The trading post at Cameron is one of the few authentic posts left in the Southwest. Founded in 1890, it remains an active center for Indians to exchange their crafts for merchandise. Its gallery offers outstanding textiles, pottery, baskets, beadwork, moccasins, rugs, dolls, and ceremonial items. The old-timers still talk about the time the Baptist mission trailer blew into the Little Colorado River Canyon during a small tornado.

When the Tuba City mission lost its missionary, that work also became the Moores' responsibility. For a year they arranged to go to Shonto on Mondays, Kaibito on Tuesdays, Flagstaff on Wednesdays, and Cameron on Thursdays. In 1966 they were officially assigned to Tuba City. During the two and a half years they served there, they continued the Shonto, Kaibito, and Cameron weekday ministries. In addition, they organized a mission at Kaibito and had Sunday afternoon services there. A favorite song of the Indians was "To God Be the Glory," and some called A. A. Moore the "Glory to God Man."

When Mrs. Moore's health required a move and doctors recommended the Northwest, they went to the Pacific Beach, Washington, FBC for four years. While there they began work among the Indians at Taholah, Humptulips, Hoh reservation, and Neah Bay, and conducted VBSs at Quinault, Ocean City, and La Push.

In 1972 the Moores were asked to return to the Flagstaff Baptist Indian Mission, which had been closed for some time. The people were eager to get the work going again and began to talk about building. The talk led to plans, financing, and work. Moore wrote, "We more than doubled the size of the mission by building an addition which was paid for upon completion. The Carlsbad, New Mexico, FBC helped with the dry wall and furnished the pews and pulpit. When the building was finished, the people bought a new piano. A number of our earlier members had graduated from college, and some had entered the ministry. We retired in 1980 from the HMB and baptized five our last Sunday in Flagstaff."

Indian camp week at Prescott every year was for the entire family, with groups coming from all over the state and down from Utah. Two highlights were the saints and sinners baseball game and the crowning of the Indian chief and princess, who were elected by the young people attending after being nominated by their missionary pastors. A. A. Moore served several times as camp director for the camp.

Irvin Dawson remembers during the invitation on the last evening at Indian camp one year, no one had responded, although the invitational hymn had been sung and repeated. Finally, a young boy came forward, whispered something in Moore's ear, and later stood beside him at the front. Missionaries lined the front of the auditorium to receive those who responded. After that little boy came, people began to come from all over the auditorium and were lined up from one side to the other. When the missionaries told why each person had come, Moore had to admit that the first little boy had whispered in his ear, "I've got to go to the bathroom."

While in GCBA, A. A. Moore was associational moderator, SS superintendent, and chairman of the missions committee. He developed his hobbies of silversmithing, leather craft, woodwork, camping, hiking, fishing, and hunting. After retirement the Moores moved back to Georgia and continued to teach literacy English-as-Second-Language (ESL) classes and work with the HMB Interfaith Witness Department. They came back to Winslow as Mission Service Corps (MSC) volunteers in 1983–1984 to teach Seminary Extension classes to the Indians and work with the White Cove and Klagetoh missions. They attended Flagstaff FSBC's fiftieth anniversary in 1995.

In Georgia A. A. Moore pastored the Cleveland Mount Yonah Baptist Church and Victory Baptist Church in Tugalo Baptist Association. He lives near the North Georgia Baptist Assembly at Toccoa and is a frequent guest speaker to various mission conferences there.

**Direct Missions Program Ends**

On January 1, 1960, the HMB direct missions department transferred all language missions work to the administrative control of the BGCA, with financial support thereafter provided jointly by the HMB and the state convention. From that time on language group missions in GCBA gave reports to the association and felt they were an integral part of the work instead of being directly responsible only to the HMB.

Irvin Dawson, state director of language missions, spent much time traveling in GCBA with superintendent of missions Bill Hunke, explaining the new organizational structure to all the language missionaries. Dawson was greatly appreciated and trusted by the language workers. By convention time in 1960, 64 language missionaries—33 among the Indians, 26 among the Spanish, and 5 among the Chinese— were added to the BGCA payroll. In 1960 the Tuba City Navajo Trail Mission, under the leadership of pastor Robert Green, reestablished the

*Navajos Marie and Lemuel Littleman served at Dry Lake Indian Mission. Her father was a Navajo medicine man.*

*Harold Baer opened Flagstaff Baptist Indian Center in 1946. HMB built the building. FIBC organized in 1989.*

*Cooper Mine Indian Mission, located on Navajo land, served a remote area. The building formerly housed mine offices.*

*Baer started the Copper Mine Mission in April 1951. Missionaries lived in the former mine superintendent's home.*

*J. D. and Virginia Back served Copper Mine, 1956–1959, in campout VBSs, classes, hogan visits, and services.*

*Navajo Trail Mission met in Tuba City Big Hogan for seven years after it began in 1955. NTBC organized in 1974.*

*A. A. and Ruby Moore led the Flagstaff Indian work fourteen years and this mission at Cameron which met in a trailer.*

*Heavy winds blew Cameron trailer into Little Colorado Canyon in 1969. A tent also blew down on VBS children.*

*Dry Lake Mission started in 1962. Alvin Wood led Flagstaff FSBC to construct a mission building at Dry Lake in 1967.*

*HMB missionaries Wilma and Calvin Sandlin started Mt. Elden BC and Tuba City Navajo Trail Mission.*

*HMB built a mission building at Tuba City on the reservation. Navajo Trail changed to Tuba City FSBC in 1980.*

*Kayenta Indian Mission met in 1962. A new mission organized as Kayenta FBC in 1988 and affiliated with GCBA.*

Red Lake mission at Tonalea with Green driving the seventy miles round trip to carry on the work.

### Spanish Work Begins: I. B. and Opal Williams

In 1953 a young Hispanic man from Williams was fatally injured in an automobile accident. At the hospital where the man lay dying, he asked the Catholic priest to wait in the hall while he begged T. J. Newbill, pastor of Williams FBC, to get his church to begin a work among the Mexicans. As a result the HMB transferred I. B. and Opal Williams from Tucson to begin Spanish mission work.

In 1944 when the Virginia WMU had allocated a salary for a missionary to establish a Mexican work in Arizona, the Williams had been appointed to work in Tucson. After Opal Williams' mother had been prevented from serving as a missionary by lack of education, she dedicated her daughter to mission work. Opal knew nothing of this until after her surrender to be a missionary. When I. B. Williams was born in 1912, his deacon father had knelt by the mother's bedside and dedicated his first son to God. God was already working to answer the pleas of the young man who died in Williams.

In Tucson the Williams had won the confidence of the Spanish-speaking people through their Christlike service. Opal taught piano lessons to any who wanted to learn to play. She invited mothers to her home to learn to sew. They started a kindergarten and enrolled one hundred in VBS their first year. As the work grew, they became increasingly concerned about beginning work in other Arizona communities. They drove to Chandler and Casa Grande to help establish work and often to preach. From this background they came to initiate Spanish work in GCBA.

At the GCBA annual meeting at Williams FBC on October 1–2, 1953, the report that work among the Mexicans was beginning in that city was joyfully received. A resolution passed "to extend our help as individuals and churches to the work of our Indian and Mexican missions." While serving in Williams, I. B. and Opal started Spanish work in Flagstaff. After SS and worship, they would eat a quick lunch, drive thirty-three miles to Flagstaff, then back again through Williams to Ash Fork for a second service, then back to Williams for evening services. In the summers they held VBSs in Flagstaff, Ash Fork, Seligman, Winslow, and Prescott.

Although Calvary Baptist Church had promised to sponsor the Flagstaff Spanish work, when it was discovered that the sponsorship had never been presented to the congregation for approval, Flagstaff FSBC agreed to extend an arm to the mission. When the work in Flagstaff showed so much potential because of the larger Spanish population, after the Williamses resigned and moved to Texas, the HMB assigned W. B. Minor to develop Flagstaff Spanish work and travel to Williams for a weeknight service.

In 1962 after LeRoy Bond started a SS in his home at Kayenta and asked for help from GCBA, Flagstaff FSBC requested that its Tuba City Navajo Trail mission receive four Kayenta members into their fellowship as the nearest Southern Baptist work, although it was seventy-five miles away.

That year Page began an Indian work in the isolated village of Dry Lake on the reservation. Lemuel Littleman served as pastor, although many times he could not get there because of muddy roads. Later, Flagstaff FSBC sent men and materials to Dry Lake to construct a building. By 1980 a paved highway ran within seventy-five feet of the building, an addition had doubled the space, and Littleman was still driving 138 miles one way to pastor the work.

On September 9, 1962, Flagstaff FSBC led in a dedication for the new Spanish mission building in the Sunnyside area of town. The Spanish work had been meeting in a rented house where pastor W. B. Minor reported a revival with a high attendance of forty-six and four professions of faith. The new building was constructed for twenty-five thousand dollars from AAEO funds and included a sanctuary and educational building on 6th Avenue and West Street. A pastorium was begun, but after funds ran out, it remained unfinished until Manny Martinez became pastor of Sunnyside in 1990.

In 1965 the Robert Greens resigned as missionaries to the Indians at Tuba City after having served effectively for a number of years. That year the HMB provided furnishings for the Flagstaff Indian mission. Important events for the language missions in GCBA included Indian camp at Prescott which registered 202 and Spanish camp which registered 142. During the two weeks, fifty-three made professions of faith, with twenty-two other decisions. Statewide Spanish fellowship meetings were begun which were well attended.

The Navajo Language School was held at Gallup, New Mexico, during August. This was an annual cooperative endeavor of the HMB and the Arizona and New Mexico Conventions to enable missionaries to become more familiar with the language. The first such conference was in

1958 at Winslow, and because it proved extremely helpful by allowing participants to learn from experts and share experiences, it continued for several years. In addition to the Navajo language, topics discussed included how to do hogan visitation and selecting an interpreter. In 1960 New Mexico executive director Harry Stagg described the Navajo Language School (NLS) as "the best mission meeting I have been to in my thirty-eight years in the West."

In the meeting attended by Navajo tribal chief Paul Jones, Allen Neshachi, a Navajo Baptist and translator, told what Christ meant to him and shared his testimony. Running for reelection, Jones commented, "Whoever said that politics at best is not so good was certainly right."

Bureau of Indian Affairs (BIA) school official Buck Dennim told a story about the President of the U.S. making a tour of the Navajo reservation. When introduced to an elderly Indian, the President asked if he had any advice to offer the nation. The old man replied, "Mr. President, my advice is that you watch your immigration laws; we got a little careless with ours." Dennim also said that when an Anglo asked a young Navajo, "Speakum English?" the young Indian retorted, "If that is the way you talk, I speak much better English than you do."

One method of communicating the gospel to Navajos in their own language was to use a small, portable, handheld record player. Gospel discs in Navajo were provided by the American Bible Society and Wycliffe translators. They were played by placing a finger in a groove and turning the player at a constant speed. The missionaries often played a portion to demonstrate the way to use the machine and then left it with Indian families. The players were inexpensive; novelty made them interesting, and most Navajos were too remote to have electricity.

A summer event involving summer workers, missionaries, and sometimes state language director Irvin Dawson was the campout VBS. Participants traveled far out on the reservation from a paved road, to a dirt road, to a path, until they came to a water tank where they parked and set up tents. These Bible schools only lasted one day but went from sunup to sundown and were attended by children and adults. They combined aspects of an all-day picnic with teaching the entire VBS two-week curriculum, and proved to be enormously popular.

In 1965 Page pastor M. K. Wilder provided preaching, Bible study, and sewing classes for the Navajos at Copper Mine mission. He wrote to Dawson that the Indians there responded to him because he came to help them in times of need such as illnesses or death. He reported fourteen members of the mission that year with average SS attendance of nine.

**Delbert and Mildred Fann**

Delbert Fann served as pastor of the Flagstaff Baptist Indian Mission from 1966 to 1968. He also served for six years as pastor of the Winslow First Indian Baptist Church before becoming director of language missions for the ASBC.

Fann testified, "My greatest contribution was in the field of theological education and ministry training, especially with ethnic church leaders. I directed up to ten different seminary extension branches each year in which hundreds of Indian, Spanish, Korean, and Anglo church leaders were trained."

For eleven years Fann was a national ethnic missionary for the HMB, leaving that position to direct an ethnic leadership development program for GGBTS. After thirty-seven years as language missionaries, the Fanns retired at the end of 1993 and moved to Shelbyville, Kentucky, where he writes and does volunteer work.

**Gerald Ross and Alice Lawton**

For about half the time of GCBA's fifty-year history, Gerald and Alice Lawton have pastored at Tuba City, far exceeding the longevity record of any other GCBA pastor. On March 27, 1937, a cold day with a light snow falling, Gerald was born in Iva, South Carolina. He attended Iva FBC from the time he was born. "In every game we played during my childhood, I was chosen to play the preacher," he remembered, "though I didn't imagine myself really becoming one. I wanted to be a carpenter like my Papa Lawton, but I never could get the hang of measuring the lumber properly or sawing straight and smooth cuts."

When he was eleven, Gerald was saved during a church revival. He took part in the church activities, including the choir, although he could not sing on pitch. "The choir director kindly told me to come to choir practice anyway and just sit. So I did," he admitted.

At age seventeen Gerald accompanied his youth group to Ridgecrest Baptist Assembly. He shared, "For several days I experienced a feeling I could not understand. I told the leader I was sick and went to bed until early evening when the others had gone to the service. Then I dressed and went to sit on the back seat of the auditorium. I could hardly wait for the invitation because I finally realized the Lord was calling me to preach to Indians, though I never had seen an Indian. As soon as the congregation began singing, 'Wherever He Leads, I'll Go,' I made my decision public. The sponsors, including my mother, told me they had been expecting me to feel God's call."

Gerald first met Alice Stuart when he was a Furman University junior, although she had grown up in Starr, only six miles from Iva. They started dating while he was a student at Southeastern Baptist Theological Seminary (SEBTS). She invited him to preach one night in a youth revival at her church, where he learned that she had volunteered for home missions.

One weekend Gerald came home to counsel a cousin who had asked him to perform her wedding. Discovering that Alice had some books he wanted his cousin to read, he invited her to join them for the counseling session. "On the way back to Alice's home, she asked me to marry her," is the way Gerald recalls what happened. "What could I say but 'Yes!'?"

When he learned in seminary about the RA missions program for boys, Gerald determined to provide that training in all the churches he would lead. His first pastorate was a two-church field in North Carolina. They started a prison ministry; Alice organized GAs and Sunbeams, and Gerald started RAs. He decided to take the boys to an RA camp at Fruitland Bible Institute. "Would you believe it? Our camp pastor was an Indian from Oklahoma. I was thrilled because this was my first contact with an Indian!" he declared.

Gerald remembers that during VBS at his next pastorate, he was teaching the mission story about Navajos, and he pronounced it "Nav-a-joes." During a school of missions (world missions conference), he and Alice had many opportunities to talk to the son of Ewell Payne, a longtime missionary to the Cherokees. For the first time Alice felt a burden for Indian work. They stopped by their associational office to ask their missionary, E. R. Eller, to pray with them. Later, Alice stated, "I'm ready to go."

When they applied to the HMB for appointment, they were turned down because of lack of experience in working with Indians. After four years of "tears and prayers," they were appointed to pastor a thirty-five-member congregation at Crown Point, New Mexico. On the way to the field, the Lawtons visited Audley and Jo Hammick and learned for the first time that the Navajos had their own language. "Audley painstakingly taught me to say 'hello' because he thought my congregation would appreciate my saying it the next morning," Gerald related. "The trouble was that the only Indians in church that morning were some children that didn't speak Navajo either." During their ministry there, the Lawtons received Hispanics, Anglos, Afro-Americans, and Indians into the church.

When they arrived to pastor the Tuba City Navajo Trail mission, Gerald and Alice found only two Indians attending. In three years attendance grew to an average of eighty in SS and 128 in worship services in a building that was supposed to seat only seventy-five. The first time he wanted to have Back Yard Bible Clubs (BYBCs), members did not think they could, but they conducted four clubs with fifty-two gathering in one front yard. The members were so excited that they wanted to have one every week the next summer.

Gerald organized the Trail Bible Institute and taught seminary classes with both basic and college-level courses. He held services at Cameron, started Bible study groups at Shonto, and taught six release-time classes for the BIA boarding schools. After three years he transferred to Shiprock, New Mexico, FBC, where he had to preach through an interpreter. When that church elected a nominating committee for the first time, the report took three hours to adopt because it was a new idea for them. He continued the Trail Bible Institute while Alice organized a WMU program and trained SS teachers. The Lawtons moved back to Tuba City two years later to find attendance had dropped back to twenty-three.

From the beginning Gerald has taken an active role in the community. He is volunteer chaplain for the Navajo police department and has served as the city fire chief. In order to enhance his counseling skills, he has taken chaplain training in crisis intervention, suicide prevention, drug and alcohol abuse, AIDS workshops, management and supervisory training, hospital and penal institution ministries, and interpersonal relations. Other special training he has received include Witness Involvement Now (WIN), prayer for spiritual awakening and revival preparation seminars, stress management, and money management workshops.

Gerald received degrees from Furman and SEBTS and certificates in clinical pastoral education from two hospitals. He attended the Billy Graham School of Evangelism and took courses at Yavapai College and the Moody Correspondence School. He is in great demand across the SBC as a World Missions Conference (WMC) speaker.

The Lawton children, Jonathan, Mary, Gerry, and Eric, grew up on the reservation and held elected positions as cheerleader, captain of the football team, class president, and student body president at the Tuba City High School. The reservation has about 80 percent unemployment; problem drinkers and teenage pregnancies are so prevalent that the high school has a special curriculum for students with children.

Tuba City FBC has been completely renovated and additional rooms built onto the parsonage. The church maintains food and crisis ministries. Not long ago when the church was on the move toward becoming self-supporting, the school superintendent fired 179 people in one day, and the BIA school fired twenty-six people. The school systems are the major source of income for the community. The church lost twenty families. The dismissals created such tension that the city has not yet recovered, and the church is still trying to make a comeback.

"In our early years we made many mistakes through ignorance," Gerald acknowledges. "I conducted my first funeral with a fifteen-minute sermon, prayed, and dismissed the group, only to learn that their custom called for eulogies by all who wish to speak and often last all day."

He remembers another funeral far out on a desolate stretch of the reservation when the mortician kept having car trouble and stopping the hearse. Gerald made repeated adjustments, but about every five miles the vehicle would die again. After the funeral, Gerald found a matchbook cover and set the points with it. When he saw the man again three weeks later, the points were still working perfectly well with the temporary arrangement.

One day when Gerald was burying some table scraps, including orange peelings, in his garden, a Navajo woman stopped to ask what he was doing. He told her, "I'm feeding my garden." The next time he visited her, he noticed that she had carefully placed a circle of whole oranges and grapefruits around each of the little cedar shrubs in her yard.

At one wedding ceremony Gerald performed, he arrived on daylight savings time, and the wedding party and guests did not show up until an hour later. "While I was talking, a sister of the bride got up from her seat three times to rearrange the wedding party. I was never sure that I had pronounced the right couple husband and wife. We saw them two weeks ago, and they told us they had just celebrated their thirteenth anniversary, so I guess they were satisfied with the spouse they got," he laughed.

Gerald and Alice have shared some helps for others who come to work with Navajos without knowing their traditions: It is highly insulting to refuse to eat with them because sharing food is a sign of acceptance and friendship. Accept all gifts with just a simple "thank you." Never point toward a Navajo. Do not whistle after sundown because whistling attracts evil spirits. Never ask a Navajo his name; ask one of his friends. Do not look into the eyes of a speaker; watch his lips. Do not ask many questions but wait patiently for information. Do not give compliments or expect expressions of gratitude. Navajos speak of good deeds only after a person has died.

Gerald is thrilled to have six students studying the "Principles and Practices of Preaching" Seminary Extension course during the 1995–1996 school year. He also rejoices that his people have caught a missions vision. "We have a special can for missions offerings in addition to the CP," he explained. "Every Sunday morning we observe a time for people to pass by and drop their offerings into the can. We have sent monies to a Navajo church in New Mexico, to an Indian congregation in Montana, to Kayenta to help with their new building, to the country of Macedonia, to Florida in the wake of Hurricane Andrew, and to India to help buy a printing press."

Gerald and Alice have been officially adopted into the Navajo nation. He has a nickname given by a Sioux who started right away calling him "chief." When the man noticed that when Gerald gets tired, the corner of his right eye turns blood red, the Indian began calling him "Chief Red Eye."

## Mike McKay: Baptist Indian Center

Language missionaries serving in pioneer missions make tremendous sacrifices to do God's will. Mike and Virginia McKay wrote concerning moving to Flagstaff from Fort Hall Indian Reservation in Idaho, "We've really had a wrestling match with the Lord. As usual, however, he won out. In spite of the huge salary, travel, and other cuts, we surrendered our wills to his and will be going to the Indian Center on May 1, 1981. I do not know how we'll be able to store furniture and pay moving costs, but we do not put a price tag on our service for God." When he accepted Christ, Mike was studying to be a Roman Catholic priest. He and Virginia retired in Alaska, where he directs the Anchorage FBC prayer ministry and preaches for a Korean congregation.

In 1982 a thirty-minute telecast over station KNAZ in Flagstaff called "The Navajo Baptist Hour" began spreading the gospel in Navajo. Designed especially for Navajos in their language, it reached to the boundaries of the sprawling reservation. A great help in the venture was the fact that the television channel manager was a member of Flagstaff FSBC who was eager to help in every way possible. The programs were all planned and produced by Navajos for Navajos. The state evangelism division added some financial support to that of the small Indian congregations who were paying for the telecast.

### *Primera Iglesia Bautista*

On February 1, 1976, the Spanish mission organized into *Primera Iglesia Bautista* after studying the "Baptist Faith and Message" and a church covenant for several weeks. The mission had started when the Williams Spanish mission conducted a VBS in Flagstaff and began week-night services in 1959. A revival that year resulted in six professions of faith. In 1960 the dilapidated building used in Williams was sold by the HMB, and the work was concentrated in Flagstaff, where eight thousand Hispanics lived. They met first in a residence at 1717 North West Street until the present building was erected on the corner of West Street and Sixth Avenue in 1962. Fifty-three charter members constituted the church family.

### Harold Boldin

In 1986 *Primera Iglesia Bautista* called Harold Boldin as pastor. Harold and his twin brother Hal were born October 16, 1934, at the family farm near Black Branch, Virginia. The family attended Black Branch Baptist Church, and in August 1944 during a revival, Harold accepted Christ and was baptized in the cold waters of Black Branch. Harold and Hal worked on the farm, graduated from Chase City High School, and attended Richmond Professional Institute until they enlisted together in the U.S. Army in November 1952. They trained with the 101st Airborne Division, but were selected for special training and assignment in the intelligence field, instead of going to Korea.

After military service, which included a two-year tour of duty in Ethiopia, Harold moved to Arlington, Virginia, to work for the National Security Agency and continue studies at the University of Virginia. There he met and married Althea Kay (Phoebe) Owens, who was employed as a cartographer at the Navy Hydrographic Office in Suitland, Maryland. They have three children: Harold Jr., Sharon Rickner, and Stephen, and seven grandchildren.

In April 1957 Harold began a twenty-eight-year law enforcement career which included seven years as a police officer in Fairfax County, Virginia, and Tucson, Arizona. In June 1964 he entered federal law enforcement where he continued until retirement in July 1985. This service included six years with the U.S. Border Patrol, three years as a U.S. Treasury Agent (narcotics), and twelve years as a U.S. Justice Department supervisory drug enforcement agent. While serving as a federal drug enforcement agent, Harold and his family spent ten years in diplomatic assignments in Colombia, Paraguay, Uruguay, and Argentina. All three children became fluent in the Spanish language and graduated from high schools in South America.

In addition to overseas assignments, Harold served in temporary duty assignments in presidential/dignitary protection and anti-terrorist duties. From 1978 to 1981, he headed a federal/state drug enforcement task force covering the state of Arizona. Twenty-two days after retirement, he suffered a massive heart attack in Flagstaff. During his six-month convalescence, Harold felt the Lord's call into full-time ministry. Following volunteer service with the FMB in a partnership evangelism campaign in Argentina, he accepted the call as pastor of *Primera Iglesia Bautista*, having previously preached in Spanish as pulpit supply for the church. He was ordained to the ministry on August 17, 1986.

Harold wrote that during his first pastorate, he learned the hard way that a pastor should always make sure he understands special requests, especially where baptism is concerned. "A four-hundred-plus-pound man requested that he accompany his two-hundred-plus-pound wife as she was baptized. I thought he meant that he wanted to go with her up to the point where she would enter the baptistry. To my surprise, just as I was about to baptize her, I looked up and saw the husband descending into the baptistry with us. The water rose to a level just under my chin and well above the top of my waders. With the waders filled with water, it was all I could do to climb out of the baptistry because of the extra weight."

On another occasion after Harold returned from preaching a revival in Argentina, he used as an illustration a remark a former Argentine man made to him about a year after his conversion. The man said, "I used to think Christian men were not very manly, but I have learned that it takes a man 'with hair on his chest' to be a Christian." Upon hearing this comment quoted, a young boy in the congregation leaned over and asked his mother, "Mama, does that mean Daddy isn't a Christian. He doesn't have any hair on his chest."

In 1987 the men of Flagstaff *Primera Iglesia Bautista* finished a major improvement and beautification project which included remodeling and a new roof of metallic Spanish tile. After serving for three years as a bilingual pastor of the Flagstaff church, Harold accepted the call to pastor Sunnyside Baptist Church in Douglas, where he also served for three years. In addition to pastoring, he guided the work of three Spanish-speaking missions, a friendship center ministry, and a prison ministry. In 1990 he became founding director and only instructor of the Douglas School of Theology, a Spanish language Ethnic Leadership Development Center, in cooperation with GGBTS.

*Primera Iglesia Bautista* reverted to mission status in January 1990 after several months when only Lilly and Juaquin Zamora and the Hunkes had met for Sunday worship. Three months later the work began anew as Sunnyside Baptist. Youth teams from Waurika, Oklahoma, Rustin, Louisiana, and Aurora, Colorado, led four BYBCs, a VBS, and evening revival services to start the new work. The VBS commencement program attracted 119 parents and children, a number of whom made decisions for Christ. Sunnyside constituted as a church with twenty-two members on October 21. Manny Martinez had come as pastor, and worship attendance reached sixty-nine, with nine candidates baptized that month.

### Manuel Martinez

Although Manny Martinez was born in 1953 in Oakdale, California, he grew up with his six brothers and four sisters in Flagstaff. "As a child, I never felt loved," Manny remembers. "I was always lonely and sad. When I was ten, I went back to California to live with an uncle for a while, but didn't feel accepted there either and soon came back home. I didn't like school and just felt confused and unhappy no matter where I was."

Manny's father worked hard, but was an alcoholic. Manny recalls coming home and finding his dad beating his mother. "She had fallen on the floor and had blood all over her face. I was scared he was killing her and began calling for my older brothers to help me stop him. Together we were able to restrain him. Other times all eleven of us children would jump on Dad and hold him to keep him from beating her," Manny stated.

Manny remembers going to bed hungry and later going to school with nothing to eat all day. By the time he was eight or nine years old, he had learned to go to the La Fonda restaurant and ask to clean rest rooms or mop the floor in order to get a hamburger and some fries to eat. When he was a little older, Manny began working there as a dishwasher and receiving a regular salary. "Every check had to go home to Mom," he recalls. "I didn't think about helping the family; I just resented handing my checks over to Mom and began to hate her. When I was fifteen, I told her I wouldn't give her any more of my money, and she showed me the door and told me to get out."

Manny lived by himself for a time in a small, unheated trailer. He was so lonely and afraid that he moved in with some brothers and sisters, but when he began to cause trouble, they told him to move out. He went to San Antonio to work for a brother, but soon began drinking and doing foolish things and had to come back to Flagstaff. At age seventeen he started back to school for his senior year, but quit just three months short of graduation because he could not stand to be told what to do.

"When I went back to work at La Fonda, God brought Angela into my life," he testifies. He was amazed to learn she could not speak English. Manny had not bothered to learn Spanish even though it was spoken in his home, and now he was unable to communicate with a person he liked very much. "We had to get my brother Vincent to interpret for us," he admitted. "We started dating and soon fell in love and learned to under-stand each other as she began to learn English and I started trying to speak Spanish."

Angela attended *Primera Iglesia Bautista* and kept inviting Manny to go with her, but he made excuses that he was Catholic and his parents would not like it although he had not cared about the Catholic church or what his family thought for years. "We were married at her Spanish Baptist church, but I told her I wouldn't have anything to do with the church or with God," Manny confessed. When he finally attended one Sunday, he was much offended when the pastor preached the truth from the Word that those without Christ were lost and going to hell. "Who did he think he was to tell me that I was lost?" he demanded.

Angela kept going to church faithfully and inviting Manny, but for six months he refused. He would pretend he had work at La Fonda's, when he actually just wasted time there waiting for her to get out of church. When a revival started, he agreed to attend and went every night. "By Friday night I realized at last that Someone really loved me with that love and acceptance I had always longed for but never felt. I wanted to go for-ward but was afraid. I had always been too scared to even answer a question or speak out in school, and now I couldn't even move!" Manny declared. "I praise the Lord that the preacher's wife came to me and asked if I would go forward to accept Christ if she went with me. When she took the first step, so did I. Pastor Fernando Martinez led me to pray the sinner's prayer and thank God for loving and saving me."

The first person Manny wanted to tell about being saved was his mother. He asked her forgiveness for all the anger he had felt, and from that moment he and his mother have had a loving relationship. "For the first time in my life I had such peace and love and joy in my heart that I loved everyone and wanted to share Christ with everyone," he shared. As soon as Richard Vera came as pastor of *Primera Iglesia Bautista*, he started having Manny greet people at the door. Soon he felt God calling him to go back to school to prepare for the ministry. Although Vera rejoiced at his call, Angela told Manny he was crazy, and his brothers teased him and predicted he would soon be back living the old life.

After praying, Angela felt the call to go with Manny to school. The Flagstaff church licensed him to preach in June 1976 before they left for San Antonio for training at the Spanish-speaking Bible institute. Adam was one and a half when they started, and Adreana was born while they were in school. Because of the high humidity, Manny suffered much with asthma. After two and a half years, when they came back to Flagstaff for a vacation and found the church without a pastor, Manny preached on Sunday. On Monday they started back to school by way of Phoenix to visit Angela's brother Guy. That day a call came from *Primera Iglesia* asking Manny to be interim pastor until they could call someone. For two years he served as interim while working about sixty hours a week at a tire shop to make a living.

When *Primera Iglesia Bautista* called Roland Lopez as pastor, he asked Manny to be his associate, and on May 4, 1980, the church ordained him. Manny felt he was not in God's will and began praying about going back to San Antonio to finish school. A call came from Dallas to be an associate pastor with a salary, place to live, and money for school. By this time Eric had been born. Manny's main concern had been how to support his family while he was in school, so he took the position in Dallas without determining whether it was God's plan. It did not work out, and he came back to Flagstaff disillusioned and bitter to work again at the tire shop. Unhappy and out of God's will, he felt he had come to the end of the road when the tire shop closed, and he could not find another job in town.

Finally, Manny moved to Tucson in order to work at another tire shop. He joined a church that Roland Lopez was pastoring and again became his associate, but he still felt he was not in God's will because he had not finished school and was not a pastor. He felt that the reason for the time in Tucson was that when the church began extension courses from GGBTS, he enrolled and was able to graduate with his diploma in theology. After trouble developed at work, he found a job in Phoenix and became active in a church.

Pastor Greg Gearing contacted Manny about starting Spanish work at Southern Baptist Temple, warning him, "We have no Spanish people coming, but the need is great." Roland Lopez told him it was a perfect opportunity for God to use him, but Manny was still scared and running from God.

Lopez cautioned him, "Manny, you better quit playing games with God. Be careful or he will deal with you." Manny accepted the mission pastorate in 1983. For six months no one came except his family and one other woman. He kept wondering if God really wanted him there. Then Israel Lopez, an eight-year-old boy, accepted Christ, and his family came to see him baptized. The whole family began attending, and one by one were saved and baptized—that helped Manny's spirits.

Two years later Satan caused Manny to feel discouraged, but when he told Greg that he felt he should leave the ministry, Greg told him the feeling was not of God. Southern Baptist Temple members began praying for Manny, and God confirmed through the Word the call to keep on preaching, teaching, and baptizing. Greg encouraged him to take his GED exam because Manny always felt inadequate from not finishing high school.

When the Spanish mission merged with the sponsoring church, Manny went back to work at the tire shop and prayed that God would use him to witness at work. He won the foreman and four other workers to Christ. "To this very day, that tire shop has gospel music playing all day long," Manny says. A year later he began praying for a door to open to be a full-time pastor again and called Don Cartwright at the state office, only to be told there were no openings in Phoenix, but a Spanish pastor was needed at the church in Flagstaff. Manny had promised the Lord to go anywhere, but now he said, "Lord, I meant anywhere else but Flagstaff."

God confirmed that he was, indeed, calling him back to Flagstaff. When Manny again called Cartwright, he was informed, "The church doors have been closed for two months. You will have to start all over again." A month later the church reopened as Sunnyside Baptist. Manny began visiting and seeing people saved and baptized from his first Sunday. After he saw an aunt and cousin accept Christ, Manny was amazed when his dad and mom started coming; they had never entered a church before.

Soon his mother came forward saying she wanted to be saved, but she would never be baptized. More aunts and cousins began to join. One Sunday his dad called him outside to tell him that he did not want to be a visitor any longer. He wanted to be part of the church. Manny went home with his parents that day, and his father prayed to accept Christ in his living room. His mother surprised him by coming forward for baptism, with his dad soon following. During the years many family members have been reached.

In January 1991 Sunnyside voted to complete the pastorium that had remained unfinished for twenty years. A call went out to GCBA churches to help raise the ten thousand dollars needed to do the job. Gifts of seventy-five hundred dollars and a loan of three thousand dollars, together with volunteer labor, enabled the home to be finished.

In April 1991 after the congregation had sung "Soon and Very Soon, We're Going to See the King," Clarence Hood asked to speak. "That is my testimony today," he shared. "Very soon I'm going to see Jesus." The next day when Manny visited Clarence to discuss the kitchen cabinets he had promised to build for the pastorium, all he wanted to talk about was going to see his King. On Tuesday Clarence died. His nephew Mike received Christ at his funeral after Manny told of his conviction that he would see Jesus soon. Clarence's sister donated $150 to build the cabinets.

On Manny's first anniversary at Sunnyside, he reported the church had baptized twenty-nine, and his family had moved into the finished pastorium. In the summer of 1992, volunteers from Williams helped pour a concrete floor for a new master bedroom and bath. Guy Meraz laid blocks and donated windows for the new room. A pack-the-pew emphasis brought 124 to worship on May 31, 1992, when an all-out effort by Manny's mother resulted in thirty of the Martinez family members attending.

Manny testified that he had not wanted to go back to Flagstaff because he was so tired of the snow, but God had caused him to enjoy snow and be thankful for its beauty. Sunnyside regularly reaches about 140 people, and members are praying the Lord will help them build a new sanctuary to seat 170 so they can use the present auditorium for fellowship. In 1995 they raised funds to purchase 170 new chairs, ninety of which are set up in the sanctuary. They donated their pews to an Indian congregation. "We are raising a building fund and continuing to trust God and experience him in a great way. We give him all the honor and glory!" Manny affirms.

### Kayenta: Virgil Stoneburner

Although LeRoy Bond had begun a mission at Kayenta in 1962, when his school teaching job did not continue and he moved away, the work closed. When catalytic missionary Virgil Stoneburner notified Bill Hunke that a new church, Kayenta FBC, had been constituted on the Navajo Reservation and wished to affiliate with GCBA, the Hunkes met with the group on September 11, 1988. Services were in a mobile chapel.

Stoneburner preached for the new church until they secured a permanent pastor. They were received into GCBA at the annual meeting at Page on October 13, 1988, when they reported attendance had reached fourteen. In June 1989 Tom Roatch, an NAU and SWBTS graduate, arrived to pastor the church. That summer a thirty-two-member team from Orangeburg, South Carolina, flew to Phoenix, rented six vans, drove to Kayenta, lived in a school, erected a 20 x 30' tent, and enrolled 132 in VBS.

In 1995 Kayenta FBC constructed a new building on the reservation after years of waiting for a permit from the Navajo tribal council. In February 1996 Rick Bond, no relation to LeRoy, came to serve as pastor.

When the Four Corners Baptist Association, which consisted of eleven Indian churches and missions, constituted October 7, 1989, Kayenta, Flagstaff Indian, and Dry Lake joined the new fellowship. Flagstaff Indian Baptist Church was constituted in November 1989. Stoneburner became missionary for the new Indian association.

Virgil Wayne Stoneburner was born April 16, 1931, at Marseilles, Illinois. He remembered, "I was saved at home at age eight after a sermon on hell. My mother led me to the Lord that afternoon. When we returned to church that night, I wanted to testify, but they said I could not be saved because I was not yet twelve years old. The next morning I took my red wagon out to the corner of Pearl and Union streets to preach to those passing by. My message was repent or go to hell." The Marseilles Baptist Church baptized him on Easter Sunday.

Virgil graduated from Dallas Baptist College. He married Donna Jean Potter, and they have four children. He served as a church starter in Illinois and pastored in California and at Mesa, Sells, Tucson, and Many Farms, Arizona. He wrote, "My mother moved to Arizona for health reasons. We came to see her on Thanksgiving 1968 and fell in love with the state. We prayed and decided in 1969 to move to Mesa. I was called as pastor of Mesa Immanuel Baptist Church. In 1970 we began working with the Indians." He was employed as missionary to the Indians in 1987. Because his territory has overlapped the GCBA area ever since, he has always cooperated with GCBA churches. Virgil retired in April 1996.

# That the Generation To Come Might Know

## GCBA YOUTH: GRAND CANYON COLLEGE, SUMMER MISSIONARIES, BSU

Through meditation on God's key works in the past, the psalmist appropriated lessons learned to meet his present needs. His remembrances of God's former dealings soothed his troubled soul like a balm. He then extolled the need to pass his recollections and reflections to the next generation. Narration of the past to our youth will help them avoid errors and recognize that God is still working in the universe. Recounting our history endeavors to lead young people and college students to prize and improve their heritage.

GCBA was especially blessed to have our Baptist college start in our territory, to have assemblies at Prescott in our territory for many years, to have student summer missionaries from all over the nation to work with our children, and to have a vital BSU program at NAU during much of our existence.

### Beginning of Grand Canyon College (Now University)

On October 30, 1946, J. N. Campbell of the Coolidge FBC delivered a moving report on Christian education at the BGCA annual meeting at Glendale Calvary Baptist Church. After adoption of the report, L. D. White, pastor of Casa Grande Calvary, moved to amend the report and add a resolution calling for the establishment of a Baptist college in Arizona no later than the middle of September 1947. When the amended report passed, White came striding down the aisle, slammed a silver dollar on the communion table, and expressed delight that he had given the first dollar for a college.

After J. N. Phillips gave the second dollar and H. R. Spraker the third, R. E. Cure, pastor at Roosevelt, Utah, in GCBA, moved that the convention receive an offering and pledges. Vernon Shipp made the first one-thousand-dollar pledge, U. R. Neely the second, and Peter Ethington gave the first check for one thousand dollars for the college. The meeting became emotional when a widow from Glendale brought a quart jar full of coins with a value of about eight dollars and presented the money for the proposed school.

As soon as news about the college became known, offers of sites on which to locate it began to come in. Two offers came from Casa Grande and others from Prescott, Yuma, Coolidge, Cottonwood, Clarkdale, Fort Huachuca, Tempe, and even Mormon Lake. The actual site was not determined until 1948 when the decision was made to locate it at Prescott. The city's chamber of commerce immediately announced on the radio that a dance would be held to raise funds. The message was, "Dance for the benefit of the Baptist college."

Willis J. Ray had to write a letter to the editor of the Prescott *Courier* explaining the Baptist position on dancing. Ray had been elected as promoter and first president of the college, sharing his time equally between it and the convention, with his $450 monthly salary paid $200 by the state and $250 by the school.

On September 13, 1949, Southern Baptists participated in one of Prescott's most impressive parades to open Grand Canyon College. About four hundred cars, stretching the length of seven city blocks, slowly circled the city square before advancing up Gurley Street to the Armory. A crowd of 750 persons attended the afternoon program to hear Governor Dan Gurley, Willis J. Ray, representatives from the city, state, and national governments, and leaders of state colleges and the university pay their respects to Arizona's newest institution of higher learning.

A hungry crowd of over two thousand consumed four beeves, mountains of slaw, and tubs of beans at the free barbecue after the program. Every available seat was filled for the evening program which was dedicated to the faculty and trustees of the college and to the pastors and state convention employees. Phoenix FSBC pastor C. Vaughan Rock brought the main address.

A total of ninety-five students from eleven states enrolled for the first semester. Thirty-three of them were ministerial students. Classes met in the National Guard Armory and in Prescott FSBC, just two blocks away.

The GCC library was in the nearby Smoki Museum. Although the school moved to Phoenix in 1951, its impact on GCBA, because of the spiritual influence its faculty and students had on the area, is immeasurable. From its beginning GCC students preached in GCBA churches and mission points, and faculty members like D. C. Martin pastored and provided leadership for associational activities. Williams FBC member Leo Atherton was listed among the first-year students for the ministry.

GCBA suffered many losses in 1951. For some time Arizona Southern Baptists had been unofficially discussing moving GCC from Prescott to Phoenix. President Leroy Smith wrote an article in the January 25 *Beacon* stating that the move would be profitable because of the availability of a larger student body and a larger job market for students who had to work. At a called meeting of college trustees that same day, a motion was adopted calling for relocation, with summer-term classes in Prescott and the fall semester to begin in Phoenix.

The first graduation exercises for GCC were on May 27–28, 1951, at Prescott FSBC with Leroy Smith preaching the baccalaureate message and Willis J. Ray bringing the commencement address. On September 17, 1951, the fall term began at 3300 West Camelback Road, Phoenix, where eighty acres of farm land had been purchased and eight buildings were under construction. Dust was six inches deep between buildings, and woolly caterpillars from nearby cotton fields covered the ground.

### VBS Summer Missionaries in 1958: Martha Goff and Ann Biffle

Early GCBA student summer missionaries paid high tribute to Troy and Katherine Brooks. In 1958 Martha Goff wrote, "Only God knows what Papa and Mama Brooks meant to me from the first moment I found myself riding up Black Canyon highway with them. Their love for the mountains, for the people of Arizona, and for the Lord was contagious. I will always cherish those precious times when I had the privilege of being with them, even the morning Papa woke us up with flying pillows. And never will I forget those homemade rolls Mama Brooks made. None of us knew we could eat so much until she made rolls."

Ernie Myers told the girls that soap and water would not be enough in Arizona, that they also would need plenty of deodorant. "He failed to mention the places we would have no water!" they said. Ann Biffle wrote, "I found what Ernie meant when he encouraged us to keep clean, although it was hard without water, and sometimes I wondered if we would ever get off all the grime. Then there were the bugs—little and big, flying and crawling. I almost got attached to some of the regulars that visited us. One night I was almost too scared to breathe when I heard footsteps outside my window. When I finally got brave enough to look out, I found myself staring a cow in the face."

Martha told of living in the back of the church at Ash Fork and the joy of working with A. A. Moore, Mr. and Mrs. James, Mrs. Farmer, and Mrs. McAbee. "I never knew before how much beginners could love Jesus," she admitted. "One day in class I had to laugh when little David turned to his friend who had just said ain't and told him, 'You ain't supposed to say ain't.'" They enrolled forty-six students that week.

She vividly remembered an experience at Seligman when the mission met in an old building with inadequate facilities. On the second Tuesday of VBS, after she attended a very sad funeral, she wrote, "The man being buried was the father of three of our VBS children who had taken his own life on the Sunday before. It was agonizing to realize he had no hope for eternity, and his family had no real Comforter."

**Eugene and Ellamae Elder**
Eugene Elder wrote of his excitement when he learned from the HMB that he and his wife Ellamae would be working on the Indian reservation. "In my mind I could see the Indians living in their tepees arranged in a circle around a centrally located campfire. I imagined them smoking their pipes and dancing around the fire, preparing for a fight as I had seen them do in the movies. When I arrived at Tuba City and started looking for the tepees, I felt a sense of disappointment, but by the time the two wonderful weeks were over, I was happy the reservation was not the way I had visualized it. My stay was filled with wonderful experiences and the blessing of souls saved. My first night was most enjoyable because I met a nineteen-year-old Navajo boy who cooked fry bread for our supper."

Ellamae added with amazement and grief, "My first day at Tuba I was amazed at the sight of the hogans and the trading post. The VBS was filled with rich and exciting incidents. I taught intermediates, most of whom were not Christians. I felt a deep concern for Priscilla who was under conviction, but did not accept Christ during the school. The last night at Indian camp we saw her step forward to make her profession of faith. Another girl I cared for deeply was Luana who had dedicated her life to medical missions. When I asked her why, she told me how sorry she felt for people who suffer and of her desire to help them. I grieved when I thought how hard it would be for those girls to be true to Christ in the culture where so many temptations like constant squaw dances, bingo parties, and drunkenness attract young people."

Eugene described the facilities since they did not have a church building in which to meet: "We met in the Tuba community center which everyone in town used for all activities. The Catholics had the building first on Sunday mornings, and as they came out, we Baptists went in. On Monday nights the Catholics had their bingo games there. The building was only one big room, which was inadequate for the seventy-one boys and girls enrolled in VBS. We conducted four large classes in the room, and it was mass confusion. I had twenty-one juniors, four of whom accepted Christ at the decision service. At Indian camp I led another of my boys to Christ."

Eugene and Ellamae also worked at the Williams Spanish VBS, a VBS at the Flagstaff Indian Center, and in east Flagstaff where they conducted Spanish school in the morning and an Indian school in the afternoon. Ellamae wrote that by the end of the Indian Center VBS, every pupil in her class had become a Christian in spite of the fact that they had Catholic backgrounds.

She continued, "My husband and I are foreign mission volunteers, but my eyes have been opened to the great need for missions in Arizona, and we feel that we may make our life's work among the Indian people. Their culture is almost foreign because they have such primitive conditions and superstitions. We also wish more people could realize the tremendous need for more workers among the Spanish people in the state."

Later, Eugene wrote, "To make a long story short, my wife and I went home with the intention of carrying out our previous commitment to foreign missions, but the call of Arizona missions needs was so heavy upon our hearts that we couldn't stay in the South and be happy. After spending two days with each of our parents, we packed up all our possessions and made the long trip back to Arizona. We are now in Phoenix preparing ourselves for work among the Indians. Our prayer is that more Baptists will respond to this same call."

### Language Missions Student Summer Missionary: Margaret Osborne

When Margaret Osborne received her HMB appointment to serve with language missions in Arizona, she was disappointed. "I had hoped for some place more glamourous like Hawaii or even California," she admitted. "All I could find out about the state centered on the terrific heat and the grasshopper plague that year."

Before her ten weeks of work ended, however, she confessed, "The summer has been a wonderful experience which I'll never, never forget.

The mission work was like being in a foreign country. It has had a great influence on my life, and I am grateful for the opportunities I had."

The five language summer workers were under Irvin Dawson, whose orientation speech included warnings against jumping cactus, snakes, and scorpions. When Margaret heard of Catholic priests who boasted that no other religious group could ever enter their towns, she expected to encounter rocks and curses, but the threats did not materialize. She did find that the work was hard and slow because opposition was so great. At one place where the only members of the mission were the pastor and family, she was shocked on Sunday when no one else came to church.

She told of a surprise one Sunday night when the workers were tired and discouraged and had decided that likely no one would show up that night. "We even put our hair up on rollers because our faith was so weak," she admitted. "Then the pastor ran in and shouted, 'Brother Sam is at church. Hurry!' We went with our hair in curlers and gave our testimonies that night. Before the meeting ended, a crowd of twenty-two persons had come. I learned to not give up on God."

### Student Summer Missionaries in 1960

Missionary M. V. Mears wrote about his first year of working with student summer missionaries: "I can say we never had a dull moment. The summer provided new experiences for each of the young people as they worked with races they scarcely knew existed and surely never expected to have a close relationship with. They came to grips with problems that pose a threat to young lives. They faced crises without faltering as they marched bravely forward with Christ's help."

"For example, when one of the young ladies learned that the income of an Indian mission was not enough to provide SS literature during the summer months, she gave me a sufficient amount from her meager wages and asked me to order what they needed. Her letters home bore such a warm message that her church sent boxes of new Bibles and testaments to give out to the people," Mears explained.

One of the most interesting and spiritually stimulating weeks of the summer for Mears came when he joined forces with the students and served as principal of a VBS in South Flagstaff which enrolled forty-four Indians, Hispanics, and blacks. "We met in a five-room house and filled it to overflowing. These children did not attend SS. We also had as helpers the A. A. Moores from the Indian Center, the W. B. Minors from the Spanish mission, and some women and youth from Flagstaff FSBC. They will try to follow up the contacts we made."

Mears summed up his feelings by reporting, "These young people took a census in two places that will develop into new missions and perhaps revive another. They worked in sixteen VBSs, enrolled 627 with an average attendance of 531, and led 30 to professions of faith in Christ. They attended and helped in five summer camps and blessed every child they taught."

### La Wanda Carlisle and Laurel Bachetti

La Wanda Carlisle was frightened when she found she would be working in GCBA without a partner in 1960. "I had no idea that any place on earth could be so beautiful as Sedona where my first VBS was to be; I wanted to just stay there the entire summer," she recalled. "When I arrived, I was told I had charge of the planning meeting that night and would also be principal of the school. No plans had been made for an intermediate department, but I decided to have one, and we enrolled eleven teenage girls. That week we had seventy students with five accepting Christ."

At Williams, La Wanda worked in the Spanish VBS, which included eight black children. "It was a joy to see them worship, play, work, and learn together about the Bible," she testified. At Seligman she found a small group of dedicated people eager to have a successful school. When she worked in the Flagstaff Spanish VBS with juniors who were mostly Catholic, thirteen of them prayed to receive Christ. "My heart echoed the prayer of a primary boy on the last day of VBS when he told God, 'Please let us do this again next year,'" she concluded.

Laurel Bachetti remembered an eleven-year-old girl who was under conviction: "When she yielded to the Holy Spirit, she was frightened about what her strict Mormon family would do. To her surprise her family came to the commencement service that evening. I felt that Satan was placing an impossible obstacle before the young girl. Imagine everyone's happiness, when in spite of parental opposition, she went forward making her faith public. When she came to me afterwards, expressing fear of what would happen, I told her she would have to rely on the Lord. That brand new little Christian looked at me with tears in her eyes and said, 'I know it's going to take faith, but that's the one thing I have now.'"

### Bob Seymour and Raymond Wilson

Bob Seymour spent the summer working with the Navajos. The first four weeks were with the A. A. Moores at Copper Mine, where sixty-three

Indian children attended. At another location where all-day campout activities had been scheduled, no one showed up. About eleven o'clock a Navajo man came by and asked what they planned to do there. Upon hearing their plans, he told them they could not have a Bible school at that place because a baby had died there about thirty years ago and that the Indians would not come.

Bob worked with the Bob Greens at Tuba City and with the Greens and Ollie Blevins at Red Lake. "At Red Lake where we had both morning and evening VBSs, I came to see more clearly the needs of the Navajos," he stated. "They are a great people, but they don't know the Lord." When he moved to Flagstaff to help in VBS at the Indian Center, he worked with Indian, black, and Spanish children, "All with one thing in common—they needed Christ."

Raymond Wilson called working at Copper Mine with the Ollie Blevins for six weeks the heart of the raw mission field. "The Navajos number about eighty thousand with about 95 percent not professing to know Christ. They are forever lost without hope unless dedicated Christians will carry them the good news," he lamented.

### Camellia Garrett, Raymona Rainey, and Faye Wilbanks

Camellia Garrett's initial thrill and excitement about coming to Arizona became overshadowed with gloom when she encountered so many needs. "I was never so shocked in my life!" she exclaimed. "Why, it's almost like being in a foreign land. I had never thought about home missions before, but now the needs are continuously on my heart." All eight weeks of VBS with Indians, anglos, and blacks brought unique blessings for Camellia.

"The Navajo boys and girls found a very special place in my heart," she wrote. "At first I felt sorry for them because of their primitive way of living. Then their need for Christ struck me when one of my junior boys asked who Jesus was. Apparently, he had never heard the gospel. How hard it was to try to explain so that he could understand," she admitted.

"Taking census was not new to me," she continued, "but it was an altogether different experience here in the West than it had been in South Carolina. How I longed to talk with Mormons and Catholics about their souls! They slammed doors in my face; I was ordered out of a Mormon home. I'll never forget asking a young Mormon girl if she was saved. She laughed in my face and said, 'How could I know? Nobody knows that.' I left her with sorrow in my heart and a prayer on my lips that she and others like her may know Christ. How appreciative I am of God's precious promises and the assurance of salvation."

Raymona Rainey also spoke of the heartaches that came with census taking because so many people believed that affiliation with some church would save them. She helped in a VBS at the Chevlon ranger station and lumber camp, where she remembered a thirteen-year-old boy who surrendered to the Lord and was an inspiration to the whole school. "His goodbye to us was, 'I'll see you in heaven,'" she said.

Faye Wilbanks began her summer at Sedona FBC, where she felt no one could help being aware of the Lord because of his marvelous works of creation. "Yet in this lovely place I met a sixteen-year-old girl who doubted that even the physical world was real," she said. "The girl reasoned that Christ could not be real either. I shall never forget the tears in her eyes as she told me that she could never believe anything is good. I rejoiced that her younger brother promised that no matter what happened, he meant to follow Christ."

Faye was impressed by her two weeks at Tuba City at the campout Bible schools. "I can still hear the Indian boys and girls as they sang *Shi K'ad Jesus Bik'ee* ("I Have Decided to Follow Jesus"), a favorite of theirs. I shall never forget the many who have not yet decided, or Rose, our interpreter, and her desire to serve him."

## GCBA Summer Missionaries in 1995

Angie Averitte of DeSoto, Texas, and Gretchen Jeffreys of New Iberia, Louisiana, wrote, "Neither of us knew what to expect, and we found Arizona very different from Texas and Louisiana. We've discovered that the wind never stops blowing, and it seems as if we can see forever with no humidity in the air. Although it's dry, the state is not one big desert as we had thought. We also had to get used to the high altitude in GCBA."

"Our experiences as summer missionaries have ranged from surprising to scary! We've done VBSs, BYBCs, youth, and construction work. Having opportunity to work with Navajo children was exciting. Moving to different towns every week caused us to run across interesting people. Each host family has made us feel at home. Although we've been attacked by a dog and swarmed by spiders, we knew God was in control and taking care of us. We have learned more about him through every situation and thank him for the opportunity to serve in GCBA."

## Reports on Youth Work at GCBA Annual Meetings

At the 1964 annual meeting at Page, missionary M. V. Mears reported an attendance of fifty-six at the GCBA VBS clinic, with seven pastors and seven churches and missions represented. Seven churches had VBSs with an enrollment of 755 and 33 professions of faith. Opal Williams, GCBA WMU director, reported that sixty-four girls attended the GCBA GA associational house party at Flagstaff FSBC; five young women attended the state Young Women's Auxiliary (YWA) house party; seventeen women attended the prayer retreat in Sedona; and nine women attended the WMU state camp at Prescott.

Mears was the volunteer pastor advisor when the BSU first organized in northern Arizona on October 29, 1956. Sid Davis, state BSU and music director, came to Flagstaff for the first meeting. Peter Hamilton of Casa Grande was elected president, and Calvin Sandlin of NAU was elected vice-president. GCBA minutes did not have records of early BSU activities until 1964 when Henry Pearson, volunteer director, reported meetings twice a month with an average attendance of twelve and high of thirty. Their special events included a sweetheart banquet, spring planning retreat at Prescott, and the BSU state convention at Phoenix. He said that the BSU had grown tremendously in initiative, interest, and inspiration, and had been recognized as a campus organization with an approved constitution. He noted they had found over fifty prospects on campus and had about thirty-five students active in Flagstaff churches and missions.

At the 1965 GCBA annual meeting at Sedona, Pearson reported that BSU membership at NAU was forty-five with twenty-five average attendance. The year's highlights included the BSU convention in Flagstaff, the spring retreat at Prescott, the student missions conference at GGBTS, and student week at Glorieta, all of which had several representatives from NAU. Of special interest was the missionary journeyman program launched by the FMB with the first volunteers going out that year.

Mears reported that GCBA hosted the two-day state summer missionary orientation. The four young people who served in this association worked in ten VBSs and took census in two Flagstaff areas. The schools were conducted at Flagstaff Calvary, FSBC, Baptist Indian, and Spanish Baptist, and at Cameron, Sedona, Williams, Fredonia, Tuba City Navajo Trail, and Red Lake, many having ten-day schools. They recorded twenty-two professions of faith. GCBA VBS superintendent A. A. Moore recommended that an effort be made to have schools in Doney Park, Happy Jack, Parks, Grand Canyon, Cedar Ridge, Kaibito, Shonto, and other locations next year.

For a time in the 1970s, the BSU met at Flagstaff Baptist Indian Mission. During those years they had a singing group called Brother Preacher's People that sang for most of the GCBA churches in northern Arizona.

I. B. and Opal Williams (lower left) led in starting GCBA Spanish work. The Robert Greens are on the right.

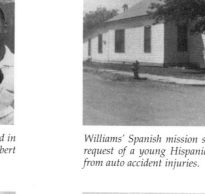

Williams' Spanish mission started at the request of a young Hispanic man dying from auto accident injuries.

W. B. Minor (left) and M. V. Mears (right) assisted in groundbreaking services for a Spanish mission building in 1962.

Flagstaff Spanish mission began with a 1959 VBS and revival. Primera Iglesia Bautista organized February 1, 1976.

Faithful Spanish-speaking families have maintained the witness. Pictured above are Lilly and Juaquin Zamora.

Harold Boldin and son Steve (4–5 from left) led Spanish services at Flagstaff in 1986–1989 and Tusayan in 1992.

NAU Baptist Student Union organized on Oct. 29, 1956. A Flagstaff BSU building, bought in 1975, was remodeled in 1995.

Marc and Lisa Hill came in 1989 as BSU directors for GCBA. Marc gave halftime to Greenlaw until 1996.

ASBC assisted GCBA by leading conferences, providing materials and financial help for projects, and employing missionaries. ASBC staff members in 1966 were: Top (l/r)—Crotts, Sutton, McKay, Brown, Wilson. Bottom—Archer, Childress, Cates, Canafax, Dawson.

Nancy, Lois, and Frank Sutton on the left. Frank served as BGCA's first state missions director, 1952–1956.

Other 1966 ASBC staff were Barnes, Parker, and Hunke. Paul Barnes and Childress joined the staff in 1966.

Although the BSU enjoyed many social activities and spent much time and energy in fund-raising, they never forgot their primary purposes of spreading God's Word and creating an atmosphere of Christian fellowship for students. In 1971 NAU hosted the state BSU convention.

### Innovators

In 1974 the HMB initiated a volunteer youth mission program called Innovators. The program was designed to encourage college students to secure secular work in areas needing missionary help during the summer. Grand Canyon National Park became a showcase of the new program, using the Innovators in retail stores, fast-food restaurants, and motels. Because living space at the park was at a premium, the park service permitted businesses to construct student dormitories. From that time to the present, students annually assist Grand Canyon FBC in Bible studies, BYBCs, music and drama groups, and in regular church services at Shrine of the Ages chapel.

At the annual meeting at Williams in 1977, GCBA WMU director Linda Pogany reported that Flagstaff FSBC had its first Acteen coronation in eight years with Shirley Pogany crowned Acteen queen. WMU organizations were meeting weekly at Flagstaff FSBC, Greenlaw, and Sedona, with other churches having monthly meetings. Williams had organized very active GA and Acteen groups that year. For the first time a Mission Service Corps report was given because the theme for the coming year was "Volunteer Involvement in MSC," with the aim of placing five thousand volunteers in the field by 1982, including many young people. Every year thereafter, the BSU raised money and sent volunteers from among its members.

### Resort Ministries

In 1978 a national Resort Ministries clinic was held at Grand Canyon with several GCBA pastors attending. That summer Grand Canyon FBC reported 21 members, 31 professions of faith, and 9 baptisms. The 8 summer missionaries and 12 Innovators and other volunteers held 37 campfire concerts with a total attendance of 3,250 and 72 Shrine of the Ages concerts with total attendance of 12,460. They also did 165 sidewalk and mini concerts with total attendance of 15,800. They hosted 11 mission concert groups, conducted 51 worship services, and built a worship/concert site in a campground near the park from logs and stones.

Bob Neeley, pastor of Page FSBC, shared results of the Resort Ministries Project which used two summer missionaries, volunteers, and

Southern Baptists they found during campsite visits. They made a total of 1,452 contacts with witnessing at each encounter. They reached people through amphitheater worship services, BYBCs, movies, campsite visits, campfire services, bulletin handouts, day camps, and an intown survey. They gave away a multitude of soul-winning tracts and 150 Bibles.

In 1979 Flagstaff FSBC sent Brian Wilcox and Jeanna Hodges as summer missionaries. Evelyn Lewis and Darrow Miller accompanied a BSU group to Mexico to do mission work. That year Jay Dorris, BSU director, reported two weekly Bible studies, four students who had been saved and baptized, and one called into full-time ministry. Other activities included retreats, international student ministry, mission projects, and helping churches reach students. Jeff Wallace from GCBA served as a FMB journeyman in Bangkok, Thailand, in 1979. In 1995 Jeff and his wife Cecilia began work as FMB missionaries on Grand Canary Island. Mike and Karla Taylor worked as U.S.-2ers with the HMB in Iowa in 1979.

Jay Dorris reported at the 1983 GCBA annual meeting that thirteen students attended the fall retreat at Grand Canyon, eleven attended the state leadership training at Prescott, and nine attended the student missions conference at GGBTS. Three students had acknowledged a call to full-time ministry, and several had made professions of faith. They raised one thousand dollars for summer missions and sent Denise Peek as summer missionary to the Globe area.

During 1984 Bill Mastriani supervised five summer missionaries and fourteen Innovators who performed night and day concerts, BYBCs, a VBS, tourist outreach and ministries, as well as working daily at concessions in Grand Canyon National Park. The BSU at NAU sponsored Friendship International House with host families caring for and sharing with a young man from Japan and a young woman from India. The foreign students visited church services and tourist sites; the woman was excited to witness her first Christian wedding. The BSU participated in the White Mountain Project with Jay Dorris and Todd Avery leading January Bible studies in Snowflake and Overgard. The students did visitation, surveys, door-to-door witnessing, and maintenance work on the churches.

In 1985 Jay Dorris reported that the BSU joined with Bethel Baptist Church and KSOJ to sponsor a Dennis Agajanian concert on the NAU campus. Their first annual Thanksgiving dinner was a success with thirty-eight students enjoying the food, fellowship, and sharing of thanks. The students found singing at the Pine Care Center a rewarding experience. Several from NAU joined four thousand students who attended Missions '85 at Nashville to hear over one hundred home and foreign missionaries. One night the NAU group attended the Grand Ole Opry together.

In 1986 Jay Dorris and Bill Creedon participated in a partnership evangelism project in Brazil. Jay thanked the churches and association for making it possible for them to go and reported, "Our two groups saw over sixty people saved. We will never forget the experience and have a slide presentation we would like to show in your church." That year the BSU raised nine hundred dollars to send Jeff Wesner as a summer missionary to Stockton, California, where he worked in VBSs and BYBCs, and helped in youth work. The BSU also formed a church ministry team with puppets, skits, and testimonies to share in the churches.

In 1990 youth mission groups from three states helped a new church get started in GCBA. Youth director Bobby Taylor brought twenty-one young people from the Waurika, Oklahoma, FBC to conduct four BYBCs during the week of June 18–22. Waurika pastor Mike Smith preached nightly revival services. Another group from Rustin, Louisiana, worked two days that week surveying the community around the church, previously *Primera Iglesia Bautista*, but restarted as Sunnyside Baptist. The Rustin youth also provided special music. Thursday night a pizza blast following evening services attracted youth from other GCBA churches, with 133 people attending the event.

A youth group from Aurora, Colorado, Mississippi Avenue Baptist Church conducted a VBS from June 25–29 and enrolled seventy-three children. Ed and Bernice Trotter, Christian Service Corps (CSC) volunteers, helped cook meals at Sunnyside for the visiting youth and worked through the summer as SS teachers at the church. Family night following VBS brought in 117 people. The new pastor, Manny Martinez, and his wife Angela, were present for the concluding service.

### Marc and Lisa Hill

When Marc Hill arrived in January 1989 to serve as director, he faced a big challenge because the BSU had been without leadership for a year; the position had moved to a half-time salary, and the students previously involved had become active in other Christian groups on campus. "I inherited only five students who had kept a Bible study going; they were Diana Bondesen, Linda Morris, Mark Shade, Paige Bruck, and Holly Cook," Marc related.

Marc was born in Albuquerque and grew up in another denomination. "Though church was a weekly event in our Christian family," he wrote, "I did not give my life to Christ until the summer after I graduated from high school. I knew I was missing what salvation was all about and was scared of death, yet I was too shy to talk to anyone about my soul. It was not until a friend who was the daughter of foreign missionaries to Austria invited me to FMB week at Glorieta that I gave my life to Christ. To this day I could show you the very pew in the balcony of that great auditorium where I was sitting when I met God."

Marc attended the University of New Mexico before transferring to New Mexico State, where he was introduced to BSU. At that time God began calling him to vocational ministry. "My plans prior to that had been to go into a financial field in order to make money, but God took that intense desire away and replaced it with a calling to serve him. I served in leadership roles in the BSU and as summer missionary youth minister in Clayton, New Mexico, in 1981. I also helped with the youth group in my church in Albuquerque during my college years," he shared.

During his final year of college, Marc met Tom Avants, the BSU director at the University of Arizona. When Tom recruited him and another student to help with the Tucson ministry, Marc became a MSC volunteer and worked for two years at the University of Arizona, beginning in January 1984. He joined Manor Baptist Church and became their youth minister as well.

On December 22, 1984, Marc married Lisa Sorensen, a blue-eyed blond he had met at New Mexico State University and courted long distance. In December 1985 he and Lisa moved to Fort Worth to attend SWBTS, where he graduated in 1988 with an M.A. in religious education. Their daughter Lauren was born in January 1988. Because God had given Marc a strong burden for BSU work in Arizona, he kept in touch with Tom Avants, who shared with him about the need for a leader at NAU.

"God began opening doors and led us unmistakably to the part-time position in Flagstaff," he testified. "After I began on January 1, 1989, God took care of our family in miraculous ways. My salary, coupled with Lisa's willingness to work in clerical positions, met our needs. I was called to serve as youth minister at Greenlaw in May 1989, about four months after we joined. Brian was born the day after Christmas that year. It is extraordinary to look back on our financial needs and recall how God was faithful to meet every one. It proves that where God guides, he provides. In January 1996 the BSU position became full-time."

Marc was excited his second fall term when ten additional students became regular BSU attenders. "Rob Chastain, Bob Smith, and Regina Jones (now married to Bob Smith), were a blessing for their entire stay at

NAU," he remembered. "God also used a student named Bryan Henson in a special way. He grew up in Flagstaff FSBC and was a gifted leader. Several helped get the BSU ministry back on its feet, but Bryan blessed not only many students' lives, but also mine. He became my close friend, confidant, sounding board, and prayer partner. He graduated in 1994 and moved to Portland, Oregon, where he still serves the Lord."

### BSU Building Renovation

In the fall of 1993 the BSU committee, chaired by Daryl Bennett, began to address the need for new facilities for the ministry. When they pursued the idea of relocating, they consistently met closed doors. Finally, ASBC church growth director Bill May suggested exploring the possibility of remodeling the 1930s house they had occupied since 1975. "Daryl became familiar with the best kept secret in ASBC—the Arizona Southern Baptist Builders and their supervisor M. C. Chancey," Marc affirmed. "This organization of retired volunteers has expertise in construction. They provide leadership in mobilizing churches to build their own facilities."

At Daryl's request, M. C. and his wife Maxine listened as Marc shared his desire to transform the "old barn" into a functional facility. After assessing the building, Chancey announced that structurally the building could be salvaged for whatever floor plan they desired. Meanwhile, the ASBC included funding repair of the three state BSU centers by the 1994 state missions offering. Because NAU's allotment of nineteen thousand dollars would not cover the entire cost of the project, the BSU made appeals to the GCBA churches and exceeded their goal.

In June 1994 the BSU received needed permits and began to gut out the building for a complete overhaul. Instead of a chopped-up floor plan with several small rooms, they built one large group meeting area and a modern kitchen. They replaced electrical wiring and plumbing and beamed the building to support the structure adequately. While tearing out sheeting, Marc noticed an old newspaper that had fallen to the floor inside the wall. When he pulled out a section dated August 10, 1941, he exclaimed, "Here is a pre-Pearl Harbor paper wrapped around a petrified tortilla!" The Baptist Builders framed the newspaper and tortilla for display in Marc's office. Because M. C. Chancey had a vision for remodeling the upstairs as well, plans included a renovation of the upstairs in the summer of 1996, also funded through the state missions offering.

Daryl Bennett reported, "When God began to move on the BSU building renovation, every door opened. After the work began, God provided people to help at just the right time. The very day we needed help to lift the beams to support the second floor, I went over to Greenlaw seeking help and found their youth team with two hours to kill. M. C. Chancey was delighted to get the call saying they would be right there. They had some really tall fellows who were able to lift all the beams and get them nailed in place."

**BSU Hears About China Trip**

Marc Hill reported the 1992 fall BSU kickoff had sixty present. The group enjoyed a tailgate party on September 12 prior to the NAU football game. The first month of the new school year also saw thirty-six in Bible study and twenty-four attending the Friday night fellowship to hear Naomi give the following report on the Hunkes' exciting and inspiring trip to China:

> After a twenty-one-hour flight to Hong Kong and a sleepless, overnight ferry trip to Guangzhou, we walked into Quian Market to encounter the incredible sights and unimaginable filth we found in open-air markets everywhere in China. Medicine aisles abounded in stalls hawking dried lizards, insects, live, writhing snakes, but worst of all, bundles of dried tiger legs stacked like cordwood. The air felt thick with bad odors.
>
> We flew to Guiyang where Dixie's university (Guida) was situated. She was the first foreign student to study at Guida because of its isolated location among the minority people. Her picture and an interview had been featured on the front page of the only paper in the capital city of over two million. We stayed at the guest house where she was allowed to live with the foreign teachers. Buildings in China are substandard with no upkeep. Our room smelled dank and had two inches of brown water on the bathroom floor. The hot water faucet was not connected to a pipe; the cold water squirted all over the room; the commode didn't work. Beds were like benches with only pads, which are used over and over without being washed, for mattresses and covers.
>
> Sharp, rocky mountains, shaped like a dragon's back, surround the city. Guizhou is China's poorest province where many people have no cash income, and seven million make less than fifty dollars a year. About the size of Arizona, it has over four hundred

rivers, all flooding while we were there. The resulting rain forest scenery, however, was breathtaking.

Each of Dixie's teachers invited us to a meal. Mrs. Zhang, who spoke no English, took us to an inn where we learned that burping, slurping, and spitting bones on the floor are practiced with gusto. We ate turtle, squid, and many unknown and suspicious looking meats, including "the best Chinese delicacy." Dixie told us that the meal cost as much as the teacher's monthly salary. That afternoon we went to Mr. Peng's home with its two small rooms and tiny kitchen, typical of what the best educated people can afford.

Another day we had lunch at Mr. Zhu's, then walked the steep trails in the city park with wild monkeys swinging overhead, screaming at us. He took us to see many shrines, Buddhist temples being restored, and the zoo where we collected crowds because we were the strangest sight of all. We never saw other foreigners in Guiyang.

The waiban, the Communist foreign affairs liaison with Beijing, walked the university campus with us and kept telling us Dixie had "excellent evaluation." He arranged a minibus trip for us and carried a document which got us by all the checkpoints where armed soldiers stopped the bus. A Summer Institute of Linguistics (SIL) teacher and her parents went along to share expenses. Our share came to forty-eight dollars for four nights' lodging, meals, renting the bus, gas, and paying the way for the driver and his girlfriend, the waiban, Mrs Zhang, and an uninvited friend who needed a ride to a Miao village.

The places we stayed had communal showers with no doors or curtains, water and electricity sometimes on, and a room for men and one for women with a trench which was hosed out once a day. We found no rest rooms along the roadway; we would stop in villages and be directed to pig sheds to use, complete with pigs.

The unpaved roads wound up and down steep mountains, getting skinnier toward the top. We hit a pothole so hard the back windshield cracked, then kept falling out bit by bit, letting in rain and dust until mud caked us and our backpacks. Mud and rock slides made the roads look impassable, and often we waited for bridge repairs. Minority villages are all located on river banks because rivers are used for washing food and clothes, bathing, toilets, drinking water, fishing, and transportation. Everything else they did in the middle of the road: herded their water buffaloes, pigs, cows, goats, and ducks; squatted to talk and smoke and play gambling games; and carried heavy burdens on shoulder poles. Consequently, our driver honked constantly while his girlfriend yelled out the window, but no one paid attention.

In Pangjiang we discovered that the "best Chinese delicacy" was dog meat. All of the dozens of sidewalk shops had dogs' hind quarters roasting on grills with tails pointing toward the street. Meals everywhere were quickly stir-fried in huge woks and served one dish at a time on a lazy Susan. We had rice (with pebbles), and usually tofu, eggplant, bok choy, and scrambled egg and tomato soup. We asked for chicken or pork. When we watched chickens being cut up, we learned that because the heads, feet, and intestines are choice morsels, the chickens are chopped from bills to claws and dumped in the wok for three minutes. Food was always served with a sauce containing big chunks of ginger and garlic which effectively disguised other tastes.

We visited a Miao village where women were dressed in festival costumes in our honor. Each of us had to go through their greeting ritual. They sang to us, poured rice wine down our throats from a water buffalo horn, then put meat in our mouths, using the same chopsticks for everyone (the concept of germs causing disease is unknown; evil spirits cause everything bad). When I couldn't swallow the meat after much chewing, I tried to drop it unnoticed into the mud, but all the chickens came running and cackling.

The Miaos showed us silkworms boiling in wash pans while women unraveled the threads, wound them onto spindles, and spun the silk on ancient spinning wheels. They demonstrated weaving, intricate embroidery, and pleating as we watched. We didn't see any men working. The unmarried young women wore elaborate silver ornaments, the wealth of the village, and danced for us using footstools to beat out rhythms. We really enjoyed everything until they decorated us with tinsel ornaments, necklaces, and crowns, and insisted that we join them in the dances. We were pitiful; they had a good laugh. We walked the length of the village along the path with buffalo, cow, pig, goat, chicken manure and human waste thoroughly squashed in the mud. We did this throughout the trip; I soaked my shoes in Clorox first thing upon returning to Hong Kong.

At another village we took a boat ride down the Wuyang River, which, with its two gorges, is considered one of China's most splendid sights. The cliffs rose thousands of feet above us, covered with bamboo, tree ferns, and jungle vegetation, with huge waterfalls coming off the top and cascading out of caves everywhere we looked. The minority people lived along the beaches and paddled up and down in their sampans. The amazement on their faces when they caught sight of us indicated that we were the first foreigners they had ever seen.

Our Chinese hosts insisted we visit the Zhinyuan Buddhist Temple, one of China's most venerated treasures. Built in a series of caves, it involved walking up hundreds of slippery steps in the pouring rain and made us late to where we had planned to take a ferry to our night's lodging. Because the river had flooded too high for the ferry, we had to retrace part of our day's journey. Fortunately, the scenery was fabulous with thin clouds swirling veils of mist around the mountains like pictures one sees of China.

When the driver was too tired to continue, we tried to get permission to stay in towns that were closed to foreigners, but were refused. We finally stayed in Kaili where we met Mr. Pan who had been imprisoned and sent to Miao villages for re-education. He had learned their still unwritten dialects, and to love the minority people. He took us to a wonderful museum where he showed us Miao, Dong, and Buyi arts, crafts, and costumes and told us about their histories and cultures.

Sunday, July 4, communion day at the state-approved church where Dixie attended, brought my best memory of China. Though we arrived an hour early after a bus ride with everyone coughing and spitting to be rid of evil spirits, the church was packed. People squatted in the aisles and stood in the rain looking in the windows. Pastor Wu, imprisoned by Communists for twenty-one years, has baptized more than two thousand since the church reopened seven years ago. The congregational song was "I Know Whom I Have Believed," the same one being sung at Falls Creek Assembly fifty years ago when I dedicated my life to missions. Although firecrackers blasted and the power went off, no one moved except to bow in prayer. At the close, Pastor Wu invited us foreigners to join them at the Lord's table.

Back in Hong Kong we stayed with Bill and Alice Peters at the International Baptist Church's pastorium and enjoyed many worship services, especially with the Filipinos. They invited Dixie to lead congregational singing for the rest of the summer. We went to Sai Kung in New Territories to meet Dixie's fellow workers. In Kowloon we visited the mission headquarters and Baptist Book Store. Gwen Crotts, an Arizona friend who is manager of Baptist Press, showed us her operation. We had a complete tour of our Baptist seminary and were blessed to meet many missionaries who were gathering in Hong Kong for their annual retreat.

In 1993 Marc Hill reported ninety-four students involved in BSU with about forty regular attenders. They raised twelve hundred dollars for summer missions. Three NAU students were youth camp staffers, and one went to the Ukraine as part of a statewide BSU partnership evangelism project. Three people accepted Christ, and fifteen students were dedicated to everyday, personal evangelism. "The most fulfilling part of BSU is seeing students get serious about walking with their Lord and beginning to minister to others," Marc concluded.

BSU saw seventy-four students involved in activities with about thirty-five regular attenders in 1994. They provided weekly Bible studies and monthly prayer nights, as well as a witness training seminar. They attended Glorieta student week and fall and spring retreats. Two students committed their lives to Christ; one rededicated her life; and two others answered the call to Christian ministry.

BSU raised eleven hundred dollars for summer missions, attended the world missions conference at SWBTS, and provided a mission project to San Diego in conjunction with the University of Arizona BSU. Two of the six staffers at the state youth camp were from NAU. The 1995 BSU year saw an abundance of discipleship, fellowship, and ministry opportunities. Over one hundred students took part in various activities. Two surrendered to Christ, and four made meaningful rededications. In addition to weekly Bible studies, two prayer nights a month, and fellowships every other Friday, the BSU launched a noonday program during spring semester. Students could come for singing, a devotional, fellowship, and a free lunch.

"We used it especially as a time for students to bring lost friends to a Christian event in a friendly environment," Marc explained. "We provided a fall retreat with pastor Pat Hail from Williams FBC as speaker, and our students joined other state groups for the spring retreat in Payson. We attended Glorieta student week and continued our weekly meetings through the summer."

Five students from NAU attended the missions conference at GGBTS, and three served on staff at state youth camps. They raised fifteen hundred dollars for summer missions and ministered to youth in the Phoenix inner city twice during the school year. Each time they rounded up children in the neighborhood of the Church on Fillmore for a one-day VBS. Phase two of their remodeling project began in the summer with the paving of their parking lot.

**GCBA Youth Program Activities**

After Daryl Bennett began serving as GCBA youth director, their first activity was a lock-in. Expecting sixty young people and sponsors to attend, they were overwhelmed when ninety-three not only came, but bought tee shirts. "We were able to get them what they ordered, but some were just a little late," Daryl reported. "The next year we ordered one hundred shirts and had only sixty show up."

Cheryl Ballew, GCBA youth director in 1995, led as Flagstaff FSBC hosted an associational VBS with thirty-six young people participating. The school featured Bible studies, eats, and "phun and gaimz." On Joyful Noise Night all activities were loud and rowdy. Gross Night everything was extremely messy. All activities were outside in the dark on Dark Shadows Night. Thursday featured Water and the Word Night with wet activities. The VBS concluded on Friday with a Christian concert by Everyday People from Albuquerque, New Mexico.

Eleven Innovators and two summer missionaries worked with members of Grand Canyon FBC in a variety of activities in 1995. In addition to BYBCs and VBS, ministries included a coffeehouse for singles, tennis instruction for tourists, Parents Night Out for local residents and tourists, a melodrama in a local campground, sports recreation night for the community, and ESL classes for Hispanics in the area.

# FORGET NOT THE WORKS

## GCBA'S MIDDLE YEARS

Forgetfulness of past mercies leads to unthankfulness, but helpful remembrance of past victories leads to nods of recognition and approval in the midst of spiritual struggles. Works of the past illustrate divine truths needed for everyday courage. We can refuse to listen to Satan's intimidations and threats and withstand his strategies through not forgetting the works that flowed from the solid faith of our fathers.

### Missionary Jackson Knox Maben

On November 1, 1958, Jackson Knox Maben began serving as missionary for Grand Canyon, Mohave, and Troy Brooks Associations. Jack was born August 2, 1910, at Rotan, Texas, saved at age nineteen through his parents' influence, baptized in 1929, and ordained in 1934 by Phoenix FSBC. He wrote, "The Holy Spirit used the concern and prayers of my mother and sisters, the preaching of pastor C. M. Rock, and the witness of friends to strike conviction to my heart, reveal to me the love of Jesus, and bring me to submission to him."

He graduated from Ray, Arizona, High School, ASU, and SWBTS, and attended University of Arizona. He shared, "I had the deepening conviction that the Lord wanted me in gospel ministry. Cities with no Baptist witness concerned me greatly. At the Prescott assembly in 1933, I finally surrendered to what I felt was God's call to preach." He pastored Southern Baptist churches at Tolleson, Phoenix, Glendale, and Prescott, and served as U.S. Army chaplain in the South Pacific during World War II. After six months as missionary, he resigned to return to the pastorate. He retired in California and now resides in San Diego.

Two missions began in 1959. Ash Fork started a work at the small town of Drake, famous for the mining of flagstone. Because a later realignment of the Santa Fe Railroad caused many people to move from the community, the mission was short-lived. Missionary Ollie Blevins of the Flagstaff Baptist Indian Center began a work among the Indian people near Cameron, which met in the home of Jimmie and Sue Crank, who are still active leaders at Tuba City.

In 1959 Flagstaff FSBC began using their new educational building in time for a revival led by Truman Webb. Dan Stringer, Buckeye FBC pastor, was guest speaker at an evangelistic prospect supper. The church reported a successful Forward Program campaign and conducted two worship services every Sunday morning.

### 1959 GCBA Annual Meeting at Williams FBC

At the fourteenth annual meeting of GCBA, the following new pastors and missionaries were recognized: T. J. Newbill, Williams FBC; Jack Goldie, Seligman; J. A. Meyers, Flagstaff Calvary; Robert Green, Tuba City; and A. A. Moore, Copper Mine. The Page FSBC reached across the Colorado River into Utah to begin a mission in the Glen Canyon City construction camp with Dora Wilder leading the SS.

On March 20, 1960, Flagstaff FSBC held a dedication, note burning, and open house with Charles KcKay, BGCA executive director, as guest speaker. They had new pews and a new organ. FSBC youth were leading out in BSU meetings every Thursday evening in the NAU Campus Christian Center. By April the church reported a special hunt for a new mission as their next major project, with the Bow and Arrow Acres area as their first target. Women of the church were saving green stamps for the purchase of a power lawn mower.

### Missionary Major V. Mears

On June 1, 1960, Major V. Mears resigned the pastorate of Flagstaff FSBC to accept the position of superintendent of missions for Grand Canyon, Little Colorado, and White Mountain Associations, an area comprising three counties and about one third of the state. Mears was born October 18, 1919, at Rogers, Texas, saved at age ten, baptized by Copperas Cove, Texas, FBC, and ordained December 2, 1941, by Brownwood, Texas, Melrose Baptist Church. He graduated from Howard

Payne and SWBTS, married Ophelia Keener, and they have two children.

During World War II Mears served in the U.S. Air Force, where he earned an air medal with an oak leaf cluster, European and North Africa theater ribbon with one battle star, and a purple heart. After his plane was shot down over Germany, Mears spent eleven months in a POW camp near the Russian border. While a prisoner, he served unofficially as the camp chaplain and led many to the Lord, including two of his German guards. Six American service men surrendered to preach during his camp ministry. Following the war, Mears pastored Texas churches at Salt Gap, Briggs, and White Deer, and Arizona churches at Buckeye and Flagstaff.

While Mears was pastor at Flagstaff FSBC, the work began on Glen Canyon Dam. He, J. D. Back, and Carrol Peaden went to the site and sat on the rim of the canyon to watch a man in a rope chair paint numbers on the opposite wall where the abutment for the bridge would later be poured. River pilots ferried workers back and forth across the canyon. Wanting to be in on the ground floor to get Baptist work in the new town, Mears drove to Kanab, Utah, to visit government employees and talked with a man named Fordham. His response to Mears was, "Man, we don't even know where the town of Page will be located yet."

Mears responded, "It doesn't matter; when Page is located, I want a Southern Baptist church in the middle of it." The man smiled and gave him a form to "apply for an application" for a church. Fordham was not a Christian, but Mears drove to Kanab so often at his own expense, having to spend the night each time, that he instructed the receptionist to put him at the head of the line when he showed up. As a result, Mears had his church request papers finalized before any other denomination had a permit.

When construction workers moved into dormitories at a temporary location, Fordham called to ask if Mears could put a preacher up there. He had no one in mind but asked instead when the trailers and families would be moving in. Given the date, he promised, "I'll have a pastor there by then even if I have to go myself."

When M. K. Wilder was called from Boulder City as mission pastor, Mears was granted the only permit in town for a trailer spot, with permission to begin a church in the trailer. Rustin, Louisiana, Temple Baptist gave Wilder a trailer and sixty dollars to install a heater in it. After articles began to appear in the *Beacon* about the new work, contributions which came in to start a "Beacon" mission provided the funds.

Two weeks before the mission's beginning date, the executive director of the Conservative Baptist Convention took a young man to Page and visited all the trailers, telling the people, "This is the preacher that has gotten the trailer site, and he will be the pastor here." When Wilders arrived, they were shoved off the site into the ditch as if they were the impostors. After waiting half a day to use the only telephone in town, M. K. called Mears, and the next morning they rushed to see Fordham in Kanab. When Fordham asked how he could help them, Mears replied, "I want to know how that other Baptist church got into Page."

"What other Baptist church?" he inquired. When Mears explained what had happened, Fordham called for his files and discovered that the Conservatives did not even have a permit for Page, much less for the trailer camp.

"He was so angry, he threatened to go to Page and throw the other preacher into the canyon," Mears reported. "I calmed him down, asked him not to move the other group out, and asked if we could have another trailer spot. I also wanted the men in charge at Page to understand exactly what had happened. I told him God would take care of the situation, and he did." When blueprints for Page were drawn, Wilder was given the choice of his church site before any other group.

Mears wrote, "I was forty years old when state director of missions Bill Hunke asked that I consider missionary service. After the official invitation came one day while I was in my office, I prayed and struggled over it for a month before accepting the challenge. I had already learned that starting missions might be difficult." He was GCBA missionary from 1960 to 1982; he also served Yavapai Association from 1966 to 1982 after the northeastern part of Arizona was reassigned, and he was relieved of Little Colorado and White River Associations.

A few years after Mears became GCBA missionary, he requested the HMB to start work in Flagstaff among the Mexicans. "I. B. Williams was already leading a Bible study, and with a larger Mexican population than in Williams, I thought we needed official work in both places," he explained. To his surprise, the HMB granted the request to have a missionary in Flagstaff, but told Mears to close the work in Williams and sell the building there.

"Very reluctantly, I did what the HMB requested," Mears wrote. "Needless to say, I wasn't at all popular among the Mexican people in Williams. We lost them to another church. The building had a large hole in the floor just inside the front door, and was in such bad shape that it was very difficult to sell." W. B. Minor was assigned to Flagstaff. The work started in an old store until Mears could find property for the HMB to purchase at some point in the future.

When he and Ophelia retired in 1982, they sold their Flagstaff home and bought a motor home in order to travel extensively in the U.S. and Canada. Eventually they spent summers in Colorado and winters in Yuma, where he pastored a mission in their recreational-vehicle park.

### Grand Canyon Mission

During the summer of 1960, Mears began leading a mission in Grand Canyon National Park, driving ninety miles from Flagstaff on Sunday nights to conduct SS at 10:00 P.M. and worship services at 11:00 P.M. Employees had requested the work, but all of them worked during the day on Sundays. The group met in the community building. When the park shut down for the winter, the mission closed temporarily, planning to resume in the spring. Because most of those who had attended did not return to work the next summer, it took two years to start worship services again, this time at the Shrine of the Ages where they still meet. From that time, SS classes have met in the schoolhouse following worship.

### 1960 GCBA Annual Meeting at Page FSBC: Fred Barnes

At the GCBA annual meeting on October 18, 1960, when no HMB report had been received, Fred R. Barnes, pastor at Ash Fork FSBC, volunteered to share some of his missionary experiences in northern Arizona. Born in Wisconsin, the oldest of six sons, as a teenager Fred became like a father to his brothers and the primary breadwinner for the family after his father was killed in a boiler explosion at a creamery. Coming from a devout, old-time Methodist family, Fred was saved at age ten and called to preach shortly afterwards. When he married Dorothy Gallagher in 1923, he was already pastoring a small church.

After attending American University in Washington, D.C., pastoring several churches, and having five children, Fred found himself struggling with Methodist doctrines and decided to leave the denomination. He moved the family to Fort Worth and entered SWBTS, where he discovered he was a Southern Baptist by deeply held convictions.

After he came to Tucson in 1944 to pastor Columbia Street Baptist Church, Fred and Dorothy discovered that her health demanded a coastal climate. They moved to San Jose, California, in 1945, where he started Southern Baptist churches in Santa Clara County and pastored until 1948. When he led music for a Phoenix FSBC revival, the church called him as assistant pastor, but again the hot climate forced them back to San Jose.

Fred accepted an appointment by the HMB to serve as the first missionary to ranchers in the northern areas of Arizona and New Mexico in an attempt to evangelize them and tie them to local churches. His work was accomplished by personal visitation, riding and working on the ranches with the owners and cowhands, and planning and conducting old-time camp meetings and other revivals. The most popular and successful of these was in Burton, where the church adopted the camp meeting and worked hard every year to make it successful. Scheduled for a week, the camp was almost always extended by popular demand. The meetings included VBS, adult Bible studies, revival services, and the "finest food anyone ever ate" provided by ranchers and the Burton Baptist Church.

Fred was known all over Arizona for his accordion playing, his rich tenor voice singing the gospel message, and his fiery preaching that left no doubt in listeners' hearts about what the Bible said about heaven and hell and how to be saved. His transportation was a Dodge panel truck with his bed on one side of the rear section and his provisions, literature, and accordion on the other. He usually cooked over a campfire and was famous for his coffee. He said that coffee did not take nearly as much water as most people thought and was greatly aided by salt and eggshells. When he later acquired an old, black Packard limousine, he converted the back into the same arrangement as the truck but had more traveling comfort.

Fred never met a stranger and was able to make himself at home anywhere. All across northern Arizona many homes were open to him as needed. He was noted for his limburger cheese aroma and the fact that he always just wanted his steaks just slightly warmed. His friends said they had seen cows hurt worse than that get up and walk away.

Soon after he resigned the ranchers' ministry in 1959 and moved to Prescott, Dorothy died. While he was packing up after a VBS and revival in Pietown, New Mexico, he suffered a heart attack and died before reaching the Springerville, Arizona, hospital. He was sixty-four. A son, Paul Barnes, and his wife, the former Barbara Hawkins, both graduated from Grand Canyon University (GCU) and have served many ASBC churches, as well being the convention's director of music and student ministries, GCU's chief developmental officer, and director of St. Mary's food bank in Phoenix.

In February 1961 Page FSBC began an Indian mission in their building on Sunday afternoons with an Indian layman leading. Pastor M. K. Wilder was conducting the work at Copper Mine on Sunday afternoons. September 1961 saw the Seligman mission constituting into FSBC and affiliating with GCBA—a pattern many missions have followed.

### 1961 GCBA Annual Meeting at Flagstaff FSBC

The following new pastors were introduced at the 1961 GCBA annual meeting on October 24: Bill James, Ash Fork; Jack Goldie, Seligman; John Jenkins, Flagstaff FSBC; Lee Cook, Flagstaff Calvary; Houston Walker, Williams; and W. B. Minor, Flagstaff Spanish.

At the request of the HMB the association voted to assume some of the missionary's travel expenses in 1962. The executive board also voted to give $150 to help construct an office for Mears. Upon a committee's report that the association must incorporate in order to hold property, the board voted to do so and elected Bill Russell, Ralph Ayers, and Bob Beckendorf to act as trustees.

Ever since the "30,000 Movement" began on June 1, 1956, a report on its progress was given at the annual meetings. By 1962 the number of churches in the BGCA had more than doubled, from 108 to 211. The state goal was to constitute over one hundred more by 1964 and triple the number existing when the program began. In GCBA four churches had been constituted, together with missions at Cameron, Tuba City, Glen Canyon, Flagstaff Spanish, Red Lake, and Page Indian. Not previously reported was the work at Standing Rock.

Missionary M. V. Mears reported a definite need of missions in at least ten more places, and urged every church to begin a new work before the end of 1962. He announced that to implement this program, fifty laymen would be coming from Mississippi for a crusade January 29 through February 4, with four working in GCBA. They would witness to the lost during the day, conduct home fellowship services each evening, and seek to establish a mission, branch SS, or permanent Bible home fellowship.

In 1962 Flagstaff Calvary began a weeknight meeting at Cameron among both anglos and Indians with pastor Lee Cook driving up to conduct the services. The group met in an abandoned tin garage with the windows broken out. The trailer belonging to GCBA was moved to Cameron for services after an agreement had been secured in writing from the Standard Oil Company in May 1969. On September 27, 1969, a tornado blew the trailer partially over the wall of the Little Colorado River Canyon. The Mearses put up money to have a custom trailer built by John L. Long and moved to a new location in Cameron. The HMB later repaid them for the trailer which was used until the mission closed.

Also in 1962, Seligman FSBC began a SS at Dinosaur Caverns west of Seligman. The first services were held in the Snowball Palace room at the bottom of the cavern because no building was available. The group moved topside as soon as a room could be secured, but had to change rooms from week to week, depending on what was open. Seligman pastor Jack Goldie led this work.

On November 11, 1962, Flagstaff FSBC restarted the work in Fredonia. Walt W. Fordham drove over two hundred miles each Sunday to lead the work. Summer missionaries who conducted a VBS there discovered that the post office would not deliver their mail even though letters were addressed to the Baker family they stayed with. An earlier work there had been carried on by FSBC, but it was short-lived with no records kept.

### 1963 GCBA Annual Meeting at Seligman FSBC: Houston Walker.

Williams FBC pastor Houston Walker took a leading role in the GCBA 1962 annual meeting. He introduced the TU report by telling of the memorable "M" Night service at Williams during a severe snow and ice storm. Five churches had brought TU members to enjoy the conferences and hear George Hook, Indian missionary from Winslow, tell of his work. Walker also brought special music twice and gave the resolutions and constitution reports. Sarah Walker brought the WMU report, telling the group that it was the seventy-fifth anniversary of the organizational meeting in Richmond when WMU received a sacred heritage of conviction, dedication, and cooperation which they pledged to bequeath to succeeding generations.

Houston Walker was born June 16, 1918, at Farmington, New Mexico. He was saved at age nine, baptized in a mill ditch, and ordained by the Farmington FBC. He wrote, "I had been under conviction for some time because of the witness of my mother and SS teacher. It was a hot July day when I went down the aisle barefooted on the dirt floor of the church tabernacle with its slat benches and few furnishings. When I put my trust in Christ that day, a peace came into my heart that has never departed. Today a beautiful building stands on that spot, but it doesn't mean as much to me as the old one with its dirt floor, slat benches, and potbellied stove."

Walker pastored six Texas and two New Mexico churches before coming to Williams FBC. He also pastored at Warren and Avondale and was active in state convention work. He wrote, "After I led a meeting as chairman of a committee on boards, Jess Canafax and Roy Sutton asked me to serve as associational missionary for Little Colorado and White Mountain associations. I told them how happy I had been pastoring for forty years, but they asked me to pray about it. I don't remember getting in my car that night or driving down Central Avenue, but I suddenly woke up, stopped the car on Central, got out and knelt beside it and heard God tell me that I should be willing to spend the rest of my ministry helping small churches and young pastors. He made me willing."

Houston and Sarah Walker retired in 1981 at Farmington. He wrote in 1986, "I am as busy as ever except that I don't get paid or have vacations any more. I have completed some interims and preach somewhere every Sunday. I very seldom get to attend my home church. We are somewhat confined taking care of my oldest sister." The Walkers celebrated their sixtieth wedding anniversary in August 1995.

In 1962 Sedona FBC, Tuba City Navajo Trail, and Flagstaff Baptist Indian Center completed the Forward Program twenty-nine-day campaign and reported that the spiritual impact on their churches was as important as the increased giving. In February 1963 Flagstaff FSBC began services in the Coconino County jail on Sunday afternoons.

### 1963 GCBA Annual Meeting at Flagstaff Calvary

At the 1963 annual meeting, missionary Mears reported that six of the seven churches in GCBA held VBSs, and seven mission VBSs were held at Fredonia, Cameron, Flagstaff Spanish, Flagstaff Indian, Red Lake, and Wild Cat Peak Indian mission, with another mission school not reporting. Tuba City Navajo Trail mission completed its new building and missionary residence. Sarah Walker reported that six of the seven churches had WMU organizations and that ninety girls had attended the GA house party at Page. That year M. K. Wilder, Page FSBC pastor, was also leading services at the Copper Mine, Dry Lake, and Page Indian missions.

In December 1962 when state leaders had studied ASBC accomplishments, they had concluded that outreach had fallen short of expectations for several years. They were so alarmed that they spent many hours formulating and implementing a plan that would focus on winning the lost and reaching them for membership and discipling in the churches. This endeavor resulted in the adoption of the People Are First campaign: reaching, winning, and baptizing new people; teaching them; developing them in stewardship; conserving the results for continued spiritual growth.

The People Are First campaign was launched at Phoenix FSBC on September 9, 1963, when representatives from sixty-one Arizona churches met to learn anew how to reach people for Christ. All churches in the state were encouraged to study the book by Charles L. McKay entitled *People Are First*. The BSSB sent sixty-one workers, and workers from other states came to assist. A statewide census the first week in September, the largest ever undertaken by Arizona churches, kicked off the program which continued through the Baptist Jubilee Revivals in 1964. Every convention entity, pastor, and church member was to be totally dedicated to the goal of reaching people.

As a result the GCBA quarterly meetings in 1964 were devoted to helping churches analyze their problems and opportunities. Leaders learned how to organize and develop their potential in order to increase the effectiveness of their Bible teaching programs to win people to Christ. The 1964 evangelism report would show that the association exceeded its goal of one hundred baptisms by six, and that the simultaneous crusades were a glorious experience, with interest and attendance high in every church, although snow was falling every night.

In addition to the People Are First challenge, messengers to the ASBC in 1963 at Kingman witnessed a visual presentation of the thirty-five-year history of the state convention. Following the report when projections of goals for the coming seven-year period were announced, they voted enthusiastically to accept the goals and to work diligently to reach them. The heart of the projected growth plan was the IMPACT Program, an acrostic for Implemented Mission Program, Arizona, Convention Thirty, which was presented and explained at length by state missions director Bill Hunke. The program planned to plant thirty strategically located new church-type missions in seven years by purchasing land, constructing a building, and funding a pastor. Each new mission would be allocated thirty thousand dollars, with the ASBC loan committee authorized to invest an average of eighteen thousand dollars in each of the thirty buildings.

In the report, Hunke told that Flagstaff had experienced growth when it became a railhead for Glen Canyon Dam. The 1950 census counted 7,663 people in the city, but the Chamber of Commerce estimated population in 1963 at twenty-three thousand. He stated, "The two Southern Baptist churches in Flagstaff need help in reaching the city. Three additional churches are needed now."

### Bethel Baptist Church
As a result of the IMPACT program, property was purchased in the Bow and Arrow Acres subdivision of Flagstaff. On May 3, 1964, Calvary had started a mission in the Lura Kensey Elementary School building of the Pine Knoles subdivision, which became inactive. When the Bow and

Arrow Acres site on Lake Mary Road became available, Calvary voted to sponsor a mission there. The mission met in an 8 x 35' trailer. Mears reported, "We paid three months' rent, and the Mitchell family, who belonged to Flagstaff FSBC, took that as a purchase price, which meant that the trailer belonged to GCBA since it had paid the rent. It was to be used as a chapel as needed to start missions until permanent buildings could be constructed."

Services began at the Bethel Baptist Mission on July 13, 1965. Mears served as pastor. Son Conally was music director; daughter Sonya played the piano; Ophelia taught the juniors. Mears wrote, "I served as contractor for the construction of Bethel. All cement and block work was contracted out. I did the plumbing, wiring, and carpenter work with help from Joe Flippin, pastor at Calvary, and later from Walt Fordham. As soon as it was enclosed and heat installed, we moved services into the building." Mears preached there until R. A. Guthrie came as pastor when the mission was constituted into Bethel Baptist Church in 1966.

In 1964 the Cameron mission and Williams Spanish mission became inactive. Page FSBC began a mission at Escalante, Utah, that remained a thriving work for several years. That year the Little Colorado Association gave up eight churches and one mission when the White Mountain Association constituted. M. V. Mears served those associations as missionary as well as GCBA. He also toured the Navajo Reservation with missions director Bill Hunke and language director Irvin Dawson to survey needs among the Indians. They found that mission work was being carried on at White Cone School, Dennehotso, and Shonto by individuals but not sponsored by churches. They noted many other places where multimillion dollar schools were being constructed by the government, and missions were desperately needed.

### 1964 Annual Meeting at Page FSBC: A. C. Miller's Report

During the years of A. C. Miller's Sedona pastorate, he brought challenging Christian Life Commission reports to the annual GCBA and ASBC meetings. The following excerpts from his 1964 report illustrate the content of these messages and demonstrate their importance:

The morals of Americans are besieged today by unprincipled forces which spare no home or community in their quest for illicit profits. The sex drive, the gambling craze, and the depraved desire for narcotics and alcoholic beverages are the major sources of these immoral indulgences and profits.

This growing depravity among our people in sexual indulgences and crimes is a matter of gravest concern to thoughtful members of our churches. Crime reports reveal a forced rape occurring every thirty-six minutes. Divorces caused by infidelity skyrocket to new heights each year. Broken homes spew children upon the streets to increase the ever growing numbers of juvenile delinquents.

This shocking and shameful state of affairs is made even more deplorable by the knowledge that obscene literature and sex crimes go hand in hand. The time for only halfhearted, oblique action against these dealers in depravity is far past. Although their despicable trade reaps five hundred million dollars a year, this diabolical business is costing the nation much more. It robs our country of plain and ordinary decency and is the seedbed of moral depravity among people of all ages.

Gambling is another potent source of immorality in our land. It soon becomes a craze to those who indulge in it. The pernicious desire to gamble emerges from the human desire to get something for nothing. Nurtured by a preoccupation with thrills, gambling idolizes material gain. It is inconsistent with the sanctity of work and honest wages and makes a virtue of covetousness. It is contrary to Christian values and harmful to the Christian life. Gambling bosses reap a profit annually that is larger than the combined profits of the nation's one hundred largest manufacturing companies. The by-products of these immense profits include corruption in athletics, deterioration of family life, bribery of officials, the promotion of prostitution, police protection for criminals, and other illicit and immoral indulgences.

Another source of immorality is the manufacture, sale, and use of alcoholic beverages and the illicit trade in illegal drugs. These are detrimental and destructive to the interest and welfare of our country and American homes; they retard business, weaken health, render unsafe our highways and airways, and destroy morality and integrity.

We must confess that these major sources of our national immorality are largely the result of our negligence in the home and our failure to proclaim and teach God's truth about them in our churches. The Christian home and church are two institutions that God has ordained for overcoming evil forces that beset us. We live in one and serve and work through the other. Let us dedicate both of them to the victory over evil that can be ours through him who has overcome the world.

New pastors introduced at the 1964 meeting were John Ramsey, Ash Fork; and Ira Day, Sedona. Mrs. Vernon Morton, WMU director, reported that three of the fifty-five girls attending the associational house party in Flagstaff were crowned queens. Average attendance at WMU quarterly meetings was nineteen. The GCBA executive board reported that the association paid for the missionary's home in Flagstaff to be connected with the city sewer system. After a realignment of missionaries, on July 1, 1966, M. V. Mears accepted the Troy Brooks (Yavapai) Association along with Grand Canyon, having been relieved of Little Colorado and White River Associations.

### Grand Canyon Mission Becomes Permanent
The work at Grand Canyon Village, which had closed in 1960, reopened for night services during the summer of 1965. On September 27, 1965, Charles and Edna Wyatt, Everett and Beatrice Robertson, Bob and Doris Roberts, and Nancy Timmons met at the Roberts' home to elect officers in order to continue the work on a permanent basis. Charles Wyatt agreed to serve as temporary pastor. They chose a committee to explain to the community church pastor why they wanted to start a Southern Baptist mission.

The first regular service came on October 3, 1965, at 7:30 P.M. At that time the group voted to call themselves the Grand Canyon FBC and pay Charles Wyatt ten dollars per Sunday. On October 24 they instructed Wyatt to ask Presley Hand, pastor of Williams FBC, to meet with them concerning sponsoring the work. By November 10 Williams had agreed to sponsorship, and missions and budget committees had been elected.

In December the mission voted to begin SS, Sunday morning and evening worship services, and Wednesday night prayer services. That month they elected a song leader and pianist, a SS superintendent, secretary, and two teachers, and a head usher. In January they worked on compiling a list of prospects in order to begin an organized visitation program and voted to organize a GA and order the girls' *Tell* magazine immediately. In February they voted to send 10 percent of their income to the CP, retroactive to include all tithes and offerings received.

Ruth and Jack Maben served as GCBA missionaries in 1958–1959. He resigned to become Prescott FSBC pastor.

Prescott FSBC hosted the 1957 GCBA annual meeting. Hassayampa Association organized after the sessions.

H. A. Zimmerman preached a revival at Fredonia in September 1941. Page FSBC continues a witness there.

M. V. Mears led a new mission at Grand Canyon in 1960 which met at 10 P.M. for SS and 11 P.M. for worship services.

After their Pine Knoles Mission closed at Lura Kensey School, Flagstaff Calvary voted to sponsor Bethel Mission.

IMPACT program of ASBC funded the start of Bethel Baptist Mission in SE Flagstaff. It met in a rented trailer.

*Heavy snow and long icicles tell of cold winters in Flagstaff. Mears' home was the GCBA office for twenty-two years.*

*Ophelia and Major V. Mears served as GCBA missionaries, 1960–1982. He had three associations at the same time.*

*Seligman pastor Jack Goldie led a SS in Snowball Palace of Dinosaur Caverns in 1962. They moved to a building later.*

*Williams started Bellemont Mission at Navajo Army Depot chapel on September 30, 1973, with M. V. Mears as pastor.*

*Mears pastored Flagstaff Bethel Mission from July 13, 1965, until 1966 when the mission organized and called R. A. Guthrie.*

*Ralph and Bettye Guthrie served as GCBA missionaries, 1983–1986. He also served Yavapai Association.*

## 1965 GCBA Annual Meeting at Sedona FBC

The executive board announced all quarterly meetings would be held at the Flagstaff Indian mission. They introduced the steering committee for organizing a citywide brush arbor revival in Flagstaff in 1966. I. B. Williams reported an outstanding year in evangelism because of participation in the simultaneous crusades. He stated, "The spirit of cooperation in GCBA is near that of the New Testament brethren. Our goal was 108 baptisms; without two reports we have gone above that goal by six."

On April 4, 1966, Flagstaff FSBC voted to see if Page FSBC would sponsor the Fredonia mission with the Flagstaff church taking sponsorship of the Dry Lake mission. That year pastor M. K. Wilder led Page FSBC to affiliate with the Utah/Idaho State Convention. After that time work at Fredonia was carried on sporadically by Page until Harold Boldin began regular Sunday afternoon services there in 1992.

Alvin Wood came from SWBTS to pastor Flagstaff FSBC in June 1966. Alvin wrote that the first thing he took part in was the purchasing of land on Switzer Canyon and San Francisco Street. Groundbreaking ceremonies for their new building took place in October 1966 with dedication ceremonies six months later. The building opened its doors for the first time on Easter Sunday 1967 to a crowd of more than three hundred persons. The church noted that when they raised the steeple on the new building, it was the highest Baptist steeple in Arizona. Of course, they began at seven thousand feet. After serving as interim pastor of Bethel Baptist Mission until July 17, 1966, M. V. Mears became interim pastor of the Seligman FSBC.

## 1965 GCBA Annual Meeting at Flagstaff Bethel

At the 1966 GCBA annual meeting the missions committee announced that any church wishing to rent the mobile trailer to start a mission should contact GCBA. Sedona indicated that they would like to try to start a mission at Indian Gardens in Oak Creek. Twelve churches reported VBSs with 636 enrolled and fourteen saved.

Other new pastors besides Alvin Wood included: R. A. Guthrie at Bethel; Bill Johnson at Calvary; Delbert Fann at Flagstaff Indian and Cameron; A. A. Moore of Tuba City Indian Trail was also conducting work at the BIA school mission, Lower Kaibito, Upper Kaibito, and Shonto; and Bob Roberts at Grand Canyon mission.

In 1967 Seligman FSBC erected a thirty-foot steeple and tore down the old building next to their church. They cleared the land, painted and repaired the inside of their building, and caught up on all back debts.

J. G. Little came to serve as pastor. Williams FBC had their first church group in the history of the church to attend Glorieta Baptist Assembly missions conferences. In September Flagstaff FSBC started construction on a new educational unit. The Mormons offered them twenty-five thousand dollars and their building in exchange for the property on Cherry and Park. Two years later Tony Galbaldon paid forty-four thousand dollars with ten thousand dollars in earnest money for it.

### 1967 GCBA Annual Meeting at Williams FBC

At the 1967 annual meeting, Missions Committee Chairman R. A. Guthrie reported a genuine missionary fervor being manifested among the people of GCBA. He noted all the work being carried on by missionaries Moore and Fann among the Indians and a new spirit among the Spanish mission members. Flagstaff FSBC bused workers back and forth each day to conduct a VBS at Happy Jack. The men of the church led by pastor Alvin Wood also constructed a new meetinghouse at Dry Lake mission. The mobile trailer was still being used by the Flagstaff Baptist Indian mission for classrooms with more space needed. Basil Holmes had come to pastor the Grand Canyon mission, and Clark Johnson was driving from Flagstaff to pastor Ash Fork FSBC. Henry Pearson reported that 675 of the 9,000 NAU students were Southern Baptists, and 50 were internationals who needed to be targeted with the gospel.

In 1968 Flagstaff Calvary changed its name to Greenlaw Baptist Church. March 27, 1968, Flagstaff FSBC empowered trustees to borrow $178,000 ASBC two-phase bonds to finance their educational building. On October 16, 1968, the church voted to ordain Clark Johnson and Bill May to the gospel ministry.

### 1968 GCBA Annual Meeting at Flagstaff FSBC

The corporation report at the October 15 annual meeting included executive board action to give GCBA's half of the missionary's home back to the Mears with sufficient funds in the budget to cover utilities, taxes, and house payments. The clerk was instructed to write a letter to the Troy Brooks Association advising them of this action.

After a busy three years and close to burnout, Flagstaff FSBC pastor Alvin Wood resigned in March 1969 to become pastor of Scottsdale FSBC. Clark Johnson was chosen to supply on Wednesday nights and Bill Parker to serve as interim pastor. After a year Wood accepted the call to pastor FSBC for the second time. Ash Fork FSBC held a mortgage-burning ceremony on October 20, 1968. Greenlaw Baptist refurnished their sanctuary, completed the remodeling of their educational building, and ordained one deacon and one minister in 1969. Seligman FSBC began a kindergarten on September 15, 1969.

### 1969 GCBA Annual Meeting at Ash Fork FSBC

Hearts of GCBA messengers to the 1969 annual meeting were moved when Troy Brooks, "our dean of missionaries," brought an inspiring and challenging message. The mobile trailer was moved to the Cameron mission, where John Gregory of Tuba City was pastor. David and Angie Benham accepted the work at Tuba City and had been on the field since March. Larry Tsingine was interim pastor of Flagstaff Indian mission; Bill May pastored Greenlaw; Jack Spurgeon was at Williams FBC; and R. K. Thompson was at Grand Canyon mission.

### 1970 Annual Meeting at Flagstaff Spanish Mission

Historical events included Sedona FBC's acquiring new pulpit furniture, choir robes, a baby grand piano, church organ, and new carpets for aisles and rostrum. Greenlaw completed building construction and paved the parking lot.

The 1970–1971 state convention theme "Thrust Missions" was adopted by GCBA. The objective was to establish sufficient new mission units that one would be within reasonable reach of every person in Arizona. Every church was challenged to start at least one Bible study home fellowship or mission. The GCBA language missions took advantage of the Paradise Valley Baptist Ranch camps which registered 183 during Indian week with 15 professions of faith and 145 during Spanish week with 24 professions of faith.

In 1970 Roy Colhour came to pastor Ash Fork, and Don Shackelford to pastor Bethel. Seligman and Williams were pastorless. M. V. Mears stated, "Things really began to move in the Troy Brooks Association." He continued to live at Flagstaff and drive to the Prescott area to pastor new missions as they started, as had been his custom through the years. He reported 8 new missions, 3 churches constituted, and 15 Bible fellowship classes in his 2 associations, but admitted, "They were all in Troy Brooks."

Grand Canyon FBC constituted on December 6, 1970, with thirty-one charter members. They voted to continue giving 10 percent through the CP, 5 percent to GCBA, birthday offerings to the Baptist Children's Home, and to participate in the LMCO and AAEO. R. A. Guthrie, interim pastor of Williams FBC, the sponsoring church, presided at the organization meeting, and Arthur K. Tyson, president of GCC, brought the charge to the church. Grand Canyon called Lawrence B. Cobb, chaplain of Phoenix Baptist Hospital, as interim pastor. He and Mrs. Cobb commuted to the field every weekend by plane.

Grand Canyon FBC held its first regular deacons' meeting in February 1971 with new pastor Steve Larkin present, together with Henry Kendall and Bill Shrode. They discussed the need for and qualifications of deacons. At their second meeting that month, the men agreed to ordain Bob Roberts and Al Kendall as deacons and have deacons' meetings each second and fourth Thursday.

### 1971 Annual Meeting at Tuba City Navajo Trail Baptist Mission

GCBA SS director David Benham, pastor at Tuba City, reported ten Bible fellowship classes started with nineteen enrolled at Grand Canyon FBC and nine at Williams FBC. Two girls from Greenlaw worked as volunteer summer missionaries, helping in a number of VBSs and other activities. In 1971 Roy Colhour moved from the pastorate at Ash Fork to pastor at Williams. Flagstaff FSBC conducted a Lay Evangelism School (LES) with many participating, which resulted in a great spiritual awakening. Brotherhood director Kenneth Bates reported active men's groups at Greenlaw and Flagstaff FSBC had held regular fellowship breakfasts with attendances averaging fifteen and thirty-five. Missionary Mears used slides and a tape recording for the first time to report on the year's activities.

Greenlaw pastor Bill May became the voluntary director of the BSU at NAU. He reported great excitement among Baptist students as their annual convention was the best attended ever; and they heard Bob Ramsey, whom they had sponsored as a summer student missionary to Alaska, give his report. They eagerly voted to sponsor five students in 1972 to Hawaii, Alaska, Florida, New Mexico, and Kentucky. In addition, they were involved in plans for a witnessing ministry on the Colorado River at Easter.

### 1972 Annual Meeting at Bethel Baptist

In 1972 no new missions or churches were reported in either GCBA or the Troy Brooks Association. New pastors included: Henry Cox at Ash Fork; John Davis at Bethel; George Wills at Sedona; and Bob Searles at Seligman. The theme "Share the Word Now" was emphasized at quarterly meetings, with "Extend Now" challenging churches to go beyond their own walls to take the gospel witness. The following Bible fellowship classes were meeting weekly: Sedona, 2 with 16 enrolled; Seligman, 1 with 12 enrolled; Greenlaw, 2 with 10 enrolled; Ash Fork, 1 with 8 enrolled; and Flagstaff FSBC, 3 with 20 enrolled.

The BSU at NAU had helped to raise over fifteen hundred dollars to send six summer missionaries to other states and were making plans to send eleven next year, including one to a foreign country. An evangelism clinic and a school of evangelism using the WIN materials were conducted in GCBA during the year. Giving to the CP by GCBA churches reached an all-time high of $7,237.29 in 1972.

Flagstaff FSBC had begun televising their morning services in 1971. The program aired each Sunday at 5:00 P.M. and was so well received that it put the church in a good position to minister in the community. By 1973 they had started a daily television program called "Coffee with the Parson" with pastor Alvin Wood. In 1972 FSBC had their one-year lease approved for the Flagstaff Co-Op Nursery. They reported that in July the Tuba City Navajo Trail Mission borrowed money to purchase a trailer home. In October FSBC began a daytime visitation program. Missionary nurse Diana Lay was guest of honor at a mother/daughter tea to start the foreign missions emphasis.

### 1973 Annual Meeting at Grand Canyon FBC

On February 12, 1973, Lawrence B. Cobb, Yuma Baptist Hospital chaplain and interim pastor of Grand Canyon FBC, wrote Bill Hunke that the church had been granted permission to use ten acres adjacent to the national park. Cobb asked the HMB to grant sixteen thousand dollars for interest on a loan and to appoint a resort missionary for Grand Canyon because national parks were viewed as priority places needing a Southern Baptist witness. That year Grand Canyon FBC began mission services outside the park at the Tusayan Forest Services property.

Danny Pritchett, a U.S.-2 worker sponsored by the HMB, arrived to direct the BSU program at NAU for two years. Nine students attended the GGBTS missions conference in January, and five helped Prescott Yavapai College get its BSU started in February. The BSU sponsored both intramural basketball and football teams. The students hosted a Western Baptist Faculty Conference at Flagstaff during the summer. Flagstaff Baptist Indian Mission joyfully celebrated its twenty-fifth anniversary on August 11. Greenlaw purchased land for a new building location, and

Sedona FBC paid off its church debt. Barry Hall, Flagstaff FSBC youth and education director, was called to pastor the Sedona church and remained until 1982. He came again in 1993 and continues to the present.

GCBA evangelism committee chairman Ken Bates rejoiced that every church reported baptisms in 1973 and stated, "It is noteworthy that several churches attached notes of a combined total of about 130 professions of faith that were not baptized. Flagstaff FSBC and Grand Canyon FBC each listed about fifty such cases, and I know that Greenlaw also reached a large number." When the 1974 theme, "Sharing the Word," was announced, Mears stated, "Speaking of sharing the Word, layman Ken Bates of Flagstaff FSBC has ordered eight hundred copies of *Good News for Modern Man* to give away through his service station in Flagstaff."

An unused army chapel at Navajo Army Depot west of Flagstaff was secured to start a mission on September 30, 1973. Williams FBC sponsored the work, which was known as the Bellemont mission. Mears served as pastor, and a woman from Williams taught Sunday afternoon SS. The missionary reported, "The mission didn't last long, but three boys were converted there."

After David Benham went to the state office to assist in language work, Gerald and Alice Lawton were approved by the HMB to serve at the Tuba City Navajo Trail Mission in 1973. The Fernando Martinezes were also approved by the HMB to pastor the Flagstaff Spanish mission. Flagstaff FSBC reported that the church had accepted the Co-Op Nursery contract and had manned a booth at the Coconino County Fair for the first time.

### 1974 Annual Meeting at Sedona FBC

Messengers came to the GCBA 1974 annual meeting with a note of victory because their record of 197 baptisms that year had exceeded by 73 the previous high of 124 set in 1957. In addition to the baptisms, Paul Milton, pastor at Grand Canyon, reported over sixty conversions among the tourists who were not baptized. Milton had come to Grand Canyon FBC from work in Texas rural evangelism and used the Innovator program to great advantage at the park. He also opened a jewelry story and used his ability as a pilot to reach people. After Mears gave the missions report, he immediately challenged the churches to baptize two hundred in 1975.

Mears also revealed that total receipts of $232,136 represented an increase of more than $19,000 over the previous year. Total missions gifts were up $16,000; CP up over $3,000; and associational missions up $1,658. He said that two stewardship meetings had been well attended and participants blessed.

Three associational SS meetings highlighted the Bible study program of the churches. Roy Sutton, George Harris, and John McBain spoke at the annual Bible conference at Williams FBC in April. A training conference for age group teachers led by local personnel was very well attended. Pastors and SS directors had an important meeting on the 1973–1974 "Reach Out" program to give help in enlistment of new members. Because the program called for bringing all class rolls up to date, some churches showed a decrease in enrollment but reported many new prospects. The CT report showed that "M" Night had to be cancelled because of the biggest snow of the season.

Mears reported that Seminary Extension classes were being taught in GCBA. The association participated in the Bob Herrington Evangelistic Crusade in Flagstaff and promoted a week of prayer for winning the lost through associational missions. The BSU had no director during the summer of 1974. During the year the students attended five retreats or conferences and did nine programs in local churches. Average attendance was seven for Bible study, eight for vespers, and twenty-four for choir and fellowship. Alvin Wood stated that the highlight of the associational Brotherhood was a steak fry held at Fort Tuthill with sheriff Joe Richards speaking to about fifty men and boys who attended. Alice Lawton reported good attendance at all quarterly WMU meetings and two new organizations started in the churches.

A new pastor in addition to Paul Milton and Gerald Lawton was Bill Crowhurst at Williams. The "value of church property" item in the Sedona FBC letter showed an interesting reflection of the rise in the cost of real estate in Sedona. The church property at first was valued at thirty-nine thousand dollars. With the construction of a building, it went to ninety thousand dollars, where it had consistently remained for about a decade until a new appraisal in 1974. In the 1974 letter, it was listed at $269,804.

In 1974 William Earl Davidson, former missionary to Chile then living on the Navajo Reservation, spoke to WMU organizations at Flagstaff FSBC. Davidson became well known to Arizona Baptists because of his writing personal letters to hundreds of foreign missionaries and his fervent missions challenges as long as he lived. In June 1974 FSBC hired Rick Barnes as youth and part-time music director. Ed Stone, NAU professor of music, was also hired as part-time music director. At Easter the choir presented Handel's *Messiah*. The church borrowed ten thousand dollars to pave the parking lot. At Thanksgiving they hosted a dinner for fifty international students. Pastor Alvin Wood went to Alaska to hold spring revival services in 1975.

### 1975 GCBA Annual Meeting at Greenlaw

Messengers to the 1975 GCBA annual meeting were pleased to hear that GCC was the fastest growing college in the state with 1,201 students from 36 states and 7 foreign countries. Ministerial students numbered 151, and 840 students enrolled in Bible courses. Jasper McPhail, medical missionary to India, presented the FMB report and enthralled the people with stories of his work and his dream of having a medical school there. Ed Stone brought a medley of hymns featuring how wonderful Jesus is, and the Pilgrim Quartet entertained with an inspirational concert before the evening session.

In 1975 the coming of Richard Vera from Utah to the Flagstaff Spanish mission bought renewed soulwinning zeal which resulted in a tent revival with forty professions of faith. The mission also started an outreach project to reach the Spanish-speaking people in Winslow. Flagstaff Indian mission constructed a 30 x 42' classroom annex to provide SS class space. Another new pastor besides Vera was Jasper Jones at Cameron. Jasper has since pastored the Flagstaff Baptist Indian Church for many years.

M. V. Mears commended the churches on their 182 baptisms and suggested a monthly fellowship and potluck meeting to help people share problems and joys and get to know each other better. The group voted to do so. At the close of the meeting, moderator Barry Hall presented a plaque of appreciation to Mears for his fifteen years of service as GCBA missionary and a bouquet of roses to Ophelia.

Flagstaff FSBC made news in 1976 with an effort to raise sixteen thousand dollars in one Sunday by passing a galvanized aluminum tub instead of the offering plates. Pastor Bill Stone explained that they were trying to catch up what they had fallen behind on their $141,000 budget. Most of the money raised would go to the CP, BSU, Campus Crusade for Christ, GCC, and their two Indian missions.

In 1976 Flagstaff Indian mission poured concrete walks and patios for their annex and grounds. *Primera Iglesia Bautista* started radio and television ministries in Spanish, remodeled and painted their building, and started a weekly Bible study in Williams. On May 23, 1976, Williams FBC ordained their new pastor, Jerry Martin, to the ministry. Bill Crowhurst, together with some Williams FBC members, had started a storefront work in Williams which became known as Faith Baptist Mission. Greenlaw extended an arm to sponsor the group.

### 1976 GCBA Annual Meeting at Flagstaff FSBC

At the 1976 annual meeting, M. V. Mears began a plea that would continue for several years for churches and pastors to pray earnestly about the great turnover in pastoral leadership which sorely hindered the work. At meeting time Ash Fork, Flagstaff FSBC, and Tuba City were pastorless. Jim Shaw had recently come to lead Seligman FSBC.

On January 23, 1977, Ash Fork ordained Jackson F. Clower, whom they had called as pastor. Jon Allen had come to pastor Grand Canyon, and Dan Sheffield was pastor at Flagstaff FSBC. *Primera Iglesia Bautista*, Tuba City Navajo Trail, and Cameron remained without pastors. Greenlaw began a television ministry on May 8, 1977. Williams FBC remodeled and enlarged their fellowship hall. Flagstaff Indian mission installed new pews and pulpit furniture, poured walks, and dedicated their building. They ordained Jasper Jones to the ministry. On September 9, 1977, Bethel dedicated a new educational building.

Flagstaff FSBC added a new ministry, a fellowship for single adults, which met each Thursday evening in the home of Evelyn Lewis. The church purchased a new van which they put to good use in their college ministry.

### 1977 GCBA Annual Meeting at Williams FBC

Earl Stallings announced that the state's first retreats for senior adults had been well attended at GCC and the Prescott conference center. He offered to assist GCBA senior adult groups in developing weekday ministries and pre-retirement planning. Ruth Stallings offered to train volunteers to conduct conversational English classes for non-English-speaking people.

### Sedona FBC Building Program

Because attendance almost trebled in the summers with visitors until the Jordan Road facility reached capacity, in 1977 Sedona FBC began planning a building program to remodel and enlarge the building. After consulting a Phoenix architect, the church felt that relocating would be better stewardship because their location was less and less visited by local residents. In its early years Sedona was centered on the Uptown and Jordan Road area, but the community had shifted toward West Sedona.

Hoping that frontage property might be available in the church's price range, pastor Barry Hall visited the office of a friend and major developer, Bill Steinbach. After ruling out other possible locations, Hall stood on the 5.342 acre parcel with 755-foot frontage on Highway 89-A and dramatic views and knew it was the right place. Its only flaw was the challenge presented by the rolling terrain. Steinbach quoted a price of $80,130 with $25,000 down.

With a sense of excitement, the building committee presented the relocation possibility to the church. On February 13, 1977, since FBC had already raised about sixty-five thousand dollars in a "Together We Build" (TWB) campaign and had received over fifty thousand dollars from the Carrie Belle McElroy estate, they decided that with the sale of the Jordan Road property, they could afford to move and rebuild. The transaction was completed on November 29, 1977. The excitement waned when problems with the local architect arose and nearly two years passed without suitable, working drawings—but significant developments would occur within a few years.

Pastor Hall traveled to Nashville to consult with the BSSB Architecture Department about the unique building opportunity and the hurdles for getting plans drawn. Hall implored architect Paul Chenowith to consider taking on the project outside of his regular work schedule. Cliff Flacy, a member of FBC and a civil engineer and engineering instructor at NAU, had offered to help. When Chenowith agreed to take on the job for a reasonable fee, Jim Coile, a landscape architect in the same department, also shared his expertise.

Work began to move at a rapid pace until it again bogged down over septic approvals. At last the building was completed, and a dedication service was held on November 29, 1981, with only thirty-seven-thousand-dollars indebtedness. The Jordan Road property had finally sold for $177,000. In 1995 the property and building were appraised for $2.7 million.

### 1978 GCBA Annual Meeting at Bethel

New pastors in the association included: Raymond Groft at Ash Fork; Stanley Daniel at Flagstaff FSBC; Bob Batchelder at Greenlaw, and Mike Stevens at its Faith mission; Roland Lopez at *Primera Iglesia Bautista*; and Bobby Neeley at Page FSBC, which had come back into the association. The evangelism report stated that almost all churches had two revivals in 1978. On September 9 the four churches in Flagstaff participated in Bold Impact Day with good results.

**1979 Annual Meeting at Flagstaff Baptist Indian Mission**

Historical events reported at the 1979 annual meeting included Faith Baptist Mission being relocated from Williams to the Parks Sherwood Forest area with the first service held July 1 in the Main Consolidated School in Parks. As a result of the missions committee studies, GCBA set goals to begin a mission in Munds Park and a VBS in Kachina Village, and missions in the Village of Oak Creek and the Continental Country Club area as soon as possible. Bethel Baptist extended an arm to save a mission in Caldwell, Idaho, with Victor Walker, son of Houston Walker, as pastor.

Ash Fork ordained Raymond Groft to the ministry. Tuba City added to their parsonage. Gerald and Alice Lawton returned to pastor the Navajo Trail Baptist Church. Williams FBC ordained two deacons, began a radio ministry, adopted a constitution and bylaws, remodeled and carpeted the auditorium, and painted the exterior of their building. Manuel Martinez was listed as a messenger from *Primera Iglesia Bautista*. On August 6, 1979, Dan Branscum came to direct the BSU, filling the vacancy left when Darrow Miller moved to Denver.

In 1980 Ash Fork ordained Conrad Roeder to the ministry. Roeder had served as deacon, pianist, and lay preacher whenever needed. The church also ordained Spencer Estus as deacon. Williams FBC installed new heating and air conditioning and started a puppet ministry and a youth choir. On June 23, 1980, Flagstaff FSBC had a potluck supper and old fashioned pounding to welcome their new pastor Clark Johnson and his family. Bill Thompson became pastor of Williams FBC. The Navajo Trail church changed its name to Tuba City FSBC in 1980.

**1980 GCBA Annual Meeting at Flagstaff FSBC**

At the annual meeting, missionary Mears reported successful BYBCs conducted in the Timberline, Fernwood, and Sunset Crater Estates areas north of Flagstaff and at Grand Canyon National Park. When a census uncovered so few prospects at Munds Park, the missions committee did not feel it feasible to try to start work there. Much time and effort were spent trying to reopen the church at Seligman, and in October the work started again. Mears expressed deep gratitude for each individual and church for prayerful concern for Ophelia's suffering over the past twelve months, saying her health had greatly improved during the last few weeks.

WMU director Linda Pogany reported that Alice and Gerald Lawton, Jon Allen, Melba Holsemback, and Bonnie Martin led conferences at quarterly meetings, and seventeen women attended the prayer retreat at the Grand Canyon with Charlotte Walter from Prescott leading. At the fall meeting, BSU summer missionaries Jeana Hodges and Karen Humbert told of their missions experiences in Germany and Lake Placid.

Associational SS director Ken Bane listed the following average attendance reports for GCBA churches in 1980: Ash Fork 25; Bethel 18; Flagstaff FSBC 114; Greenlaw 134; *Primera Iglesia Bautista* 59; Sedona 50; Tuba City 40; Williams 64; Flagstaff Indian mission 22; and Parks Faith mission 22.

On March 17, 1981, the annual associational evangelism clinic met at Bethel with J. P. Dane, George Webb, Bob Batchelder, and M. V. Mears as speakers. Attendance was good from all the churches. April 5–11 was Scripture distribution week throughout Arizona. Special marked copies of the Gospel of John were handed out door to door in an effort to place God's Word in every person's hand. With the churches in GCBA participating, the northern part of the state was blanketed with copies of John.

Mears rejoiced that the work at Seligman was going again with a healthy spirit with the help of Bethel Baptist Church. Bethel also was sponsoring a Bible fellowship class at Bellemont. Greenlaw had voted to sell their building and property and relocate. New pastors in 1981 were Mike and Virginia McKay at Flagstaff Indian mission, Bill Mastriani at Grand Canyon, Vancil Gibson at Sedona, and David Wallace at Williams FBC.

After Bill Hunke preached a fall revival for Mike and Virginia McKay at Flagstaff Indian mission, he wrote the following members to thank them for meals and gifts and to encourage several family members who had followed the Lord in baptism during the revival: Joe and Cindy Crank, Margaret Fredericks, Miriam Torivio, Tanya and Clarence Lomayma, Jasper and Theresa Jones, Lemuel and Marie Littleman, Jack and June Smith, Shirley Barlow, Sally Spencer, and Reuben and Juanita Lomayesva.

Flagstaff FSBC added a Keenagers senior adult group to their thriving singles groups, which included one called the "Availables." They hosted a youth choir from Tucson and "Eternity," and presented a multimedia musical, "Listen to the Butterfly," and Christmas music by "The Music Makers."

### 1981 Annual Meeting at Ash Fork FSBC

Messengers to the 1981 GCBA annual meeting were saddened to learn that M. V. and Ophelia Mears were retiring on December 31 after they had served twenty-two years and seven months as missionaries and forty-two years in the ministry. During his tenure in the three associations he served, Mears saw forty-seven missions started, sixteen churches constituted, and drove a half million miles in the work. GCBA would be without a missionary until R. A. Guthrie came in June 1983.

Linda Pogany reported an inspirational WMU prayer retreat at Sedona studying spiritual gifts and a leadership training seminar at Flagstaff FSBC with good attendance. She had developed a foreign mission booth about French West Africa for the WMU house party at GCC in preparation for the week-of-prayer study. At WMU week at Glorieta and the executive council at Prescott, she had learned about the StarTeam program soon to be initiated.

Messengers learned that GCC's Samaritan College of Nursing had received accreditation and had ninety students with a nursing major enrolled. The Antelope baseball team captured the world series crown for their third consecutive championship. The group also enthusiastically listened to missionaries Gerald Lawton, Mike McKay, and Bill Mastriani tell about their work.

### 1982 GCBA Annual Meeting at Sedona FBC

In 1982 Page FSBC officially came back into GCBA. Ray South was its new pastor. The GCBA executive board had spent much time discussing the search for a new director of missions. At the annual meeting the board's goals and desirable qualities for a missionary were accepted. Messengers voted on plans for a special service for the Mears and increased missionary travel expenses for pulpit supply. Missions committee chairman R. A. Guthrie told how the association had helped Bethel with travel money for a supply preacher for Seligman for about eighteen months. After the church closed and reopened as a mission, a bivocational pastor came on the field for six months. A small group there was currently meeting for SS and Wednesday prayer meetings led by members of the mission.

During the GCC report, Joyce Parker announced that Willard and Katheryn Hardcastle of Sedona had been made honorary members of the alumni association. State evangelism director Irving Childress said that 90 percent of Arizona churches had revivals in 1982, and that his department was scheduling fifty tent revivals for next year. *Baptist Beacon* editor Wendell Freeze reported 174 churches received the paper through their budgets. Earl Stallings shared that 126 senior adults had attended a special meeting during the state convention. Childress presented awards to Tuba City FSBC, Grand Canyon FBC, and Flagstaff FSBC for out-standing missions giving.

Flagstaff FSBC pastor Clark Johnson was elected president of the ASBC in 1982. The church exceeded their LMCO goal of $1,600 by $173.10. Bill and Linda Clark, missionaries from Chile, shared slides and testimonies with the congregation to help promote the offering. On May 20, 1983, Carolyn Weatherford, SBC executive director of WMU in Birmingham, spoke to FSBC women.

**Director of Evangelism and Missions R. A. Guthrie**

The highlight for the executive board came on February 14, 1983, at a special called meeting at the Afton House Restaurant when ten pastors and several laymen unanimously approved R. A. Guthrie to serve as the new director of evangelism and missions (DOEM) for GCBA. Ralph Anson Guthrie Jr. was born February 29, 1924, at Spartenburg, Texas. He was saved at age twelve through his parents' influence, baptized in a stock tank in 1936 by Pettit, Texas, Baptist Church, and ordained July 13, 1952, by Hamlin, Texas, Hitson Baptist Church. He wrote, "I had been aware for more than a year that I was lost. When we had a late summer revival in 1936, I trusted Jesus to save me during a morning service." R. A. married Bettye Jo Petree on June 5, 1943; they have two children.

He graduated from Sundown, Texas, High School, Hardin Simmons University, and SWBTS. He wrote, "I had never been to Arizona and did not know anyone in the state when a letter came from the pulpit com-mittee in McNary asking me to come in view of a call. I had no idea where they got my name. I was not looking for a change since I had been in my present pastorate only a few months. We prayed about the request and felt impressed to investigate. They called and we accepted. Two years later we left McNary for seminary in Fort Worth feeling we would return to Arizona. We did and have been here ever since." After pastoring in Flagstaff, he served as DOEM for Grand Canyon Association from 1983 to 1986 and Yavapai Association from 1983 to 1989.

**1983 GCBA Annual Meeting at Flagstaff *Primera Iglesia Bautista***

During 1983 Greenlaw sent Harold Miller out to pastor the Parks Faith Baptist Mission. Miller was the first black pastor in the association. The Seligman FSBC was reorganized and trying to establish a presence in the community. Ross Woodruff served as interim pastor until September 1983. He led the church to pay off all its outstanding debts in the com-munity. In the fall Woodruff became pastor of the Flagstaff Indian mission. Paul Reed served as pastor at Page FSBC, and Don Greenwalt, a member of Bethel who was a graduate student at NAU, became pastor there.

SS director Dave Wallace shared that nine churches and missions reported VBSs with an enrollment of 634, 180 new prospects discovered, and 14 professions of faith. GCBA enlisted a SS ASSIST team which was used in April at Sedona to train teachers.

The missions committee reported that on May 6, 1983, R. A. Guthrie and Bill Mastriani did a house count in the Doney Park, Sunset Crater Estates, Mountain View Rancheros, and Winona communities. They found 748 dwellings; to get an estimate of the resident population, they multiplied the houses by 3.2 persons. With only one evangelical work established in the area, they agreed it was a potential site to begin new work. In June GCBA gave three hundred dollars to the Flagstaff Indian mission for a special statewide Indian fellowship.

WMU director Linda Pogany told about attending Glorieta and hearing Helen Jean Parks, wife of FMB president Keith Parks, teach her book on intercessory prayer, *Holding the Ropes*. The theme for WMU was Partnership in Prayer and Ministry. Linda was in charge of a special table at the state house party, showing new materials, and she also sang the new hymn of the year. In the association, state director Beverly Goss installed WMU officers at the annual meeting, and Jay Dorris preached the missions message. The culmination of their year's activities was a training seminar with state WMU president Dorothy Rinker leading.

On January 1, 1984, Flagstaff FSBC welcomed the Frank Jackson family. Frank pastored the church until 1988 when he entered the chaplaincy. During his time with the church, Frank was especially grateful to be able to participate in the singles' ministries, the purchase of additional property using the TWB program, the college ministry with their retreats at Sacred Mountain and Grand Canyon and leading out in visitation and VBS, and the youth ministry. He wrote, "The youth mission trip to Chula Vista illustrated their commitment. They prayerfully and diligently prepared to lead BYBCs and door-to-door visitation. What great times we had encouraging one another!"

## 1984 GCBA Annual Meeting at Greenlaw Baptist Church

Missions committee chairman Bill Mastriani welcomed the Ollie Bryants, MSC volunteers from Louisiana, who came to lead the Seligman mission. On June 21–22, 1984, six teams of four each met at Sedona to do a PROBE study of the populations of GCBA.

In January 1985 Flagstaff FSBC called David Cox as associate pastor of religious education and outreach. Carol Cox became director of the media library. The church went over their LMCO goal of $2,500, receiving $4,184.88. By October the TWB program had received $27,658 towards the purchase of ten acres adjacent to the church.

### 1985 GCBA Annual Meeting at Bethel

In 1985 Seligman became a community church, and Parks Faith Baptist ceased operation. WMU director Linda Finley reported that the April Women in Evangelism and Lifestyle Witnessing workshop led by Fayly Cothern at Sedona was such a success that a repeat was scheduled for February 7–8, 1986, in Flagstaff with Fayly joined by Gaylon Cothern, who would lead a conference for men.

Dave Wallace announced that most churches had their SS teachers present at the Glorieta Flagstaff conference. The ASSIST team had responded to every church that requested their help in training teachers. The seven churches that reported their VBSs had over six hundred enrolled, but only about half had mailed their reports to the GCBA office.

### 1986 GCBA Annual Meeting at Williams FBC

At the 1986 annual meeting GCBA voted to dissolve the partnership with Yavapai Association in the sharing of a DOEM. Missionary R. A. Guthrie sold his Flagstaff home and chose to move to Prescott Valley to serve Yavapai Association, requiring GCBA to secure its own missionary for the first time since it was reduced to the present boundaries. Evangelism director Gerald Lawton reminded messengers that the evangelism clinic had been snowed out and reset for February when a film on prayer with Dr. Orr attracted a large number.

Gerald told the group to think about the story of Aunt Sophie, a converted scrub woman who said she was "called to scrub and preach." When she was ridiculed by someone who said she was seen talking about Christ to a wooden Indian in front of a cigar store, Aunt Sophie retorted, "Perhaps I did. My eyesight is not so good. But talking to a wooden Indian about Christ is not so bad as being a wooden Christian and never talking to anyone about the Lord Jesus."

Linda Finley shared that the GCBA WMU held monthly meetings with state leaders and special speakers each time. Highlights were a spiritual awakening seminar led by Dave Wallace in preparation for the Good News America revivals, and a pastors' appreciation night, a time of fellowship and fun enjoyed by all who attended.

# Split Rocks in the Wilderness

## GCBA under Doem Bill Hunke

God told Jeremiah that his Word is the hammer that breaks in pieces the rocks of even the most stubborn resistance. He promised Ezekiel that when the people were so stubborn of heart that they would not listen and obey the Lord, he would make Ezekiel's face and forehead strong and hard against them, as hard as an adamant flint or a diamond point against sandstone.

Although obstacles to starting churches in GCBA have loomed before the missionaries and pastors, God promised they cannot permanently paralyze their efforts. Advance of the gospel has always been in the face of adversity, but ever "it is required of stewards that a man be found faithful." The hammer of God's Word can break down resistance in unregenerate hearts and crush defiance in antagonistic lives. It can smash the illusions and falsehoods of false doctrines and cults, for it is a powerful and dynamic force. However great the determination of communities to reject it, even greater will be the power of the message.

### Sedona Becomes the Worldwide Center for the New Age Movement

In the early 1980s, New Age gurus had identified seven vortexes, or energy focal points, in the Sedona area, with Bell Rock becoming the most prominent. Suddenly, it was no longer just a picturesque piece of beautiful sandstone, but a sacred site where thousands gathered, especially on nights of the full moon, to absorb cosmic vibrations. Stone prayer wheels and altars began to tattoo its flanks, and humming in harmony with the vibrations of the spheres became its hymn of praise to the god of this world.

A highly publicized "harmonic convergence" in 1987, attended by up to thirty thousand New Agers, helped establish Sedona as their mecca. The New Age teachings are most evident in crystal and book shops, healing pyramids and psychic readings, rolfing, chakra cleaning services, books on human potential and meditation techniques, and advertisements promising spirit guides and channeling. Local evangelical pastors state that about 75 percent of the people they counsel are trying to break away from the New Age movement after becoming disillusioned.

New Age beliefs include monism—the concept that all reality, including God, man, the universe, time, space, and energy, is One. This belief leads to pantheism, which states that everything is God: "You are God, and the aim of life is to awaken to the god within you." Every person is divine and, therefore, wonderful. Secular works on self-esteem are largely based on this fallacy.

Another basic teaching is reincarnation or many lifetime progressions to reach ultimate unity. Positive or negative benefits, the "fruits of actions," carry over to the next life cycle as good or bad karma. Eventually one will accumulate enough good karma to enable him to leave the cycle of rebirth through the experience of enlightenment, or fully realizing one's true self, his inner being.

New Agers teach that people's biggest problem is the illusion that they are limited, finite human beings. They say religion creates the primary obstacle to obtaining true spiritual experiences. They advocate a transformation of consciousness through practice in yoga, meditation, mind-altering techniques, past life regressions, and out-of-body experiences. Worst of all is channeling—contacting spiritual guides from other dimensions. In reality, channeling is deliberately opening oneself to possession by demons.

Jesus, to New Agers, is one of many manifestations of God during history. Christ is different from Jesus and represents the perfect awareness of the god within. Jesus, they say, had more Christ awareness than others, but everyone can have the same Christ or cosmic consciousness that he had. The world is constantly being changed by an evolutionary process into a better place, and a new age is dawning when humanity will make a great leap forward and emerge as entirely new creatures.

New Age buzzwords include peace, human potential, rainbow, pyramid, holistic, networking, unity, global, and personal growth. Their techniques may involve changing consciousness, or how to perceive reality; finding all solutions and answers within oneself; and use of harmonizing, integrating, or balancing energies or polarities. They emphasize experience over faith and deny revelation of truth outside oneself.

New Age beliefs are making inroads into the educational system by such avenues as values clarification, which teaches children to discover their own values and not accept values imposed by parents or churches. They emphasize "transpersonal" education under the label of centering or relaxation exercises. They instruct through visualization which tells children to imagine themselves filled with light, their essential goodness or god within. Many corporations are employing consciousness raising or human potential techniques to improve productivity. Health professionals may practice the therapeutic touch, a healing concept based on trying to tap universal energy and channel it into the patient's body.

Because these practices have a strong grip on the Sedona area, our Southern Baptist church members find themselves confronting Satan who defies efforts to disengage his hold on minds of men. Many residents have been "taken captive through hollow and deceptive philosophy, which depends on human tradition and the basic principles of this world rather than on Christ" (Col. 2:8, NIV). The oldest temptation is still the most alluring—"you shall be gods." The hammer of God's Word must be applied to the rocks of false doctrines until they split asunder.

### DOEM Edmund William Hunke Jr.

On December 2, 1986, GCBA called Bill Hunke to serve as DOEM. Because Hunke was employed by the HMB as western regional coordinator, and the board was without a director, its leaders asked him to remain in his position until a new director was selected. The HMB and ASBC permitted him to serve as a consultant to GCBA on his days off, weekends, and vacation, anticipating that he would assume the full position on October 1, 1987.

Bill Hunke was born September 22, 1924, in Taylor, Texas, and saved at age twenty when fellow serviceman Clifford Clark witnessed to him while serving in the U.S. Air Force at Van Nuys, California, during World War II. He was baptized in the San Joaquin River in 1949 by California's first missionary B. N. Lummus and ordained by Madera, California, FSBC. He married Naomi Ruth Savage in Fresno, California, on August 29, 1946, the day the GCBA constituted in Prescott, Arizona.

Bill attended Baylor University, Southwest Missouri State, University of Wisconsin, University of Illinois, Georgia State, and Yavapai College.

He received degrees from Pacific College, Fresno State, GGBTS, and Arizona State, where he earned a doctorate in educational administration and supervision. Bill served as University of Alaska dean of Elmendorf and Fort Richardson extensions, as a major in the Civil Air Patrol, and later as Canadian Southern Baptist Seminary interim president for seven months.

Bill pastored Clovis FSBC and Pittsburg Baptist in California and Vernal, Utah, FBC. He served as missionary for Gila Valley, Yuma, San Carlos, Mount Graham, and Estrella Baptist Associations in Arizona from 1954 to 1956. He was elected as assistant executive secretary and superintendent of missions for ASBC from 1957 to 1966 and as executive director for Alaska Baptists 1966 to 1971. The HMB employed him as the first western regional coordinator with responsibility for the western state conventions and Canada from 1971 to 1987. He served as DOEM for GCBA from 1987 to 1992.

Naomi Ruth Hunke taught world literature and English at Grand Canyon University, Alaska Methodist University, University of Alaska, and DeKalb Community College in Clarkston, Georgia. She has written the history of Alaska Baptists, *In This Land*; about experiences in the Holy Land; the biography of missionary B. Frank Belvin, *God's Warhorse*; the 150-year history of Stone Mountain, Georgia, WMU; and *Volunteer Missions Opportunities for Senior Adults*. She also has written for BSSB and WMU publications. The Hunkes, who traveled over Europe and the Orient, enjoyed participating in overseas partnership evangelism crusades. They retired September 30, 1992, at Sedona, Arizona. They have three children and five grandsons.

### 1987 GCBA World Missions Conference

One of the first GCBA activities the Hunkes participated in was the 1987 WMC. Pastors and church members met the missionaries and received packets of materials at a noon luncheon at Flagstaff FSBC on Saturday, March 14. Snow began falling the next day, and by the following Sunday, missionaries from Malawi and Guatemala found driving so hazardous that they were held over for extra sessions, to the great delight of their host churches.

In spite of the late snow, attendance in GCBA churches for the WMC meetings totaled 1,292 with 56 decisions recorded. All who attended learned much about HMB and FMB activities and programs, and many responded to the important challenge to pray for and regularly support our missionaries and to try to win at least one person to Christ during the year. The following missionaries shared their experiences.

Ross Collier from Malawi told about a ninety-year-old man who was beaten for almost three hours and left for dead because he taught from the Bible. The man then walked barefooted for 351 miles over mountains nine thousand feet high because he heard that Ross gave away Bibles. If he had been found carrying the Bible Ross gave him, he would have received an automatic death sentence. He said that he would cut the pages out of the Bibles with a razor blade and distribute them to friends who would memorize all their pages so that they would never again lose God's Word.

Yvonne Helton wore a beautiful costume from Guatemala and chose some persons to model other clothing as she told about the customs of her country and showed a movie using a VCR. Yvonne taught Christian education classes for pastors using Master Life. She also taught special classes for pastors' wives, other women, and children. She gave her students two months to read through the Bible. Manuel, one of the students she won and taught, now pastors a church and has started nineteen other churches in the past fifteen years. In 1992 Yvonne joined Dixie Hunke as a Cooperative Services International (CSI) representative to an unreached people group in East Asia.

Charles Jolly told of his work in the Puget Sound area of Washington. The Jollys helped develop home Bible studies into fully organized churches. They had started six missions in the past eight years. One mission was for the deaf. Others offered Bible studies in twelve different languages. The Jollys worked with an ethnic church with services in four languages: Japanese, Korean, Filipino, and mixed. Of the two and a half million people in their area, approximately 80 percent are not saved.

Tom Draper told how everyone present could become a missionary, either under full appointment, as a missionary associate, or a missionary volunteer. He shared experiences as a field-worker with the BSSB, area missionary in Orlando, and member of the HMB of directors. He now works starting new SSs. Tom's son has worked a number of years trying to start the first Southern Baptist church in Boston. So far the group has five members. Living expenses are so high that his rent is more than his income.

Bill Hunke told of typical converts, cities, and experiences in missions. He told of building a church in the arctic, of eating moosehead stew with the eyes looking at him, and of a young nurse in Hawaii who won fifty-two friends to the Lord and begged for a church in her hometown.

Naomi Hunke told of extremely old Eskimo women who found and served the Lord, learned to read so they could read the Bible, and witnessed to the whole town of Fairbanks during the 1969 floods. She told of the faithfulness of older Indian Christians who were willing to walk twenty-five miles through the snow to attend church services in order to set an example for the youth, and of an old woman in Oklahoma who walked many miles as keeper of the church building key and never missed any services although she was deaf and never heard a word that was sung or preached.

### Ash Fork FSBC: David and Carol Cox

On January 19, 1986, Ash Fork FSBC ordained their pastor, Randy Randall, who left in September after serving for a year. Deacon Spence Estus carried on the work the following year until Dave and Carol Cox responded to the church's call. Early in 1987 the church purchased two small houses adjacent to the church property to provide room for future expansion. In July 1987 several families from Santo, Texas, FSBC led VBS, put siding on the building, and replaced a number of windows.

David Cox was born in Winfield, Kansas, on October 25, 1953. When Dave was five, his grandfather died, and subsequent discussions about his eternal destination left Dave confused. He went forward in response to an invitation after hearing a sermon about hell, and was baptized, but had no real understanding of salvation. From that time, however, he considered himself a Christian, especially since he grew up in a pastor's home.

When he was seventeen and a student at Casa Grande High School, a Bible study group attended by fellow students caught his attention. Because some of the leaders had previously been known as drug users, Dave felt the need to investigate. To his surprise, he found a group of saved young people with a joy, peace, and enthusiasm that were foreign to his experience. When one of them asked him if he were a Christian, Dave responded indignantly that of course he was. The response shocked him: "Man, you sure don't act like it!"

Convicted of his need for salvation, Dave came to Christ shortly afterwards on February 19, 1970. Because he had been baptized as a young boy, it was not until years later when he was a seminary student that he realized his need to be baptized as a genuine believer. He was baptized by the Fort Worth Southcliff Baptist Church in September 1982. Dave's call to preach came during an intensive prayer time in July 1970. Although becoming a pastor had not entered his thinking, when he became convinced that pastoring was the Lord's will, he surrendered and was licensed to preach in November 1970 at Prescott Miller Valley Baptist Church.

Dave's college and career plans were to go to NAU and become a forest ranger because more than anything else he loved being alone out-doors. In the summer of 1971, God began leading him to attend GCC to study for the ministry, but Dave struggled against the decision, arguing that he could go to NAU and become a pastor to the forest rangers. Eventually, he yielded to God's will, started to GCC that fall, then later graduated from SWBTS. He and Carol, a native of Phoenix, were married on June 11, 1974.

Before becoming pastor at Ash Fork, Dave served as minister of education at Flagstaff FSBC for two years. He was in the U.S. Army from 1973 to 1976. During college and seminary days and as a bivocational pastor, he has worked at a variety of jobs, including maintenance super-visor, machinist, typographer, appliance repairman, and custodian for Ash Fork schools. He enjoys leatherwork and hunting.

### Mysterious Odor

Carol Cox wrote that a memorable week at the church that was defi-nitely not a spiritual highlight came when a funeral was scheduled. "The evening before, I went over to make sure the church was ready and was met by an overpowering stench of something very dead. I looked under tables, behind boxes, even in the baptistry, thinking that perhaps a mouse had fallen in and died."

She worried because the deceased's family had chosen not to have the body embalmed and feared the sanctuary would be filled with mourners sniffing surreptitiously the following day. She located a can of lemon fur-niture polish and lavishly applied it to the pews, threw open all the windows, and went to tell Dave and Spence about the problem. The next morning the sanctuary smelled like lemon, but the bad odor had traveled to the kitchen as strong as ever. A search revealed no source. With the mourners discreetly kept away from the kitchen, the funeral went well.

On Wednesday the stench had permeated the nursery and fellowship hall so badly that prayer meeting was held in the parking lot, using car headlights. Carol wrote, "Someone suggested the smell might be coming from underneath the building, and we even went over the possibilities of anyone from the area who might be missing." A careful search revealed a small hole leading underneath the church that a rat or other small animal might have crawled into and died. They never determined why the odor kept changing from one location to another inside the building unless changing wind currents periodically relocated it. Any ideas, readers?

In December 1989 a Flagstaff church donated clothes and toys for Ash Fork to distribute to needy families. This ministry has continued to the present with donations coming from local people as well as from out-of-town individuals and groups. Carol wrote, "The clothes closet has proven to be a most effective ministry tool. It is set up on a voluntary donation basis. If a person has a need and cannot pay, everything is free. If he can donate something, he chooses the amount. This money goes into a travel fund used to help people passing through Ash Fork who need food or gas."

Spence Estus' scrapbook of old minutes indicates that at least sixteen men have served as pastor during nineteen periods since 1952. A few highlights include an open house and mortgage burning held on October 20, 1968. The loan was paid off under pastor Clark Johnson. Early pastor O. R. Moore was the principal speaker for morning worship, with ASBC executive director Charles L. McKay guest speaker for the open house. Flagstaff FSBC ordained Clark Johnson on November 3, 1968. On October 20, 1981, GCBA held its thirty-sixth annual session at Ash Fork. In November 1991 church attendance averaged fifty.

### Greenlaw: Steve May

Steve May returned to Arizona from the pastorate of the Gillette, Wyoming, Antelope Valley Baptist Church in 1987 to serve at Greenlaw. Although he had been born in Holbrook, November 23, 1957, Steve lived in Flagstaff from ages three months to seventeen years and graduated from Flagstaff High School. His father Bill May was a former Greenlaw pastor who now is president of the ASBC Church Growth Board.

Even though he said yes to questions about knowing Jesus when he was eight, Steve wrote, "God dealt with me strongly around age ten about my personal relationship to him. I realized then that I needed to be saved. At age eleven, at Glorieta, New Mexico, in July 1969, I personally invited Christ into my life." He was baptized by Greenlaw Baptist Church in May 1974.

"I believe God was dealing with me about a call to ministry even before I was saved," Steve continued. "During an invitation at Flagstaff FSBC, pastor Alvin Wood asked if God might be calling anyone to be a missionary or pastor. The thought arrested my attention. Riding home from church, I asked my father how I could know for sure that God wanted me to be a minister. The conviction remained in my mind and led to a lengthy time of prayer, searching, and public surrender at age twelve."

While he was a ministerial student at GCC, Steve pastored the Dewey Humboldt Southern Baptist Chapel. Prescott FSBC ordained him on January 21, 1979. He pastored the Mill Creek, Oklahoma, FBC while he was attending SWBTS, and upon his graduation the Morenci, Arizona, FSBC called him. From there he went to the Wyoming church. Although his first pastorates were two years each, Steve has remained at Greenlaw until the present. He served on the ASBC committee on boards from 1987 to 1990 and on the ASBC executive board from 1990 to the present. As GCBA SS and TU director, he led VBS leadership training and music and motivation events for a number of years.

By the end of 1987, SS attendance, which had dropped into the teens and low twenties while Greenlaw was without a pastor, had increased to the seventies. In December 1995 it reached 161.

Steve and Jayne have four children: Chris, Amanda, Emily, and Becky. Steve is a gifted pianist and is also greatly used of God as an expository preacher. Besides reading and travel, his interests include aquariums and photography.

### Moenkopi Bible Study

Tuba City pastor Gerald Lawton initiated a Bible study among the Hopis at Moenkopi in October 1987. After water from a frozen pipe caused damage in 1989, the Tuba church installed new tile and carpet and painted the interior. Members distributed Christmas bags at their own expense in 1989. Shortly thereafter, a Seminole Indian joined the church. Lawton stirred up community interest when he announced plans for an alligator tail cookout. In January 1992 Gerald reported the most snow and coldest weather during his twenty-two years on the Navajo Reservation.

Sedona FBC completed and occupied their new Hardcastle Fellowship Hall and youth recreation area in 1987. They added land area to their parking lot by removing a hill. Williams FBC paid off their debt, held a note-burning service, and completed their new pastorium.

### 1987 GCBA Annual Meeting at Tuba City FBC

Brotherhood president Harold Boldin reported that the *Primera Iglesia Bautista* men had undertaken a major improvement and beautification project which included remodeling and a new metallic Spanish tile roof. "If the Lord provides us with a few more days of good weather, this project will be completed before May 1," he stated.

A digest of church letters showed the following summaries for the 1986–1987 year: baptisms 61, membership 2,632, SS enrollment 1,004,

Church Training (CT) 149, music 228, WMU 149, Brotherhood 39, and grand total mission gifts $102,958. Bill Hunke announced that monthly pastors' breakfasts for fellowship and mutual encouragement would begin January 4, 1988.

Gerald Lawton reported that Tuba City had had an excellent revival with Al Campsen from Winslow preaching. The meeting was blessed with decisions in homes and large attendance. On Friday, November 27, 1987, Gerald, Alice, and son Eric hit a horse in the road about thirty miles west of Shiprock, New Mexico, and totaled their van. Gerald sustained a back injury that required years for recovery.

Flagstaff Indian Mission had fifty in attendance at a Thanksgiving fellowship meal and service. At Sedona FBC a large crowd enjoyed Thanksgiving dinner on November 18; afterwards, pastor Troy Capps presented an appreciation plaque to Willard Hardcastle. Williams FBC participated in a community Thanksgiving service. The church received an organ from a Las Vegas, Nevada, church and planned to donate their present organ to a church that needs it. Steve May said that eighty attended Greenlaw's celebration of Thanksgiving and the pastor's birthday.

In November Flagstaff FSBC held a worker appreciation banquet at Mt. Elden Conference Center. Their JOY Bunch traveled to Phoenix Metro Center for shopping and fellowship. JoAnne Polk taught the foreign missions book on Korea and led in a missions fair to prepare for the LMCO. Pastor Don Greenwalt wrote that Bethel hosted the Titus group from Denver who presented a musical program on Saturday night and Sunday morning. They had thirty for their Thanksgiving potluck.

Page FSBC hosted the "M & M" night rally with the seven churches represented enjoying a delicious meal. Michele Cason led the program which featured a CT fashion show led by Gerald Lawton; Bible drill led by Dave Wallace; testimony by Harold Boldin; and music by Hope Keyes, Susan Sanders, Carl Krigbaum, Marian Kallock, and the Lawtons.

**Pastors and Wives' Retreats**
From 1988 to 1992, during March the Hunkes hosted an annual, three-day pastors and wives' retreat at Arroyo Robles resort in Sedona which featured a fellowship banquet at Shugrue's, picnic by Oak Creek, Bible study, conferences, music, sharing and prayer times, and recreation. Attendance averaged twenty-six. Some of the speakers were LaVern and Bobbie Lewis, Clyde and Judy Billingsley, Glen and Erma Braswell, and Judy Rice; speakers came from Alaska, Colorado, Utah, and southern

Arizona. A check list revealed the retreat was the highlight every year for promoting fellowship among GCBA pastors.

Fifty members of the HMB board of directors spent two days in GCBA during May 1988. Several expressed a desire to return to spend time helping in the work. Grand Canyon FBC received a check for ten thousand dollars from the HMB to help build a pastorium, and East Valley received a box of Bibles for distribution. One HMB board member asked that he be considered to pastor a GCBA church. Another member, Hal Boone, returned to spend a week in the Village of Oak Creek to check out possibilities of beginning a church.

### Munds Park Mission Begins

On June 10, 1988, a Bible study started in the home of Dori and Eddy Emerson at Munds Park. A week earlier the Emersons, Bill and Naomi Hunke, and Harold Boldin had met to discuss starting an SBC work as the result of a letter Bill had received from Phoenix pastor Jerry Martin telling of the Emersons' imminent move to the area. When Eddy and Dori arrived, the first letter in their mailbox was from the Hunkes, welcoming them and asking if their home would be open to begin a new mission.

Within a month a telephone census had been taken, and attendance at the Friday night services reached thirteen. Vaughan Rock, who had a vacation home at Munds Park, directed the early studies. Rock, a pioneer of Southern Baptist work, was eighty-three years old. He had retired in 1973 after pastoring Phoenix FSBC for thirty-seven years following the death of his father C. M. Rock, who founded the church—the first Southern Baptist church in Arizona—in 1921. "To begin missions, you have to be willing to give up members," Rock stated in a 1973 interview. Phoenix FSBC's family tree comprised over one hundred churches in five generations of church starts. Rock had served as a trustee for the BSSB, GGBTS, and the HMB, and as a member of the SBC Executive Committee and many SBC committees.

GCBA moderator Harold Boldin led Flagstaff *Primera Iglesia Bautista* to sponsor Munds Park. When Vaughan Rock returned to Phoenix at the end of summer, Harold led the Bible studies. Linda Brown was the first convert; she and her husband Jim and son Darrin were the first to join by baptism.

On December 23, 1988, fifteen persons braved the snow and ice to go caroling. Arizona's lowest temperature of minus twenty-two degrees had been reported at Munds that week. In February 1989 Harold Boldin resigned *Primera Iglesia* and Munds Park to accept a pastorate in Douglas.

Bill Hunke became interim pastor, with Naomi leading Bible studies on Friday nights at the home of Ronnie and Faye Callicoat.

Sunday services began on Easter 1989 with thirty-two present and an AAEO of $1,475 the first week in spite of a snowstorm. The Pinewood Fire Department building has always been made available to the mission free of charge. Services included SS at 1:30 P.M. and worship at 2:30 P.M. In May pulpit committees of Bethel and Munds Park issued a unanimous call to Steve Martin, a GGBTS student from Cornville, to serve as pastor. Steve began his ministry on July 16 with Bethel sponsoring the mission. In the summer of 1990 an ASBC "saturation witness" event brought 80 people from Phoenix Hillside Baptist who visited 550 homes and discovered 56 prospects in the Munds Park community.

### Bethel Baptist: Steven Louis Martin

In 1988 a group from the General Baptist Convention (Swedish) was scheduled to meet with Bethel for the purpose of drawing the church away from Southern Baptists. Bill Hunke met with the pulpit committee to urge that the church be allowed to hear GCBA church members tell why they are Southern Baptists. On November 6 the following persons from seven churches shared why they believe in the SBC: Ernie Stebbins, Glenn Young, Harold Boldin, Eddy and Dori Emerson, Daryl and Julie Bennett, Steve and Carol May, Kathy Nation, Pat Welch, and Bill and Naomi Hunke. Bethel decided to remain in the SBC by an eleven-to-seven vote and called Steve Martin as pastor; he arrived on the field in July 1989.

Steve Martin was born December 14, 1953, in Ennis, Montana, where his father had worked as a cowboy for several years. Because his mother is a native Arizonan, and his father grew up in the state, in the spring of 1956 they returned to Arizona, where Steve's earliest memories begin. Settling in the Verde Valley, his father had to give up ranch work because he could not support the family on cowboy wages. Steve remembers, "We always had food to eat, but I worked in grade and high school cafeterias for the meals we kids ate during school. We did a lot together as a family like fishing and picnicking, but we never went to church."

While Steve was growing up, the family always had relatives living with them; so he was taught early to share. "I felt it was a big adventure when a new cousin or aunt or grandparent came to live," he wrote. "I also spent much time visiting with relatives who lived nearby, and if anyone had a need, we all banded together to help. The calls for help ranged from house fires, to unemployment, wood gathering, and medical bills."

Steve loved school and excelled in his studies, graduating from eighth grade as valedictorian and from Mingus Union High School in Jerome as co-valedictorian. The fact that his parents set rules with a price to pay if they were not obeyed helped to shape his behavior and decisions. He and his two sisters had regular chores and study time which had to be observed. He remembers that he could always count on his parents to support and back him up in every situation.

He listed examples of their support, the first coming during elementary school days when the school district decreed that those living within a mile of school could not ride the bus. "Although straight across country we were fifteen-sixteenths of a mile from school," he wrote, "by the roadway we were one and a quarter miles away. Dad stood up to the school board and told them if we were to walk cross country, we needed a path, or we would ride. We rode the bus for years until a developer bulldozed a path we could walk on."

During Steve's third semester at college, he lived in a trailer house with a roommate who began dealing drugs from the trailer. He wrote, "I was clean, but I knew if he were busted, my future career with Arizona Game and Fish would be forfeited. I called my parents to explain my predicament. At 6:00 A.M. the next morning when I heard a knock on the door, I found my dad had driven all through the night to be there for me. I moved into a small motor home, then into a house trailer they purchased so that I could finish college. It was this kind of structure and support which shaped my philosophy on life and family."

When Steve's dad began a truck-driving job, and his mother started working full time, the children became latchkey kids. In fourth grade Steve saw his first basketball game and fell in love with the game. After that he had a basketball in his hands every waking moment he could spare. He made the school's freshman and junior varsity teams, but a friend told him at the start of his senior year that the coach had decided to cut him from the varsity team.

"I knew I had to think of something and decided the only way to make the team was to impress the coach with my effort," he affirmed, "so I ran every drill twice. I was first to run it and the last. I made the team and started in over half the games. I learned a valuable lesson—that hard work can overcome a lack of skills."

After basketball season he realized he had no scholarship offers to play college ball. The strenuous training schedule had kept him from partying during high school. He admitted, "Now that excuse was gone, and I began to party and drink regularly. My academic efforts began to fade, a pattern that haunted me for years. I used alcohol to escape life's problems and pressures. College became a time of socialization. It took me five years to earn my degree in agriculture and fisheries science."

During his fourth year at University of Arizona at Tucson, Steve met Loralie Ward and fell in love. When they went for pastoral counseling before their marriage, and Steve told the pastor he was not interested in God, the pastor responded that he should see that their children had a chance to know God. Loralie worked in a bank to enable him to finish his college degree.

After Steve worked a while at a Prescott water-softener company, his father convinced him to help him start a backhoe business. Although he did not know how to run a backhoe, in December 1976 they formed Ben and Steve's Backhoe Company. "For five years I gave the business everything I had," Steve asserted. "It became very successful. Our family began to grow also as Tara and Amber were born, and we moved into our own house. By the world's standards, I had everything anyone could desire."

When Loralie told Steve she wanted to take the girls to church, he was adamant that if she did, no one from the church was to visit him, and she must have his lunch ready at noon on Sundays or she could not attend. From the day she took the girls to Cornville FSBC, the members began to pray for Steve's salvation. "For nine months I argued with the Holy Spirit that I was a good, redneck, alcoholic boy, and didn't need church," he admitted.

Then two elderly ladies from the church visited him. He told them he did not need church, and he could send his money with his wife. They replied that the church was not the building but the people, and they did not need his money. "Because God's Spirit had prepared my heart for those words, I agreed to go with Loralie the next Sunday. One of those little, old, redheaded sweethearts met me at the door with a big hug. During the sermon I heard for the first time that Jesus died for my sins, and would have died for me if I had been the only sinner needing salvation. I learned of another lifestyle far different and better than the life I was leading, and I wanted to be a part of it. I went forward and told Brother Joe Fredericks that I wanted to accept Christ." He was baptized by the Cornville church in 1981.

Steve testified that God began to work overtime with him to make him clean up his language and quit drinking after ten years. He wanted to serve God and soon led youth on Wednesday nights, taught adult SS, and directed the CT program. He quit working seven days a week in order to do things with the family, which now included Lucas, and soon felt God's call to do something more. He took the youth to Show Low to work on a church education wing, thinking that perhaps construction volunteer missions was what he was being called to.

In early 1986 as he was preparing a sermon for a lay revival, he felt God telling him that preaching was what he should do for the rest of his life. Without discussing his decision with anyone, he went forward the next Sunday morning, declaring his call to the pastorate. A number of people confirmed his call and began to pray with him about how to fulfill it. He wondered if he should go to a Bible college or to seminary, and if he should sell his business and equipment or plan to be bivocational.

After much prayer, he and Loralie knew they should leave the business behind and go to GGBTS. "It was at Golden Gate that God made major changes in me, not only at seminary but also in my ministry!" Steve declared. "As director of Project Hope at San Francisco FBC, I did outreach in the five-block area surrounding the church. I worked with twenty-one different language groups, homeless people, prostitutes, and homosexuals. I tutored in a black housing project where no white man had gone before. We wrote letters to and visited everyone who came to church and anyone else we could find addresses for. God blessed and in eighteen months the church grew from 250 to 650 people. I felt such an urgency from God that I completed my M.Div. in two years. Samuel had been added to our family. We spent time and drew together more than ever although I was totally devoted to my studies."

Toward the end of his seminary work, Steve became interim pastor at Comptche Chapel of the Redwoods. The pastor shared that he wanted to retire and hoped that Steve would become full-time. The church began to grow as the Martins developed a closeness with the members. At that time Bethel and Munds Park contacted them about pastoring one or the other. When the Comptche pastor decided not to retire, and Bethel and Munds Parks agreed that Steve should pastor both instead of choosing between them, they knew God had led them back to Arizona.

Steve maintains that pastoring two congregations has the distinct advantage that when one is down, the other is up. Bethel soon began to grow and saw many baptisms the first two years. They expanded from only one children's, youth, and adult SS class to four children's, one youth, and two adult classes. They began Discipleship Training on Sunday evenings; youth and children's mission groups with RAs, GAs and Mission Friends on Wednesday evenings; and a prayer ministry. Worship attendance grew from fifteen to twenty to seventy to eighty. Ed Troxel and Nancy Frick started a hospital ministry in 1990. In 1992 Bethel's VBS enrolled one hundred, and a Moss Point, Louisiana, youth group conducted four BYBCs in Kachina Village with forty-eight enrolled.

Meanwhile, Munds Park was struggling. In the fall of 1989 after summer visitors had left, a business relocation caused the loss of almost every member. "That first winter was bleak as one member and I met for worship; sometimes I was alone. In the spring we had a breakthrough and went from two to fourteen coming regularly. Attendance grew rapidly during the summers because Munds is a summer-resort community. After three years when state convention pastoral support ran out, the mission experienced financial difficulties, and I questioned if it could continue."

When a choice property with a house that seemed perfect for a church building became available, attendance rose and giving jumped dramatically as people became excited about raising thirty thousand dollars for a down payment. During that time at Bethel, losses occurred as 175 people passed in and out of the church in four years, with only few members still living in Flagstaff. Baptisms dropped to only seven or eight a year. Activities were curtailed because of lack of leaders, and SS attendance dipped to the thirties.

After four and a half years as pastor of both groups, when Steve felt impressed to begin work on a D.Min. degree and knew he could no longer serve both churches, he became full-time pastor at Bethel, where he continues to serve. He chaired the GCBA missions development two years and the DOEM search committee that called Si Davis. Hunting is his favorite hobby, together with fishing and gardening. For five years Steve was a member of the Coconino County Community Action Board and coached little league.

### East Valley: Daryl Bennett

East Valley met for their first service with thirty-eight attending on Christmas Eve 1987 during a snowstorm. Daryl Bennett, newly graduated from SWBTS, has served as pastor from the beginning. For four months Daryl knocked on doors and sent mailouts in preparation for the new mission start. In addition to Sunday services at Sturgeon Cromer School, he led weekly Bible studies in Christmas Tree Estates and on Silver Saddle Road. Before Easter he mailed four thousand fliers to homes in the Doney Park area. In October four more four-thousand-piece mailouts led seventy-five people to attend a special service. During

*Naomi and Bill Hunke took early retire-*
*ment to return to Arizona. They served as*
*GCBA missionaries, 1987–1992.*

*Naomi Hunke initiated the Kachina Point*
*Nursing Home ministry in 1987. It*
*reaches about twenty-five persons weekly.*

*Bell Rock Baptist Church met at Bell Rock*
*Inn and organized August 17, 1990, with*
*Darwin Welsh as pastor.*

*Anita Welsh (left) visits neighbor Edna*
*Maxson. Edna painted the scene used on*
Remember the Wonders' *cover.*

*Flagstaff East Valley Mission began on*
*Christmas Eve 1987 and organized August*
*16, 1992, with Daryl Bennett as pastor.*

*Pittsburg, Kansas, Trinity Baptist Church*
*sponsored Flagstaff Trinity Church in*
*1992 with Mike Rasberry as pastor.*

*Munds Park started June 10, 1988, with a Bible study led by Harold Boldin. The mission meets in the local fire station.*

*C. Vaughan Rock, pastor emeritus of Phoenix FSBC, also led Munds Park Bible study in the Emersons' home.*

*Munds Park Baptist mission charter members: Bill and Naomi Hunke, Jim and Linda Brown, Dori and Eddy Emerson, Ron and Faye Callicoat. Weeknight Bible studies met in Callicoats' home. Hunkes, Browns, and Eddy Emerson had lived in Alaska.*

*Sunnyside Mission started with a revival and VBS led by youth. Commencement services reported 117 people present.*

*Bernice and Ed Trotter of Tulsa, CSC volunteers, spent their summers with GCBA missions, 1989–1992.*

"Outreach Month" in October 1989, four mailouts of three thousand each were sent, and one thousand phone calls were made. East Valley mission reached ninety-three in attendance in October 1990.

East Valley incorporated on August 16, 1992, with fifty-nine charter members. The constitutional service was on Sunday afternoon, August 30. Mesa Brown Road Baptist and Holbrook FSBC, that have assisted the work, took part on the program. Volunteer Jess Neil, who was scheduled to give the benediction, passed away August 27.

After seeing six possible sites for a church building fail, East Valley purchased twelve-plus acres north of Flagstaff on Highway 89-A on August 1, 1993. August 1995 saw the original ninety-thousand-dollar debt down to seven thousand dollars, with contributions coming in from across the U.S. By the close of 1995, the debt was completely cleared. "Prayer meetings at the site during the summer months with the most beautiful, majestic sunsets possible have been a highlight for the group," Daryl said. "We've even had Dutch-oven, open-pit potlucks out there."

Every Sunday the congregation hauls materials to the Cromer school, and then packs them up again after services, leaving the building cleaner than when they arrive. One week the fire alarm went off in the middle of SS. "We didn't know what to do," Daryl remembered. "The commons is completely open, and we didn't see anybody out there moving around. We found the alarm had self tripped in the gym where we met."

A continuing problem has been to provide a pianist and song leader. "Many times we began singing several notes apart, but always ended up together by the end. God answered prayers several times and provided musicians for us. We've seen three young men surrender for the ministry," Daryl said.

Daryl Bennett accepted Christ on August 12, 1973, when he was fifteen years old, under the ministry of George Webb at Holbrook FBC. After he felt called to preach in his senior year of high school, he attended GCC and graduated in 1980. He graduated from SWBTS with M.A. and M.Div. degrees. Before coming to his first pastorate at East Valley, he served as youth director at Apache Junction FBC in 1980–1981. He and Julie have two children, Benjamin and Katie, who have been born during their time at East Valley. In 1994 they purchased and renovated a home near their church location.

### Grand Canyon First Baptist Church
Dick Underwood from Fairbanks, Alaska, wrote to Bill Hunke, "Back in 1958–1960 I lived at Grand Canyon Village where Patsy taught school.

One day I received a copy of the *Baptist Beacon* in the mail and delivered it to the family that it had been addressed to. They were glad to find another Southern Baptist family and said they missed singing the old hymns they were used to back home. I suggested that we meet at their home for singing and Bible reading. Being an ordained preacher, I couldn't help speaking a few words of exhortation from the Scriptures. We continued to meet every Sunday until school was out. Because my wife did not renew her contract, we moved on to Oklahoma. I've heard there is now a church at Grand Canyon and thought you might like to hear how the beginning of that work was due to a mistake by a postal worker."

Grand Canyon FBC shares the Shrine of the Ages chapel with several other denominations because no church buildings are allowed in national parks. Ron and Kathy Nation went to Louisiana in December 1987 to try to raise thirty-five thousand dollars for a new pastorium in Grand Canyon Village after securing a long-term lease for a lot. On February 21, 1988, the church broke ground for the new home. The sale of the trailer in which the Nations had lived brought $12,500 and made possible continued work on the four-bedroom structure when two Louisiana volunteer work teams came to assist the villagers. A record attendance exceeded four hundred during the summer of 1989. The HMB presented Grand Canyon FBC the nationwide "Resort Church of the Year" award at the 1991 state convention meeting.

Page FSBC SS entered a float in the 1987 Christmas parade and won first prize in the church category. A highlight of the Christmas season was seeing three young people baptized during the Christmas program. Bob Cason was serving as interim pastor.

In January 1988 Grand Canyon FBC deacon Harvey Howell began leading a home Bible study for ranchers living near his home on Cataract Ranch, located about forty miles south of Grand Canyon Village. Greenlaw set SS records when attendance reached ninety-four the last Sunday in January and exceeded one hundred in February. Tuba City had sixty-five in morning worship in February. Bethel pastor Don Greenwalt took nineteen youth to the ski and prayer retreat at Sunrise Ski Resort.

Jimmy Hart, music and youth director at Sedona FBC, reported ninety attending on Easter Sunday, with interim pastor Tom Holland preaching. Pastor Frank Jackson reported 180 at Flagstaff FSBC on Easter. Holly Cook served as an Innovator at Grand Canyon in 1988; Jennifer Wingles and Dawn Wells went to Indiana with an Intervarsity team. FSBC voted to sponsor East Valley mission where pastor Daryl Bennett announced fifty-six in Easter services. Bennett also ministers to the juvenile detention center, counsels with young people seeking help, and serves as chaplain at the Flagstaff Medical Center.

Joe Berna of the Kingman Golden Valley Baptist Church accepted the call to pastor Sedona FBC. Joe accepted Christ in 1973 and was called to preach at Scottsdale Coronado Baptist Church. He graduated from SWBTS. Joe, his wife Marilyn, and children Chris and Angela arrived in Sedona on June 25. Page FSBC's new pastor, Jim Ayers, his wife Karla, and month-old son Joshua arrived on the field July 4. Baptized by Tucson Rincon Baptist and licensed by Tucson Morningside, Jim graduated from GCC and GGBTS.

Lemuel Littleman reported a full house at Dry Lake all week when a Tennessee youth group conducted VBS for fifteen adults and thirty-five children. Four children and two adults were saved. "The people prayed for rain, and we were almost flooded out of church on Sunday," he laughed. Fort Worth Benbrook Baptist sent twenty-nine youth and nine sponsors to conduct VBSs at Page and Kaibito. The group slept in the Page church building and showered at the school across the street. Such youth groups greatly assisted VBS mission work.

Steve May directed thirty Tempe Southside youth as they held two neighborhood BYBCs. Greenlaw's VBS enrolled 162, with two saved. Pastor Harold Boldin announced that July attendance at *Primera Iglesia* reached forty-five and fifty on two Sundays, with thirteen adult professions of faith during the summer. The church voted to sponsor Munds Park mission where Harold led Bible studies. In August Naomi Hunke led Utah-Idaho senior adult leadership conferences and California WMU leadership conferences, attended a Christian Social Ministry (CSM) meeting in Casa Grande, led Munds Park Bible studies, and taught a WMU mission study for Phoenix First Indian Baptist. Two of her Kachina Point group passed away.

Daryl Bennett's five mailouts to four thousand homes in northeast Flagstaff brought seventy-five people to a special service at East Valley. Pastor Jasper Jones of Flagstaff Indian hosted the all Indian fellowship on November 5. Kevin Notz of Many Farms preached. Seventy-one people from nine churches participated in "M & M" night at Greenlaw. The *Primera Iglesia* choir was a hit as they sang two numbers in Spanish, as was the fun and refreshment time after the program.

### 1988 GCBA Annual Meeting at Page FSBC

DOEM Bill Hunke recognized the following new pastors and wives who had arrived since the last annual meeting: Joe and Marilyn Berna,

Sedona; Jim and Karla Ayers, Page; Daryl and Julie Bennett, East Valley; and Gerald Raynor, Flagstaff FSBC. The Kayenta FBC was received into the association with a request that messengers be sent next year for a formal seating.

In the executive board report Harold Boldin emphasized the increased efforts to start new work which had resulted in East Valley and Munds Park missions. The board voted to transfer to Yavapai Association full ownership of all office equipment and supplies jointly owned by the two associations.

Discipleship Training director Jim Ayers shared that Bethel hosted the Bible drill with eleven contestants participating. WMU director JoAnn Polk announced she and Linda Pogany represented GCBA at the WMU Centennial Celebration in Richmond, Virginia, in May 1988. Seventeen women from four churches attended a missions prayer retreat in Flagstaff, and four attended the WMU leadership training seminar at Prescott. Marc and Lisa Hill of Fort Worth, Texas, arrived January 1 after graduation from SWBTS to lead the BSU. Marc had worked two years in BSU in Tucson and has committed his life to student work.

Joe Berna's evangelism report revealed that half of GCBA baptisms came from VBSs and BYBCs in 1988. Our Navajo churches and missions had eleven church groups from across the nation working with them during the summer. Billy Hines, ASBC evangelism leader, directed a lay evangelism study in February. Our churches took part in the state evangelism conference and the "Make Waves 88" youth conference.

Northern Arizona catalytic missionary Virgil Stoneburner reported visiting every Indian and Spanish church in 1988. He had led in establishing the Kayenta FBC which began with only two but was now reaching sixteen in SS. For years the church had petitioned the Navajo Council for land on which to build. It was not until 1995 that a site was granted and a beautiful building erected with the help of M. C. Chancey and the Arizona Baptist Builders. VBSs were held in Kayenta, Halchita, Dennehotso, Black Mesa, Kaibito, Dry Lake, Page, Flagstaff, Spider Rock, Many Farms, and Chinle. The VBSs enrolled over seven hundred; Spider Rock baptized twelve, and Many Farms baptized six VBS converts.

A young man at the Halchita, Utah, VBS had asked, "What is a Bible?" Stoneburner commented, "How sad that a child in our country has never seen God's Word." He asked prayer that the Page VBS might result in a regular Bible study for the three thousand Navajos in that area.

A group of fourteen singers from NAU, led by Trei Watters, joined the Sedona FBC choir in a Christmas service on December 14. Pastor Joe Berna led a candlelight service on December 21, and Dixie Hunke, dressed as Lottie Moon, dramatized the Lottie Moon story for the Christmas Day service. Flagstaff FSBC, Greenlaw, Williams FBC, and Ash Fork FSBC also reported candlelight services. Tuba City reported every seat filled on Christmas and sixty attending worship on New Year's Day. *Primera Iglesia* had sixty in attendance on Christmas Day.

Daryl Bennett led the first GCBA youth workers meeting on December 10 with leaders from Bethel, Grand Canyon, Greenlaw, East Valley, Tuba City, and Flagstaff FSBC attending. Grand Canyon laymen Ron Clayton, Norm Hicks, Harvey Howell, Robert McNelly, Rick Boucher, and Bill Barber filled the pulpit while pastor Ron Nation attended GGBTS January session.

Pastor Dave Cox and family moved from Flagstaff to Ash Fork in February to live on the church field. Marc Hill reported that five hundred students on the NAU campus listed "Baptist preference." The BSU sent out a mailout entitled "Under New Management" to 230 students. East Valley's SS enrollment reached seventy-one in January, with three persons saved and three baptized. Daryl Bennett directed the GCBA youth snow party, "Crazee Olympics," which attracted forty young people and many sponsors to the Snowbowl on February 25. Films of the activities were shown at the youth lock-in rally April 14–15.

After Flagstaff FSBC started a new bus ministry, SS attendance reached 165. A Wanda Jackson concert attracted over 400 persons in 2 meetings with 28 decisions, including 16 saved and 6 additions to the church. The Ambassador Singers from Daejon, Korea, presented a concert on February 23. Greenlaw's LMCO was $4,010, twice their goal. *Missions USA* featured Ron and Kathy Nation and the work at Grand Canyon.

Steve Martin, GGBTS student and native of Cornville, Arizona, preached a revival for Page FSBC which resulted in four additions. An Easter sunrise service at Wahweap Marina brought two hundred worshipers to hear Steve. A youth team from Sierra Vista FBC assisted the church in a summer mission program. Sedona FBC called Ralph Barham as music and education minister in January. Their western barbecue on February 15 saw eighty in attendance. Tuba City pastor Gerald Lawton did his reserve training time at Fort Bliss, where he was appointed Chief of Chaplains of the Individual Mobilization Augmentee. Even though Flagstaff dipped to a minus thirty degrees chill factor, about seventy-four brave souls turned out for the January GCBA board meeting and rally at Bethel—expressing intense interest in the association's work.

### Volunteers Ed and Bernice Trotter

On March 3, 1989, Ed and Bernice Trotter, CSC workers from Tulsa, Oklahoma, Immanuel Baptist Church, arrived in GCBA to help churches; visit prospects; prepare mailouts; do secretarial and carpentry work, including building Caraway Street sets; teach VBS and BYBCs; be Mom and Pop to student missionaries; cook for visiting youth groups; and whatever else they could find to do. They returned for three more summers and also came to Cochrane, Alberta, Canada, the year the Hunkes served at the Canadian seminary.

They wrote later, "One of our highlights in GCBA was helping restart *Primera Iglesia* as Sunnyside after it had been closed. We remember how glad Lilly and Juaquin Zamora were to have their church open again. Another joy was helping Manny finish the interior of the parsonage and getting it ready for them to move into. We also have fond memories of the East Valley tent revival on the parking lot on the north side of town."

"Another memorable experience was the tremendous turnout for some of the Bethel BYBCs held by the youth group from Clarksville, Tennessee, and the response to the sports clinics they conducted," they continued. "A great thrill was to see Munds Park get started in Eddy and Dori's home, then watch them grow large enough to move to the fire station. What a disappointment when they could not move into the house they bought! Our greatest reward was getting to know and love the GCBA people." Every winter Ed and Bernice serve as volunteers for ten weeks, helping Ross Hanna with the Tucson CSM programs.

Pastor Steve May reported that a February SS attendance of 121 and average of ninety-nine broke a Greenlaw record that had stood since 1981. On Easter they counted 155 at morning worship. Their VBS enrolled 190 with 156 on high attendance day and eight professions of faith. Grand Canyon had four student missionaries and twenty-four Innovators at work during the summer with record attendances reported at all services and more than four hundred one Sunday morning. Six evening Bible studies were reaching more than one hundred people each week. Bethel sponsored a GCBA youth revival with the Waco, Texas, youth choir leading.

Tuba City services continued with the building full, SS enrollment at 159, and $8,223 contributed to mission causes by September. Four BYBCs enrolled eighty. An ice-cream social attracted a large crowd. Turmoil on the Navajo Reservation resulting in thirty-one resignations at the high school severely impacted the church.

Hollis and Eunice Bryant, the Maurice Flowers, and Charles Melton, interfaith witness specialists from Mississippi, came to GCBA in June and led seminars to help in understanding other religious groups. Loren and Becky Kennedy of Flagstaff FSBC launched a prison ministry in Winslow with thirty-one in attendance. The church's Caraway Street ministry was underway by the time school started and had twelve workers and thirty to forty children attending each Sunday.

The Anchorage, Alaska, Grandview Baptist Church sent a twenty-one-member youth handbell choir to Page FSBC. The group conducted five concerts: three at Lake Powell amphitheater, and one each at Grand Canyon and Navajo Mountain. In August Page had twelve saved and eight baptized. Bill Welsh, a pilot killed in a Grand Canyon crash, attended Grand Canyon FBC and was the church's fourth pilot in an air crash.

A thirty-two-member team from Orangeburg, South Carolina, flew to Phoenix, rented six vans, drove to Kayenta, lived in a school, erected a 20 x 30' tent, and enrolled 132 in VBS. Pastor Tom Roatch reported that children were wall to wall. Roatch, who had attended NAU, completed work at SEBTS. He and his family lived in a mobile home while he taught school.

The following Canadian leaders and pastors from Alberta Baptist churches led Lay Evangelism Schools and revivals in GCBA in September: Al Schmidt, executive director of the Canadian Convention of Southern Baptists, at Flagstaff FSBC; George Knight of Calgary Freedom Baptist at Grand Canyon; Robert McGrann of Calgary Willow Park Baptist at Greenlaw; Billy Heath of St. Albert FBC at East Valley; Paul Peacock of Grand Prairie New Life Baptist at Bethel; and George Bojackly of Cochrane Bow Valley Baptist at Williams FBC. All churches reported subsequent increases in attendance and prospects.

**1989 GCBA Annual Meeting at Grand Canyon Baptist Church.**
Moderator Ron Nation read a letter from Al Schmidt expressing appreciation on behalf of Canadian pastors who assisted GCBA in the LES. The BSU report included forty contacts made at NAU's open house. Their retreat at Shoshone Point reached seventeen students, and a discipleship seminar enrolled fifteen.

DOEM Bill Hunke reported he had preached in most of the GCBA churches, served as interim at Munds Park and *Primera Iglesia* for four months, and led a Baptist heritage study four Sundays at Flagstaff FSBC.

He and Naomi led a revival at Eloy, Bible studies for 160 Utah pastors and wives, and escaped injury from an auto accident in a snowstorm. Bill had two surgeries during the year.

GCBA had ten monthly pastors' breakfasts, four board meetings, a youth lock-in, the annual pastors and wives' retreat, three rallies, and an interfaith witness emphasis led by three Mississippi couples. Jim Coldiron from the HMB led eight churches and seven Canadian pastors in LESs. On PEAK Sunday GCBA churches had an 8.8 percent increase in SS attendance with 539. Every church contributed to the CP and associational missions. On October 7, 1989, three GCBA churches and missions helped establish the new Fourcorners Association: Flagstaff Indian Baptist; Kayenta, FBC; and Dry Lake Indian mission.

The senior adult "Get Together in Sedona" had 115 attending from twelve churches, four in Yavapai Association. As the GCBA senior adult representative, Naomi Hunke emceed the senior adult convention luncheon in Tucson, spoke to sixty-five attending the Prescott FSBC annual birthday party, led conferences at the state retreat in Phoenix, directed leadership workshops in Pinetop and Williams, and led the senior adult State and Associational Leadership Training (SALT) meetings in Phoenix. Every Thursday she leads advanced reorientation for residents of Kachina Point Nursing Home and urges every church member to develop a personal witnessing ministry.

Grand Canyon FBC baptized its first adult Navajo Indian in January 1990. Ron and Kathy Nation were commissioned as home missionaries at special services in Atlanta. The HMB conducted a conference for state directors of volunteer work at Grand Canyon in March. Bethel initiated an operation foodshare program. Sedona FBC offerings one month exceeded twenty-eight thousand dollars. Their special January missions emphasis featured foreign missionaries Charles and Jenny Garcia. Page pastor Jim Ayers began leading a weekly Bible study at Shonto.

### Williams FBC: Pat Hail

At the foot of Bill Williams Mountain, Williams sits among stately pine forests at an elevation of sixty-seven hundred feet. Known as the "Gateway to the Grand Canyon," it was named for mountain man Bill Williams who explored the area. It was the last town in the nation along Route 66 to be bypassed by the interstate freeway system. Seven high-country lakes within minutes of downtown attract vacationers throughout the year. The Grand Canyon Railway, a turn-of-the-century steam train, conducts tours from Williams to the national park.

Williams FBC pastor, William Patterson Hail Jr., was born January, 1958, in Henderson, Nevada. As a child he attended the Las Vegas West Oakey Baptist Church. Through the influence of a SS teacher, he recognized his need to receive Christ and accepted him as personal Savior and Lord when he was nine or ten. He was baptized by the West Oakey Church and vividly recalls his baptism and the youth fellowship afterwards.

Pat gradually fell away from church and did not return until he was eighteen, when he began to attend a college and careers class. Through the class he realized God was calling him to be a minister of the gospel. He testified, "Having very little background and no comprehension of what that meant, just knowing that God was yanking at my heart, I surrendered to preach in January of 1979." His ministry began at West Oakey where he led children's church and even filled the pulpit for a Mother's Day service. He preached on two occasions at Indian Springs Baptist Church. When Mel White, pastor at St. George, Utah, became so ill with emphysema that he was unable to preach, Pat welcomed the opportunity to preach twice on Sundays and on Wednesday nights.

When he was not preaching, Pat worked at installing heating and air conditioning ducts. Through this vocation he met David White, who was attending GCC. He shared, "David helped me discover that the Lord was leading me to go further in my ministry by getting more education. I only considered three schools, California Baptist, Baylor, and Grand Canyon. I sent letters and applications to each of them after praying for God's guidance. I literally laid my hands on the envelopes and said, 'God, whichever of these schools you want me to attend, let that be the only school I hear from.' I was working at my uncle's gas station one day when my aunt brought me a letter of acceptance from Grand Canyon. I never heard from the other schools."

Pat entered college full-time in the fall of 1979 where he had opportunity to live in the dorm and cook in the cafeteria. Even better, he met Janet Baldwin, who soon became his date, his fiance, and eventually, his wife. During their engagement, Janet embarked on a nationwide Christian entertainment tour while Pat served as interim summer youth minister at St. George FSBC. They married in 1981, and Pat was called as minister of youth and custodian at Phoenix Bethany Baptist. In 1982 Mission Drive employed him as minister of youth, at first part-time, then half-time, and finally full-time. The ministry grew from four to more than forty youth. He remembers, "A lot of ministry, discipleship, and baptisms happened during that time. Also, Courtney and Caleb were born."

In 1986 the Hails served at Tucson Emmanuel Baptist for nine months. He said, "There we got our first lesson in church politics. I listened to the Lord, and we returned to Phoenix without a job." Janet went to work for a law firm while Pat spent three years as a laborer pounding nails, finishing concrete, and becoming foreman of his brother-in-law's concrete company. During those years, he worked as interim youth minister at Apollo Baptist, served as a division SS coordinator at North Phoenix, and worked with young marrieds as a volunteer at Hillside Baptist.

Jerry Bowling, his pastor at Hillside, asked Pat one day why he was not in the ministry. "After I shared all my war stories, he basically said that I needed to go back to what God had called me to do. For two years, Jerry kept asking if I were ready yet to return to the ministry, but I kept declining," Pat related. "In August 1990, Williams FBC requested my resume, and the Lord laid on my heart during a devotional time that this was the time. In November 1990, when the church called me as pastor, I accepted."

In August 1992 the church baptized seven; SS attendance averaged ninety-eight with a growing children's ministry adding three classes; VBS enrolled 122 with five saved; and worship services were reaching over one hundred persons. They used two rooms in an adjacent hospital to expand and planned to soon enlarge their youth ministry.

Williams FBC celebrated its fiftieth anniversary November 24, 1992, with one hundred in SS and 150 in morning worship. Former pastors Jerry Martin, Dave Wallace, and R. A. Guthrie told tales of the past. Former missionaries M. V. Mears, Guthrie, and Bill Hunke also took part on the program. Truett Baker and Bob Warren from the state office spoke, and current and past members Thelma Jackson, Bob Davis, Carl Winslow, and Steve Jiminez shared special memories.

The children's choir sang to start off the morning service. Martha Menne of Flagstaff and Jerry Martin brought special music in the afternoon. Pastor Pat Hail stated that when he came, only one child was in the nursery, his son Dylan. Now from nine to sixteen are there every Sunday. "There aren't many Southern Baptists in our community of twenty-five hundred people," he added. "We have to lead people to the Lord and baptize them to add members to the church."

### Sunnyside Baptist Church

At the suggestion of ASBC leaders, *Primera Iglesia Bautista* discussed reverting to mission status and seeking sponsorship when unpaid bills threatened closure of the church. In April the church voted to close for three months in order to launch a new work and qualify for assistance from the ASBC. In July a youth team from Waurika, Oklahoma, conducted four BYBCs in the area, and a team from Aurora, Colorado, conducted a VBS at the church with 117 present on commencement night and twenty-five professing faith in Christ. Those participating in the activities were equally divided among anglos, blacks, and Hispanics. Manny Martinez, who had been secured as pastor by Don Cartwright at the state office, began services the following week. The work was renamed Sunnyside Baptist. During the first month, attendance averaged thirty-six, and they baptized four and had ten join by letter.

Sunnyside honored Manny and Angela Martinez with special recognition on his first anniversary as pastor. The church baptized twenty-nine people his first year. Manny and his family moved into the completed pastorium and gave thanks for gifts of seventy-five hundred dollars and loans of three thousand dollars that made the move possible. On October 21, 1990, Sunnyside constituted into a church.

The aggressive GCBA summer program involved more than three hundred volunteers. Peter Chen of the HMB led a study of the New Age movement. Dixie Hunke, California WMU director for ten years and daughter of Bill and Naomi Hunke, resigned her post for an overseas CSI career assignment in China. Both her grandmother and parents had volunteered for similar work, but were prevented from going by health problems. Dixie met with GCBA pastors before leaving for the field, and during her first furlough in 1995, she spoke in nine GCBA churches.

Grand Canyon FBC pastor Ron Nation reported three melodramas and five BYBCs each week during the summer. In June the church saw five saved, two baptized, and ten additions. The Bob Trotters and Ralph Renfrows, CSC volunteers, led twenty Innovators and four summer missionaries in the summer program. SS enrollment increased from 45 to 134, and Sunday evening services were attracting in the eighties. Sedona FBC gave five hundred dollars to purchase Bibles for Romania. Oldham Little Church Foundation provided funds to Bethel for a new roof and new carpet. On Labor Day thirty-six persons attended Munds Park.

### Bell Rock, Village of Oak Creek

A new church, Bell Rock Baptist, was organized August 17, 1990, in the Village of Oak Creek, with Darwin Welsh, former executive director of Utah-Idaho State Convention for twenty-five years, as pastor. Charter members were Darwin and Anita Welsh, Bill and Naomi Hunke, and Lee Zwink. A twenty-two-hundred-piece mailout and local newspaper ads announced services in the Bell Rock Inn conference room. The twenty-two people attending the first Friday evening meeting gave a $812 offering.

In addition to Friday night services, ministries of the church included a weekly Bible study by pastor Welsh and the "Remember When" group led by Naomi Hunke at Kachina Point Nursing Home, a Big A club at La Vista apartments led by Lee Zwink, a Hispanic children's class led by Anita Welsh, and Tuesday night Bible study at the home of Edna Maxson led by Naomi Hunke.

After Bell Rock began reaching a number of Hispanics in the Village of Oak Creek, Manny and Angela Martinez of Sunnyside started coming down every Friday evening with a group of their members to conduct bilingual services. More than twenty made professions of faith, but none accepted baptism because of strong Catholic backgrounds. The meeting place later changed to the Nazarene Community Church. Attendance averaged around thirty during the next three years. In 1991 Sedona FBC asked Darwin Welsh to serve as interim pastor in addition to his work at Village of Oak Creek.

Delores Barragan accompanied Manny and Angela to the Bell Rock service every week and brought pinatas she made out of paper cups or toilet-tissue cylinders for all the children. They eagerly gathered after their Bible class to see what goodies and candies she had brought. They knew she cared for them and joyfully responded with love and hugs.

For three years Bell Rock observed the AAEO and LMCO mission studies in the Hunkes' home with attendance averaging twenty. The Welshes hosted frequent fellowship dinners at their home with old-fashioned hymn singing after the meals. In the early years, ESL lessons from the Bible preceded the sermons. The Hispanic children learned English quickly and were soon teaching their parents.

After Lee Zwink married and moved to Colorado, the Hunkes went to Canada for seven months, and the Welshes moved back to Utah, Manny and Angela kept the work going until the Hunkes came back to help. When Bell Rock applied to the state convention for pastoral aid for Manny, leaders asked that the Hispanic work be moved into Sedona with the Sedona FBC as sponsor and Manny as mission pastor of the *Primera Bautista Mision*. Bell Rock continued the Kachina Point Bible studies, which averaged around thirty in weekly attendance.

### 1990 GCBA Annual Meeting at Greenlaw

Moderator Ron Nation announced that petitionary letters had been received from Flagstaff Sunnyside and Village of Oak Creek Bell Rock, that the GCBA board had approved their requests for affiliation, and that messengers from both churches were present to be seated.

DOEM Bill Hunke reported that fifteen pastors and associates serving in GCBA have come since 1987, with only Ron Nation and Gerald Lawton here before that time. Over half of the pastors are in their first pastorate. The GCBA newsletter was mailed to 5,660 people in 26 states and 5 foreign countries in 1990. More than three hundred volunteers helped GCBA in mission work during the summer. VBSs and BYBCs enrolled over eleven hundred, almost double PEAK Sunday's attendance. GCBA had leadership training for youth, senior adults, music, Discipleship Training, VBS, BYBCs, and a study of the New Age movement.

Marc Hill stated that sixty-three NAU students were involved in BSU work. Only two hundred of the fifteen thousand students on campus consider themselves evangelical Christians. Six of the nine GCBA churches reported 256 enrolled in Discipleship Training. GCBA youth had three events in 1990: a spring meeting, a banquet with video films of their activities, and the April lock-in. GCBA senior adults attended their rally in Sedona, the Phoenix SALT meeting, the ASBC luncheon, and the ASBC retreat at Cooke Theological Center in Tempe. The missions committee reported youth teams from Oklahoma, Louisiana, and Colorado had started Sunnyside. Munds Park attendance had doubled since last summer. Bell Rock had constituted, and the Pittsburg, Kansas, Baptist Church is working to start a new mission in southeast Flagstaff.

### Tusayan Mission

Tusayan mission started on May 8, 1991, after Ron Nation and Manny Martinez had spent three days visiting the community and led twenty-six to accept Christ. The first service at Best Western Squire Inn attracted fifty-four people. The first candidate for baptism was immersed in the indoor spa following the meeting. Manny led an onlooker to the Lord during the baptismal service. Loren and Julie Ward, who are CSC workers, interpreter Jose Avila, and the Gil Gabaldons led services for Tusayan until a pastor was called.

In January 1992 Steve Boldin, pastor of a Spanish SBC church in Casa Grande, came as the first pastor. The Squire Inn provided space for three Sunday services. A day care center, food bank, SS lesson, and Tuesday BYBC afforded nine services weekly.

**Flagstaff Trinity Baptist Church**

The initial partnership committee meeting for beginning the Flagstaff Trinity Baptist mission was held December 8, 1990, when a group from Pittsburg, Kansas, Trinity Baptist Church visited Arizona to discuss plans for a mission they wanted to sponsor here. Pastor Wayne Tope affirmed, "I have wanted to begin a mission in Arizona ever since I returned to the U.S. after serving as a missionary in the Pyrenees Mountains in Andora."

The group met with Ken Belflower and Coy Wilkerson of the ASBC, and GCBA DOEM Bill Hunke, to discuss finding a pastor. The Kansas church presented the ASBC with a seven-thousand-dollar check to help the church-starting process and signed an Arizona partnership covenant agreement. The group toured Flagstaff to view possible sites for the new work. Other partnership committee members included Steve Martin and Alan Anderson of GCBA, Elijah Touchstone and Ruth Coble of Pittsburg, and Gerald Raynor and Doyle Bain of Flagstaff FSBC, which will serve as the local supporting church.

After several prospective pastors looked over the new field of work without feeling called to accept the pastorate, Mike and Diane Rasberry arrived in Flagstaff from south Texas in January 1992 to lead the new mission. The first service in February 1992 saw twenty-four attending and a $252 offering. The sponsoring Kansas church called the pastor. Pastor Wayne Tope and his members helped launch the mission by making phone calls from Kansas to survey the community.

Kansas missionaries Tom and Ruby Thorne led a youth team in the summer of 1992 to conduct a VBS for the mission. Youth from Memphis Bellevue and Grand Prairie, Texas, FBC also helped survey three thousand homes, distribute two thousand Bibles, and lead eight BYBCs. The church saw twenty saved its first year. Trinity constituted into a church with twenty-five members in July 1992.

**1991 GCBA Annual Meeting at Flagstaff FSBC**

GCBA completed long-range strategy planning as one of twenty-nine associations working with the HMB in a program called TACT (Town and Country Thrust). Charles Crim, Wyoming general missionary, led the two-day event, which attracted forty-four to the banquet and thirty-nine in the planning sessions. Ten churches and missions participated. The group agreed that promoting and facilitating outreach evangelism in the churches, in new work, and in GCBA was their main objective.

Other objectives considered important were training opportunities targeted at the needs of each church; producing an awareness of individual church needs with an attitude of committing resources, time, and prayer to meet the needs; and encouraging pastors and lay leaders to stand for Christian beliefs by being informed and actively involved in the community and government.

Some specific needs cited were recreational-vehicle, mobile-home ministries; single-parent, latchkey, and parenting help; tourist evangelism; financial counseling; literacy and ESL classes; and ways to open church buildings to the communities. The group wanted GCBA to recognize churches needing help; communicate churches' needs; share talents by helping other churches; lead out in interfaith witness seminars; encourage pastors to stay put; challenge members to commitment; and recognize differences in communities. Gerald Raynor appointed five committees to develop objectives and lists of specific goals for each of the next five years, leading up to the fiftieth anniversary of GCBA in 1996.

The $20,760 given to GCBA in 1990–1991 was a record, an increase of 31.8 percent over last year. Baptisms increased from sixty-seven in 1990 to 128 in 1991. The senior adult rally at Sedona was attended by ninety-seven persons from sixteen churches. Dan Stringer, ASBC executive director, shared personal experiences from forty years of working with Southern Baptists. Earl Stallings reviewed his book, *Seniors Reaching Seniors*, and Joe Berna led a conference on understanding the New Age movement. The newest organization was the Humdingers of Williams FBC. Glenn and Corky Young led the Greenlaw seniors, and the Paul Grays led the Flagstaff FSBC JOY Bunch. Sedona FBC had provided a monthly birthday party for residents at Kachina Point Nursing Home for many years. A senior adult choir from Tulsa, Oklahoma, Eastside Baptist Church gave concerts at Grand Canyon and Tusayan mission last summer.

During the winter of 1991–1992, Wanda Jackson gospel concerts and evangelistic meetings brought good results in GCBA churches: Williams FBC reported 175 in attendance and nine professions of faith; Sedona FBC had 140 with two saved and four rededications.

Harold Boldin became pastor of Page FSBC March 1, 1992. He was elected moderator of GCBA four times, served two terms as chairman of the ASBC border ministry council, and is currently a member of the ASBC committee on boards. He feels that the most significant things which have taken place during his years at Page include the fact that the Page church has been a catalyst in the initiation of many community-wide programs and events, such as fifth-Sunday hymns sings, gospel concerts, an association of evangelical ministers, and a police chaplain program.

The work at Fredonia was reinitiated and continues as a mission of Page FSBC with Harold and Phoebe driving back and forth on Sunday afternoons to conduct services. Fredonia sits against a background of vermillion cliffs on Highway 89-A, just a stone's throw from Utah, but separated from the rest of Arizona by the Grand Canyon. In spite of its notorious history of polygamy, it seems like a peaceful place for family life, but in 1995 a school principal was fired and two school board members recalled. The Kaibab Industries sawmill, the staple source of income for the town for generations, closed in February. The blow would have killed some communities, but Fredonia's twelve hundred residents are determined to hold on. Harold wrote, "In spite of the closing of the industry which employed 90 percent of the men in town, our Baptist work has continued until the present and is finally beginning to grow."

In addition, more than fifty thousand dollars was raised by Page FSBC without incurring any indebtedness. The money has been used for remodeling and improvements. They erected a new, truss-supported roof with a cupola and a cross. They built two handicap access bathrooms with shower facilities and installed new carpet and floor tile, ceiling fans, vertical venetian blinds, and a state of the art sound system for the sanctuary.

Best of all has been a notable increase in the number of conversions and baptisms. Harold shared, "This is our area of greatest blessing; in fact, we had twenty-two baptisms in one year which was more than were baptized during the previous ten years."

Before entering the pastorate, Harold was ordained a deacon at the Tucson Twenty-second Street Baptist Church in March 1964. He served in preaching, teaching, music, and youth ministries in Virginia, Arizona, California, and South America. He graduated from Cochise College (A.A.), International Bible Institute and Seminary (Th.B. and Th.M), Plymouth, Florida, and attended the Universities of Virginia and Maryland and American University in Washington, D.C.

Harold testified, "During fifty-one years following my conversion, I have survived armed shootouts, assassination attempts, a massive heart attack, and other serious illnesses. But through it all, I've had a sense of well-being which the apostle Paul referred to as the 'peace which passeth all understanding' because of a personal relationship with Jesus, my all sufficient Savior and Lord!"

In 1992 the first VBS in several years at Page FSBC enrolled fifty-seven with nine saved and nine new members added to the SS. A Blackwood Brothers quartet program attracted 350 people. When the Page mayor

proclaimed September 12 "M. K. Wilder Day," 150 people met to celebrate. Three Navajo families joined the church in August.

On September 26, 1992, Flagstaff FSBC hosted a noon luncheon retirement party for missionaries Bill and Naomi Hunke. ASBC director Dan
Stringer entertained the group with amusing experiences he and Harriet
have shared with the Hunkes.

### 1992 GCBA Annual Meeting at Sedona FBC

GCBA messengers welcomed new pastors Mike and Diane Rasberry
and Harold and Phoebe Boldin. Steve Martin reported that the DOEM
search committee is talking to Si Davis of Tucson. All program chairmen
gave encouraging reports. Pastors shared outstanding events of 1992 in
the churches. In August Williams FBC baptized seven. Bible study attendance averaged ninety-eight with a growing children's ministry adding
three classes to the SS. VBS enrolled 122 with five professions of faith.
Over one hundred regularly attended worship services. Pastor Steve May
was honored by Greenlaw Baptist Church on completion of five years as
pastor. Their 1992 VBS enrolled 152 with four trusting Christ. Marc Hill
took fifteen Greenlaw youth to camp. An old-fashioned camp meeting
saw one hundred attending.

After Grand Canyon FBC pastor Ron Nation resigned to return to
Louisiana in July, ASBC leaders provided pulpit supply. Local members
continued the ministry at Tusayan mission. A Tennessee youth group
assisted at Bethel and Munds Park with VBSs, eight BYBCs that enrolled
222 and had fifteen saved, and a sports clinic that enrolled ninety-six.
Munds Park received four new members in September, reported six
saved, and baptized one, a fifth-generation Mormon.

Grand Prairie, Texas, youth assisted in Sunnyside's summer programs. The BYBC enrolled sixty-five with fifty attending one day. Manny
Martinez led workers in adding a master bedroom and bath to the pastorium. The church purchased a new van to use in mission work.

# Drink Abundantly

## FROM THE COMING OF SI DAVIS TO THE PRESENT

Water is an essential ingredient to sustaining life on earth. Today we turn on taps, and running water gushes out. In early days providing water was difficult. Oak Creek, which drops over two thousand feet from the top of the switchbacks through the canyon that splits the red rocks, has long furnished water for drinking, irrigation, and electricity to the Sedona area. In the 1930s waterwheels were used to generate power.

When the rocks of the wilderness yielded to the rod of God in the hand of Moses, life-giving streams of water sprang out, falling in great curtains that shimmered in the desert heat. Divine blessings can come from unlikely places as surely as water once flowed from solid rocks. Christ's death on the cross opened the floodgates for the Holy Spirit's living waters to pour forth to quench the thirst of the souls of men for the things of God. God offers plenteous redemption, grace abounding, peace like a river, and righteousness as the waves of the sea. Jesus promised that he would satisfy longing hearts, cleanse and purify thoughts and emotions, and revitalize lives that partake of his abundance. Today we need the Spirit to break down demonic opposition and pour his saving power abundantly on our communities.

### DOEM Silas Emory Davis

Si Davis became DOEM for GCBA on January 1, 1993. Born at Jessieville, Arkansas, on September 12, 1927, he had nine sisters and three brothers. He attended the University of Arkansas and graduated from the University of Phoenix. He served in the U.S. Navy from 1945 to 1947. He wrote, "I was an unsaved church member for twenty years, actively involved in the church, but not satisfied with my relationship with Christ. I trusted Christ in an evening worship service at Phoenix FSBC in 1956 when Vaughan Rock was pastor." Si served as a deacon, SS teacher, and CT leader in the church. He enjoys fishing, golfing, hiking, and gardening.

In 1969 he and his family moved to Tucson and were members of Emmanuel Baptist Church. He managed Arizona Door and Sash Company. For three years he conducted a hotel ministry every week and served as pulpit supply for vacationing pastors. "My preaching ministry began when Irving Childress suggested that I serve as a lay pastor of Emmanuel's mission. For five years I worked as a bivocational pastor at the mission that became East Tucson Baptist Church. At first I had no salary, no doubt one of the deciding factors in choosing me. It was an opportunity to offer the gospel without charge and one of the high points of my ministry," Si testifies. He pastored the church full-time from 1979 to 1992.

Regarding becoming a missionary, Si shared, "I was planning to retire and find a church in the Phoenix area where I could serve as pastor on a part-time basis for part-time salary. Brother Bob Warren asked me to consider the position of DOEM for GCBA. After prayer with Yvonne, I decided that was God's will for me."

Si Davis served as president of the ASBC from 1984 to 1986, a member of the SBC Committee on Boards in 1984, a trustee of Midwestern Baptist Theological Seminary from 1985 to 1990, and a trustee of the SBC Brotherhood Commission for five years. In Catalina Association he was on the pastoral ministries committee for five years and associational vice moderator for two years. He is married to Yvonne, and they have four grown children and two grandchildren.

Yvonne Talbott Davis was born in Phoenix. She graduated from Baylor University, received her M.A. from Arizona State, and attended SWBTS. She grew up in a Christian home and stated, "I talked and sang about Jesus as far back as I can remember and was in church from the cradle roll on up. I first went forward to receive Jesus into my heart at age five and again at age nine to make sure. I was baptized at that time. I surrendered for full-time service in 1965."

She has been a SS teacher and VBS worker for over forty years, a choir member for sixteen years, and was WMU president for three years. She enjoys gardening and hiking as well as crafts and cooking. She and Si have hosted the GCBA pastors and wives for delicious meals in their home ever since coming to the association.

## Sedona FBC: Barry Hall

Sedona FBC called Barry Hall on January 10, 1993. By May about twenty children were attending the Wednesday evening program designed for them. Barry testified, "I think of my walk with Jesus Christ as a journey of confidence that has always been rooted in his person, power, love, and saving ability."

Barry was born in Annapolis, Maryland, where his father became acquainted with W. C. Wood, pastor of the College Avenue Baptist Church (later renamed Heritage Baptist because it is one of the oldest churches in the SBC). Through the encouragement and guidance of Wood, his father accepted Christ. Barry remembers, "Our whole family soon felt the effect of Dad's decision and his respect for the pastor and began to attend church faithfully."

As a young child Barry developed a simple and sincere openness to God and readily learned truths taught in SS and preaching services. After pastor Wood talked with him at home, he went forward at the invitation, together with his father and mother. He and his father professed faith in Christ and requested baptism, and his mother moved her membership from South Carolina. Barry was nine years old.

"Before I received Christ, I used to sleep with the bed covers over my head because I was afraid in the dark. Also, I often looked out the upper windows of our house and noticed elderly people passing by. I was concerned that I would soon get old like them and die. Everything seemed hopeless," Barry confessed. "But all those fears disappeared, and I realized that Christ Jesus took that dread of darkness and death from me the moment I accepted him into my life."

"That early confidence that came with conversion has continued intact throughout my life. Although at times sin has interfered, repentance has served well to keep my love relationship with Christ on track. He is the central focus of my life and my best friend. I want to follow him all the days of my life," he concluded. When Barry was thirteen, he moved to Florida, where he attended high school. He attended William Carey College in Mississippi and GGBTS. He graduated from California Baptist College and NOBTS, where he did post-graduate work in pastoral counseling.

## 1993 News From the Churches

In January 1993 Bethel's choir resumed rehearsals. The church saved four hundred dollars in heating bills by adding insulation in the attic. Greenlaw had packed the auditorium for their annual Christmas cantata. When Ed Stone retired as music director after almost seven years of service, Greenlaw called Alan Guthrie as the new music leader. Sunnyside baptized seven persons on January 17. Pastor Manny Martinez rejoiced in a record high attendance of 143 in worship on February 7. Seven children accepted Christ in summer BYBCs.

Gerald Lawton reported that Tuba City obtained an "ecumenical" coal-fired furnace for the church. An Assembly of God pastor and two Mormon laymen helped build and install the unit. A volunteer group from Alabama conducted two BYBCs. Munds Park licensed Eddy Emerson as a minister on February 14. In June they moved Sunday worship into the fire station engine bays to accommodate increased attendance, which ran as high as seventy.

Page FSBC pastor Harold Boldin restarted the Bible study in Shonto, and attendance was growing. They ordained Ray Elmore as a deacon with Si Davis, John Vest, Steve Ballew, Harold Boldin, and Dick Barton on the council, and Peter Valk, deacon trainee, an observer. During a reroofing project when church members had special prayer that God would stop the wind so that the work could be completed, the wind ceased. The summer beach ministry gained popular approval. Pat Hail preached a revival that resulted in a number of salvation and rededication decisions. Other churches in the city participated by providing special music.

Grand Canyon FBC's lay members kept services going and the fellowship sweet as they searched for a pastor. Williams FBC counted fourteen professions of faith during their VBS. Trinity Baptist Church disbanded with Mike, Diane, and Kevin Rasberry leaving Flagstaff for a new ministry in Korea.

### Flagstaff FSBC: Stephen Dale Ballew

In 1993 Steve Ballew came as pastor of Flagstaff FSBC. Steve had been born on January 8, 1962, in Roswell, New Mexico. He graduated from Clovis, New Mexico, High School, New Mexico State University, Las Cruces, with a degree in accounting, and SWBTS in 1988.

"I grew up in a good, but non-Christian home," Steve wrote. "A friend invited me to attend Sandia Baptist Church with him in Clovis. I went forward during an invitation and was baptized the following Sunday, but didn't truly give my life to Christ at that time. Though I was not saved then, God honored my desire to know him. In my second semester in college, through the constant witness of three Christians, most prominently, David Brown, I gave my life to Christ on Friday, February 13, 1981, by my bedside." He was baptized on Easter Sunday 1987 by the

Mansfield, Texas, FBC, and ordained by that church August 14, 1988.

Steve and Cheryl Nail were married August 6, 1983, in Las Cruces. In the spring of 1988 as he was facing graduation from seminary, and he and Cheryl were praying for God's direction in their lives, they felt led to stay in the Southwest, anywhere from western Oklahoma and Texas westward. "I sent resumes to every DOEM in those areas, together with a cover letter expressing God's leadership and our desires," Steve shared. DOEM Charles Tyson called from the Yuma Association to ask if Steve and Cheryl would meet with the pulpit committee of Wellton FSBC. The church called, and the Ballews served there from 1988 to 1992 until Flagstaff FSBC called them.

Steve worked in public accounting and bookkeeping for six years. He has served on several ASBC committees and on the state executive board from 1990 to 1995. Since coming to GCBA, he has been actively involved on committees and is presently moderator for the association. Cheryl directs the GCBA youth ministry program. Their children are Joel Aaron, age four, and Tiffany Ann Cole, a foster daughter.

On high attendance Sunday in December 1993, FSBC reported 197. Ninety-three participated in the FMB study of Indonesia, with $3,701 received for the LMCO. In February 1994 the church replaced major kitchen appliances and took a special offering for the Los Angeles earthquake relief fund. They also began Discipleship Training courses in "Parenting by Grace" and "Covenant Marriage." Mike Latham led a traditional Seder service to celebrate the Passover on March 31.

A highlight of the year came at the close of VBS when pastor Steve Ballew swallowed a gold fish as he promised if three hundred dollars were raised in offerings; over five hundred dollars came in. From October 1993 through September 1994, FSBC members received credit for completing 333 study courses, making them number one in the state. The December LMCO brought in $6,397. The debt-free church property was listed as having a value of $1,165,237 in 1994. The church budget for the following year was increased by over forty thousand dollars.

FSBC's April 1995 revival resulted in eight professions of faith and worship attendance the Sunday following revival exceeding Easter attendance by 13 percent. The church celebrated its fiftieth anniversary with homecoming activities on June 23–25, 1995. The programs included inspiration times, with open house and displays; a picnic, games, and fellowship day at Fort Tuthill; and a continental breakfast and Sunday services at Flagstaff High School. Former pastors Frank Jackson, Clark Johnson, and Alvin Wood spoke at the various events. Music personnel were Lisa Baker, Dan Brady, the Deibels, Linda Pogany, Ed Stone, Helen Schwichtenberg, and Ruth Wood.

### GCBA Volunteers: Lois and Jesse Neil

After Lois and Jesse Neil retired from the pastorate and school teaching, they began spending summers at Kachina Village and serving in GCBA churches wherever they were needed. They attended Munds Park mission in the Emersons' home, and when the fire station opened to the group in 1990, Lois became the pianist. She recalled, "We had wonderful fellowship with pastor Steve Martin and the people and saw the work grow. Dr. Hunke presented us with an appreciation certificate for helping start Munds Park."

When Sunnyside had its first service in July 1991, Lois played the piano. "Pastor Manny Martinez asked if I would play for them all summer," she said, "and I loved it. We had a unique wedding for a couple who were too poor to afford to pay for the usual trimmings. The Sunnyside people provided everything. Ruth Clark played for the ceremony, and I sang a solo. The members brought food for the reception. I experienced such love that day, and have ever since, by those dear people! Brother Manny gave us a certificate of appreciation for helping start Sunnyside. We love being a part of these new church starts."

When pastor Daryl Bennett asked Lois if she would mind driving farther to play for East Valley in the summer of 1992, she agreed to make the forty-mile round trip for services. On August 27 Jesse became very ill and was taken to Flagstaff Medical Center. Lois said, "I called brother Daryl to meet me at the hospital. He sat with me from 7:00 A.M. until 2:10 P.M. when Jesse went to be with the Lord. This was Daryl's first pastorate, but I told him that if he had been pastoring fifty years, he could not have been more help to me in those hours of watching Jesse slip into eternity. He prayed, read Scriptures, and comforted me. I can never thank him enough."

She loves to remember little Katie Bennett playing around her daddy's feet while he preached. "When Daryl and Julie sang with four-year-old Ben and two-year-old Katie, they knelt on their knees to be on the same level with them. Daryl even played the accordion on his knees. It was precious to see that young couple training their children to serve the Lord."

During the summers of 1993–1995, Lois was back at Sunnyside. She shared, "I love playing for them because they are such a warm, loving people. We've had wonderful worship services with many saved. They always stand by to help each other. If someone has a need, the members have a car wash or bake sale to raise money or do whatever is necessary to meet the need."

### Garnett and Uma Ridenhour

Garnett and Uma Ridenhour are noteworthy examples of volunteers who represent GCBA across the nation. Ever since they moved to Page in 1962 to teach school, they have worked in many capacities at FSBC. Uma led singing and was WMU president, and Garnett served as a deacon. They find opportunities to minister and witness to individuals and help with religious services in campgrounds as part of the Campers on Mission program and continually seek to enlist new Campers on Mission members.

During 1993 they helped several campgrounds secure hymnals and Bibles. Sabino Road Baptist in Tucson gave large boxes of hymnals for the Arizona Twin Lakes RV Ranch and the Gunnison, Colorado, Blue Mesa Ranch. Uma inscribed them, "A gift from Arizona Baptists through Campers on Mission." The Twin Lakes park manager requested one for his desk and began attending worship services.

The Ridenhours are advocates of the Arizona Children's Services, Baptist Foundation, and Baptist Village. When they saw field rocks at a tourist gift shop labeled, "Pet Rock Orphanage," with a sign urging: "For a dollar you can adopt a rock and feel good," they developed a new endeavor. "It occurred to us that we could pick up free rocks, add a nose, tongue, eyes, and ears, and offer them to any takers," Uma explained. "When they buy a rock, people can help provide hope and loving care for needy children. We have shown our pet rocks at craft sales, in churches, and at associational meetings, and have collected many dollars for the children. We have encouraged those who have inquired about copying the idea to do so."

After the 1992 national Campers on Mission rally in Illinois, the Ridenhours joined a twenty-nine-recreational-vehicle caravan for Alaska. When they arrived at North Pole FBC in time for the town's Fourth of July parade, they decorated an RV for a float and set up blood-pressure checks, cups of cold water, clown activities, and puppet shows at the church, which was on the parade route. "We were able to quickly acquaint large crowds with our Campers on Mission ministries, witness to them, and pass out Scripture portions," Uma said. "We even enlisted a couple to join our caravan to help with the summer's projects."

In addition to her construction and cooking duties at their Delta Junction mission work site, Uma made twenty-mile trips to a youth camp to teach Bible studies because the student summer missionary had broken her leg while directing games. "I didn't try to play any games," Uma laughed. "In addition to the benefits of fellowship and joys of service, we also enjoyed some of Alaska's bounties as church members shared fresh vegetables, salmon, moose meat, and strawberries to offset our food costs."

All along the way people came to the Ridenhours' trailer to learn about the crafts they displayed or just to visit or discuss problems, giving Uma and Garnett a chance to share Jesus. "We are so grateful to be involved in a program that allows us to serve 'as we go,'" they said. "We are also thankful for family members who look after our property, and for pastor Harold Boldin and the loving church family at Page who keep us uplifted in prayer because they consider us their missionaries." Although Uma and Garnett are now in their eighties, they recently purchased a new trailer and are eager to get back on the road. "There's nothing like keeping busy in missions to keep you young," they advised.

### 1993 GCBA Annual Meeting at Flagstaff FSBC

Moderator Harold Boldin introduced the following missionaries who would be speaking at WMCs in ten GCBA churches after the annual meeting: state missionaries Ken Belflower, ASBC new church extension, and Jerry Jones, ASBC ethnic catalytic; Charles Morris, emeritus to Malaysia, Philippines, and Singapore; Luke Nguyen, to Asians in California; Kevin Sigsby, Salt Lake City resort; Earl Jolly, to Argentina; and Steve Burke, to Paraguay. Charles Morris shared an exciting and sobering testimony to start off the program, with Earl Jolly giving his testimony later.

The executive board report revealed they had approved the DOEM compensation package and purchase of office equipment. Vice moderator Lee Zwink had resigned to be married and move to Colorado. Later he and Cathy went as International Service Corps (ISC) volunteer missionaries to Ecuador for two years and opened their files to serve as career FMB missionaries. The board approved a partnership with ASBC, GCBA, and Munds Park which provided for funds from the HMB for pastor's salary and expenses.

Missions development director Steve Martin announced that Munds Park was in the process of raising thirty thousand dollars for down payment on property and a house to be converted into a church. Steve had resigned Munds Park, effective October 31, to pastor Bethel full-time. Munds Park was GCBA's only active mission in 1993.

SS director Steve Ballew reported Pat Hail led a GCBA panel discussion at the national SS directors' seminar at Greenlaw. A VBS ASSISTeam was recruited and trained in Phoenix. The GCBA clinic at Bethel saw five churches with thirty-three in attendance for training, and a BYBC clinic hosted by Williams had nine attending from nine churches.

Corky Young, senior adult director, shared that speakers for the fifth annual fellowship rally at Sedona included Dan Stringer, Gene Virt, and Clyde Taylor, with Wendell Freeze leading. Paul Gray led a summer program for seniors in the Flagstaff area on alternate Saturdays with many activities and speakers. All featured potluck meals and were greatly enjoyed.

Evangelism director Manny Martinez announced that twelve out of thirteen churches in GCBA have a weekly visitation program. Seven churches had revivals, and seventy baptisms were counted. DOEM Si Davis disclosed that the GCBA office had been set up with a computer, filing cabinet, and telephone with answering device. A committee had written job descriptions for all associational officers, program directors, and committee members.

### Grand Canyon FBC: Steve Burke

Grand Canyon FBC called Steve Burke with a unanimous vote. His first Sunday on the field was November 21, 1993. Steve received Christ as Savior during the summer of 1971. "Although I grew up attending church every week, I heard for the first time the plan of salvation before my senior year in high school," he testified. "I did not receive any follow-up during that year, but I was determined when I entered college, I was going to be involved in a Christian campus group. When I began my second year at Biola University in southern California, I received my call to the ministry. I was involved in ministry projects in Mexico during school breaks at that time, which made it natural for me to go into ministry full-time. I had to; there was no alternative!"

After graduating from Biola in 1977, Steve received his M.Div. from GGBTS in 1980. He was associate pastor of the Pomona, California, White Avenue Baptist Church from 1981 to 1983 and pastor of the Jones, Oklahoma, FBC from 1983 to 1986. He and Mary were SBC foreign missionaries to Paraguay and Chile from 1986 to 1993, when he resigned to become pastor of Grand Canyon FBC and resort missionary for the national park.

Over two hundred people came to the fifth Sunday Hymn Sing sponsored by Page FSBC on October 31, 1993. Other evangelical churches joined and brought special music. In December Harold and Phoebe led the group at Shonto in their first community caroling. Page hosted the Heavens Above quartet with a full house attending, including twenty-five from the Shonto Bible class, on January 16. With a vision for missions, Page revived and sponsored the Fredonia mission. The first service on February 6 had twenty present. A BYBC in June discovered many prospects in the Mormon community. Volunteers Danny and Renee Causey came to serve in the mission.

Pastor Boldin's ministry now stretches over a 150-mile area. By Easter the church was ministering to a large Navajo extended family who had begun attending. Two of the Native Americans have been baptized and are witnessing to other family members.

Bethel elected Randy Smith outreach director and designated Tuesday as outreach night. An average of fifteen have joined in visiting and reported good results. They put in a drainway and completed paving their parking lot. Once a month the church took their evening service to the home of a shut-in. Pastor Steve and Loralie Martin attended the Billy Graham School of Evangelism in North Carolina. Bethel held a sports clinic with sixty-five attending and saw twelve saved in BYBCs. VBS enrolled 107 with one saved.

Williams FBC observed Thanksgiving with a church dinner which 108 people attended. Sixty people joined input dialogue as they began detailed drawings for their remodeling project. They had 150 at their musical on Sunday evening, December 19. Pastor Hail baptized nine during the first quarter. In the summer they began conducting a Bible study in an RV park. A total of 170 attended VBS family night. Attendance averaged 96 children, with 27 decisions, 16 for salvation.

Sunnyside had 125 attending in October with six saved and baptized. A good number joined with Flagstaff FSBC for the January Bible study. They had 130 in worship on Easter and already had exceeded their goal for baptisms for the year and for the AAEO.

During the spring East Valley averaged around fifty-five in SS every week. They conducted special activities at the school gym to attract the unsaved to church. They directed a sports clinic in June with the help of youth and leaders from Abernathy, Texas, and concluded the week with a barbecue. As a result, they discovered twenty-eight new families as prospects for the church. Daryl and Julie Bennett bought a home near their church field and moved into it in December.

Sedona FBC agreed to assume sponsorship of the Spanish work begun and carried on for four years by Bell Rock church. An average of twenty-five Hispanics who live in the Village of Oak Creek regularly attended the Friday evening services held at the community church. Manny Martinez continued to pastor the group with bilingual Bible studies. With a new name, *Primera Mision Bautista*, they began meeting at Sedona FBC church on Thursday evenings. Bernadine Blucher and Diana Wyatt used ESL classes as a form of outreach. Four men began attending along with the women and children.

Bell Rock was without a pastor for over two years. During that time, they continued their weekly Kachina Point Nursing Home ministry with Naomi Hunke leading. In April attendance reached a high of forty. Bill Hunke finished six weeks of radiation for prostate cancer with a good report. He filled pulpits in GCBA as needed and preached often for the Korean International Fellowship in Flagstaff.

Munds Park had to sell their recently acquired property because the local home association rejected their use permit application. They called Art Meirose as pastor. He moved on the field in June, but only remained with the church for a brief period. In December they called Eddy Emerson as pastor. When Eddy declined in order to complete his seminary training at the Canadian Southern Baptist Seminary, the mission suspended services until a pastor could be found.

Pastor Steve Burke and Grand Canyon members revived the Tusayan mission on March 20. They met in the rent-free banquet room of the Quality Inn and provided worship for tourists as well as for Hispanics and Anglos in the community. ESL classes for Denny's employees opened doors of ministry and evangelism.

## 1994 GCBA Annual Meeting at Bethel Baptist Church

Moderator Harold Boldin presented the executive board's report. During 1994 they adopted a goal of five thousand dollars to assist with remodeling the BSU building; conducted a "People Search" at Greenlaw; and hosted a pastors and wives luncheon at Little America. Evangelism director Pat Hail reported eighty-six baptisms and a building witnessing relationships seminar and viewing of the "Roman Road" training video at Greenlaw. He challenged the churches to soul-winning preparations for the Here's Hope simultaneous revivals. Missions development director Steve Burke reported on the renewal of work at Tusayan and Fredonia and the sponsorship of *Primera Mision Bautista* by Sedona FBC.

Pastoral ministries director Barry Hall told about the pastors and wives' Christmas retreat at the Living Water Center in Cornville, with eighteen attending the two-day event. SS director Steve Ballew reported that GCBA's nine-member ASSISTeam and eleven-member VBS team were available to train workers in the churches. The VBS clinic was attended by fifty-eight workers. A SS growth seminar reached forty-one from eight churches for training. Corky Young reported that eighty-five attended the Western Meetin' senior adult rally in Sedona which featured an outstanding dramatic presentation. Eight GCBA churches have representatives to promote senior activities in the association and state.

In November 1994 Flagstaff FSBC had 182 present on their high attendance day. The WMU entertained foreign students and exchanged national customs for celebrating Christ's birth. The church ranked first in Arizona for the number of study courses completed. Pastor Steve and Cheryl Ballew purchased their own home with the help of a gift of five thousand dollars from the church. The student SS departments of FSBC and Greenlaw began meeting together in the newly remodeled BSU building.

Grand Canyon FBC sponsored an outreach trip to Mexico during Thanksgiving week. Fifteen members worked with missionary Ross Hanna in Tucson, packing boxes delivered to needy Hispanics. Pastor Steve Burke preached at the community-wide Christmas service on December 24. During the summer of 1995, thirteen Innovators helped in ESL classes for thirty Hispanics, a coffeehouse ministry for singles, parents' night out for local residents and tourists, tennis lessons, and BYBCs at three locations. Lisa Oldenburg was sent as a FMB journeyman from Grand Canyon in 1994. In March 1995 Peter Valk and his wife Amy were called to work with the Oklahoma Baptist Convention children's services.

As GCBA Arizona Baptist Builders representative, Daryl Bennett directed the razing of the Stone Forest Industries Building to acquire materials to help in the construction of East Valley's proposed building. The materials are stored on the church property. They rejoiced to learn that a water line runs adjacent to their property.

Sunnyside surprised pastor Manny and Angela Martinez with a pastor appreciation Christmas banquet attended by around one hundred. Because their insurance company refused to pay for Angela's surgery and left them with a six-thousand-dollar bill, the people presented money gifts to them. The church installed new carpet and exchanged their pews for chairs. A high attendance of 140 was present on July 23.

Page FSBC completed installation of new carpet in the sanctuary. Summer missionaries conducted three BYBCs at Page, Fredonia, and Le Chee. The Le Chee hostess had been baptized the day before the BYBC began. When Harold Boldin served as chaplain for the Page rodeo, he met

Ben Tso, a saddle bronco rider. Ben began attending church, was saved, and baptized on October 1. Pastor Boldin also became involved in the police chaplaincy program. The church completed its remodeling project (at fifty thousand dollars) without borrowing money. It included a new roof, carpet, sound system, and rest-room facilities with showers.

Bethel began a Yokefellows class to train church members to become encouragers of new Christians. A total of ninety-five attended a concert presented by the Spiritual Genes. The church paid Steve Martin's seminary registration fee as he works toward his doctorate. Cooperating in a mission project at Bethel, ten members of Topeka, Kansas, Covenant Baptist Church and nine from Sun Valley, Nevada, FBC painted the exterior of the building and completed a reroofing project. After Bethel sponsored BYBCs in Winona, an outreach ministry began in the area on October 3 with Loralie Martin leading a weekly Bible study.

Greenlaw conducted a groundbreaking ceremony for their new worship center on June 25, 1995. They reached 130 children in VBS in July. Ash Fork FSBC began ministering to Hispanics using a computer program to translate pastor Dave Cox's sermons from English to Spanish, and a Hispanic congregation began sharing the church facility. After the church prayed for Christian teachers to fill vacancies in the local school, five of the eight teachers hired were Christians.

### Bell Rock, Village of Oak Creek, and Munds Park:
### Marty and Lenni Nordloh

Bell Rock and Munds Park entered a partnership with GCBA, ASBC, and the HMB to call Martin Nordloh as pastor. Phoenix Hillside Baptist and Starlight Park Baptist Churches also assisted in the pastor's salary. Marty and Lenni began their work on April 30, 1995. The Bell Rock services were held in the chapel of Verde Valley School for several months. When the building became too hot during the summer, services moved to the Canyon Diablo Assisted Living Center in the center of Village of Oak Creek.

Marty was born January 5, 1947, in Denver, Colorado, to parents who were good people but seldom attended church. He wrote, "The times I remember attending church were during VBS and at the death of a ten-year-old girl who was my friend in school. I do not remember ever hearing about Jesus, though this may have been due to my lack of attention."

Lenni Roberts Nordloh was born October 17, 1947, in Grand Junction, Colorado. At age ten she was led to the Lord by a street evangelist.

*After Corky and Glenn Young retired in 1984, they served several years as GCBA senior adult director and treasurer.*

*Flagstaff Greenlaw Baptist Church is building a $700,000 addition in 1996. Steve May serves as pastor.*

*Many tourists and Grand Canyon FBC members worship at Grand Canyon's Shrine of the Ages Chapel.*

*Ash Fork FSBC translates the pastor's message into Spanish by computer and maintains a food and clothes closet.*

*Garnett and Uma Ridenhour serve as HMB volunteers and Campers on Mission who witness "as they go."*

*Page FSBC sponsors gospel concerts, fifth-Sunday sings, rodeo ministries, Fredonia mission, police chaplaincy.*

Flagstaff FSBC employed Jason Stone-ketter as associate pastor in 1995 in an effort to reach new people.

Yvonne and Si Davis began serving as GCBA missionaries in 1993 after he retired as East Tucson pastor.

Bell Rock Baptist Church transferred a Spanish ministry to Sedona FBC to reach Spanish people in West Sedona.

Sedona FBC reached fifty youth at skate-night programs on its basketball courts behind the church building.

Bell Rock expanded nursing home work to Canyon Diablo. Marty Nordloh came April 16, 1995, to start Sunday services.

Flagstaff's housing boom centers near Bethel church. Pastor Steve Martin has led sustained growth for eight years.

Although her mother refused to allow her to attend church, she occasionally went with her father, who was a believer. Marty and Lenni met and married in 1947. When the minister asked them about their relationship to Christ, Lenni acknowledged that she knew him, but Marty responded with "not now."

After marriage they lived a carefree military life for six years until a friend of Lenni's confronted her with her walk with the Lord, and she rededicated her life. In Sacramento, California, Marty attended a Billy Graham crusade and accepted Christ. A year later while stationed in Alaska, Marty felt the call of God into the ministry. It took almost ten years for him to surrender, and then he thought he would go into a music ministry. In 1983 he enrolled in GGBTS as a music major but changed to a theology program when he realized he must preach the gospel.

After seminary Marty and Lenni went to Wyoming where their first full-time ministry was devoted to starting a church twenty miles west of Cheyenne in a rural community. After four years there, they moved to Florence, Arizona, and stayed over four years until the church's fiftieth anniversary. The fact that Marty plays the guitar, and both he and Lenni are gifted musicians, enhances their ministry at both Bell Rock and Munds Park.

In August 1995 Bethel worship attendance averaged seventy-one. Pastor Martin wrote that two new subdivisions were beginning near the church, one to have eleven hundred homes. A new apartment complex was being built between Lake Mary Road and I-40, with three hundred apartments. He told his people, "We need to expand our vision to be prepared to minister to all these new people God is placing in our neighborhood. Please begin to pray for him to reveal his plan for our church for the next five years. God wants to bless us even more than he has, but we must be prepared." Early in 1996 Bethel ordered new chairs for additional seating.

Si Davis wrote that worshipping at Tuba City FSBC during their revival with evangelist Ray Sheldon was a delightful and uplifting experience. "The service continued for two and a half hours with activities following. Some highlights included Marie Perry singing 'Safe in the Arms of Jesus'; Gloria Bonnahe playing 'He Hideth My Soul' on the harmonica, then singing it in Navajo; the Sunshine Boys singing 'Victory in Jesus'; and Wayne Benally telling what Jesus had done in his life and singing 'How Great Thou Art' in Navajo." Tuba City conducted three BYBCs with twenty-nine professions of faith. Attendance during the summer was excellent, and enthusiasm was high.

In May, nine GCBA pastors and wives participated in the retreat sponsored by the Baptist Foundation. PROBE consultants recommended six church-type missions in the greater Flagstaff area. Sedona FBC reported their summer Friday night skate program was a great success, reaching more than fifty youth each week. After the superintendent of the Parks school joined Williams FBC, he and his wife began working with youth.

### 1995 GCBA Annual Meeting at Sunnyside Baptist Church

Harold Boldin, chairman of the GCBA fiftieth anniversary committee, announced a banquet with a time for reviewing the struggles and victories of the past planned for October 25, 1996. The next day the annual meeting would continue the celebration of the past, present, and future. The music led by Jason Blackketter and Dan Brady, with Lynn Johnson at the piano, blessed the messengers, as did Tillie Yazzie singing "How Great Thou Art" in Navajo and Angela Martinez singing "You Have Given Life to Me" in English and Spanish.

Missions development chairman Steve Burke shared the following areas revealed by the church PROBE as strategic missions opportunities: University Heights, Cheshire, Winona, Kachina Village, and Elk Run/Fox Glen. Harold Boldin reported the pastors and wives Christmas banquet at Little America saw twenty-two in attendance with excellent food and fellowship.

WMU director Jayne May shared that on March 25, 1995, over fifty women from GCBA gathered for a luncheon at Greenlaw that featured CSI representative Dixie Hunke as guest speaker. Two GCBA women taught workshops at the annual Woman to Woman conference. Joint training with Baptist Men for all age levels was held at Greenlaw on November 18.

Daryl Bennett delivered the annual sermon that reminded messengers how God has done great things through people who were not considered important by worldly standards. He focused on the thought that although we cannot see the completion of God's plans in our lifetimes, we should be encouraged to continue the work he calls us to do and trust him with the results. We will not know the impact of our labors until we appear before his throne.

In her senior adult report, Corky Young announced that state leadership had passed to Baptist Senior Life Ministries, Inc., with a new director, Roger Hauser. Corky now has a mailing list of 132 senior adults in GCBA. Steve May reported that continued emphasis on Discipleship Training resulted in raised enrollments and participation. "The LIFE series from the BSSB has been a blessing with issues ranging from child abuse to weight loss, addressed lovingly and effectively," he stated.

In November 1995 Daryl Bennett reported East Valley had the conduit run for the electrical and telephone connections and began work for the septic system on their property. Neighbors to the north brought in utilities by boring a tunnel under the highway and allowed the church to tie in with them. The highway department was not allowing any further overhead electrical crossovers. Because the phone company provided its conduit in the same trench as the electrical wiring, it only cost fifty dollars.

By the end of 1995, the purchase price of the property was paid off. Baptist Builders director M. C. Chancey promised a construction team from Texas in June 1996 to put up the proposed block building and roof. Daryl and Kevin Notz, pastor of Winslow Indian Baptist Church, are working together to plan a facility that can be utilized both by East Valley and a proposed new Indian congregation.

### Williams FBC: Pat Hail

Pastor Pat Hail wrote, "I am proud to say that because Williams FBC has a very positive influence, it has become a leader in this community. Financially, we are in incredible shape. In 1995 we were just under a one-hundred-thousand-dollar budget which the Lord provided. We have a full-time pastor, a part-time secretary, a paid custodian, and a full-time children's, youth, and adult ministry. Our worship team includes three flutists, a drummer, pianist, guitarist, and four or five vocalists who lead us on Sunday mornings. Our youth ministry has been revived and is growing."

Williams FBC ran twenty-five to thirty in SS and worship when Pat came as pastor and now regularly enjoys attendance in the eighties and nineties. Because growth emphasized the need to remodel and add onto the existing building, in January 1995 the church began to rebuild the old facility in three phases. Phase one included remodeling the education area on the south side of the building.

After that was completed, phase two began on Easter Sunday, when they broke ground for the twelve-hundred-square-foot new addition, which included a new foyer and a 20 x 20' carport in front. Phase three began in September 1995 and included a new fellowship hall and bathrooms, complete with shower stall. In October they began to pour 140 yards of concrete on the parking lot on the north side of the building. The building dedication date was January 1996.

Other improvements have included the purchase of a nine-thousand-dollar sound system during the summer of 1995. The entire building was recarpeted. A new marquis advertising worship times, special guests, and upcoming events was installed on the west side of the building. The remodeling and building were done under supervision of the Baptist Builders after contacts with M. C. Chancey and Ken Belflower of the ASBC. Local building consultant Jim Forbes worked alongside the Baptist Builders. Funds were secured through a $125,000 loan from the HMB, with interim financing obtained from the Arizona Baptist Foundation's New Church Ventures fund. Most of the renovation was completed through the dedication of volunteer labor.

Pat rejoiced, "Our church has been truly blessed. I praise God that we have been chosen to lead so many to Christ in Williams. From November 1990 to November 1995, we baptized eighty-eight persons into our fellowship."

Although no information can be found on pastors between November 23, 1941, and November 1, 1944, since that time twenty pastors have served Williams FBC, with fourteen of the twenty serving two years or less. Five served from two to six months; five served one year; and four served two years. T. J. Newbill led in construction of the present building, then served the church as pastor a second time five years later. The first building was sold to the Church of Christ, moved to the north side of town, and is still being used by them. Houston Walker led the church to purchase a parsonage and lot east of the present building for $3,856. In 1964–1965 the south wing was added to the building. Attendance grew to one hundred during Walker's time with the church.

Presley Hand served from 1964 to 1968, with attendance nearing two hundred during his ministry. In 1966 the church restarted the work at Grand Canyon which had closed down. The first pastor of record was Walter Platt, who stayed for six years. Only Dave Wallace stayed longer, eight years from 1982 to 1990; during that time the old parsonage next to the church was torn down and a new parsonage built on Fourth Street. The church parking lot was blacktopped during that time as well. Pat is in his seventh year as pastor.

As the 1996 church year arrived, Pat announced, "The focus for the year is relationships—both among ourselves and with those outside the church. You will be amazed at results as you begin to develop and build relationships," he challenged. "During the last two months, we have had two church families who have been establishing a relationship with our family. One called up one night and said they would bring us dessert. The other recently had us over for dinner. What a wonderful time of fellow-ship and a real encouragement to me as a pastor!"

This kind of reaching out is what Hail has in mind for all FBC members this year. "We need to grow into as close a family on earth as we will be in heaven. I want to encourage you to leave your comfort zones and take time out of busy schedules to build up a family relationship, men to men, women to women, children to children, with whomever God lays on your hearts. The investment of time with bring an immense reward, spiritually and personally. As this closeness grows, we are going to see more people coming to Christ and more coming back to the Lord's house. I look forward to seeing what God is planning for our church," he concluded.

### Greenlaw's Building Program

In the November 1995 Greenlaw *Announcer*, pastor Steve May shared that God has blessed ever since the church started the process of building for the future back in May 1994: "Attendance saw some good increases; so did our giving. But around August, we saw an unusual jump in both! Previous average attendances were between ninety-five and one hundred in SS. In August, however, we saw 110; September, 118; October, 115. Right before August, building plans looked defeated. Bank One approved a loan, but then made it contingent on a guarantor (not allowed in our Articles of Incorporation); the HMB again rejected even a smaller request. And Dailey Hicks, our volunteer general contractor, fell seriously ill and could not do the work. Using Dailey had seemed to be the only way we could afford the building if we could arrange financing. We refused to give up, knowing that God never asks us to do something he doesn't equip us to do."

Greenlaw members now stand poised on the threshold of a new day of ministry. In December the Goodman Church Builders secured their Arizona General Contractor's license and collected bids from local labor forces. Construction began early in 1996. It has been a monumental task, but God has provided miraculously. The financing has been arranged with $442,000 coming from debenture sales, and $265,000 from the bank loan. The builder can construct what they want, within the budget—a miracle in itself. The estimated date of completion is September 1996, just in time for the GCBA fiftieth anniversary celebration.

On a rainy, Sunday autumn afternoon, Ed and Kathy Shaver gave their witness through baptism in the cold waters of Oak Creek. The climate soon went unnoticed as smiles and words of praise rose from the Shavers. Ed was saved years ago; Kathy, only months earlier; but this time of testimony was a picture of their faith as a result of their decisions claiming Christ as Lord. They previously were part of the unchurched community of Flagstaff, but found their way to a vital commitment to Christ through the ministry of Greenlaw Baptist Church. The main reason for the labor of love to expand the walls is that more Eds and Kathys are waiting to be reached.

Flagstaff FSBC helped fund the Rimrock Beaver Creek Baptist Church, which held a dedication service October 1, 1995, in its new location on Beaver Creek Road. It was the fifth anniversary of the church and first anniversary of its groundbreaking. The church, located in Yavapai Association, had been organized and supported through the partnership Arizona process. The building, which still needed much work to be finished, had been largely constructed from materials reclaimed from the Flagstaff Stone Forest Building, which Daryl Bennett had helped demolish to salvage materials. Bell Rock pastor Marty Nordloh helped work on the Beaver Creek building. Attendance at the dedication was 247, including pastors and members from sister churches in Flagstaff and the Verde Valley.

### Glenn and Corky Young

Throughout GCBA's history, dedicated laypersons have stood shoulder to shoulder with pastors and missionaries in bearing responsibility for ministries undertaken. Glenn and Corky Young represent many who have served in various capacities.

When Glenn and Corky married on May 11, 1943, she was already a Christian, but he did not accept the Lord until 1953, while they were attending Winslow FBC. Their son Ray, who was nine, had been saved and kept urging his dad to become a Christian and join the church with him. "He talked me into going into the baptismal waters with him, and I've always been so happy he did," Glenn explained. The whole family became involved in all the church activities, a lifestyle they have followed ever since. Glenn was ordained a deacon in 1963.

"After thirty-one years of working however many hours it took to get the job done, usually twelve or more a day, for the Santa Fe Railway, Glenn's retirement came as an industrial strength shock to both of us," Corky admits. They began looking for an ideal retirement location two years before he retired in 1984 at La Junta, where he was Santa Fe division superintendent for Colorado. It came down to a choice between Pinetop and Flagstaff. Corky wanted to live in the mountains among pine trees, and Glenn wanted to be near a golf course. They liked the medical facilities in Flagstaff, and when they heard that Clark Johnson, a preacher they knew and appreciated, was pastor at FSBC, they decided to buy a lot in Flagstaff's Fairfield area. There they designed a lovely home with windows that soar skyward and seem to bring the golf course inside. The day they joined FSBC, Johnson resigned to become pastor at the Phoenix Royal Palms Church.

"Although we were strangers in town, we knew we would find friends and fellowship as soon as we became a part of a Southern Baptist church family," Glenn testified. "I believe that if a retired couple doesn't stay deeply involved in a church program, all the benefits of retiring will be destroyed," he added.

"I always thought retirement was for old people ready to sit down and do nothing," Corky chimed in. "I'm like my friend who was ninety-four when she told her daughter, 'Honey, when I get old, then I'll quit coloring my hair.' We felt we still had places to go, work to do, things to accomplish for the Lord." They have, indeed, gone places: *Love Boat* cruises to the Caribbean and Mexico; month-long tours and salmon fishing trips to Alaska, Canada, and Colorado; trips to Europe—all the places Santa Fe trains could not travel.

While working for Santa Fe in California for twenty-three years, Glenn served three terms as a trustee for California Baptist College and also on the CSBC Foundation board. Since retiring, he has served six years on the ASBC executive board. Corky has finished a number of years on the state Senior Adult board. "We enjoy being in on the big things Southern Baptist are doing," they confess.

Glenn has served as treasurer of GCBA for about six years and shares, "I like doing it. I've really enjoyed watching things happen in the association, working with the missionaries, seeing the churches grow. It isn't at all like a hammer over my head, but a privilege to be able to help." Corky is finishing four years as GCBA senior adult director and has provided excellent programs for the annual senior adult fellowship rally.

At Greenlaw where Glenn serves as a deacon and sings in the choir, the Youngs team teach the senior adult couples class. They agree that the class provides the biggest blessings in their lives. One couple has a log home about thirty miles out in the forest where they have parties. Their group spends every New Year's Eve together, having soup suppers and planning more happy times.

A few years ago a fellow deacon got the Youngs interested in the Gideons. "We've really appreciated the Gideon work because it broadens our Christian base to work with evangelicals from every walk of life in this worldwide outreach program. They all understand that my responsibilities to my church, association, and Southern Baptist state work come first," Glenn stated. He was president of the Flagstaff Gideon Camp for three years.

Living on the golf course, Glenn walks the eighteen holes four or five times a week and nine holes the other days, except never on Sundays. In the winter they walk the malls or come down to Beaver Creek or Village of Oak Creek courses. Corky also keeps busy sewing. When she was seven and an only child, her mother gave her a box of scraps, showed her how to peddle the Singer sewing machine, and walked out of the room. "I've been sewing ever since," she laughs.

"She has saved us lots of money making all her own clothes and most of our daughter's," Glenn agrees. The Youngs feel blessed in their children. Ray, who was one of the first to serve in the journeyman missions program of the FMB, pastors Fresno, California, Harvard Terrace Baptist Church. He led the church to start a mission in nearby Clovis. The church also has ministries to Chinese and Hmongs, with both groups using the church facility. Daughter Tami gave up her family counseling job to work toward a doctorate at Loma Linda University as a full-time student. In 1994 sorrow came to the family when their only grandson, a college freshmen, was killed in an automobile accident.

Corky added, "It's marvelous to be a part of what God is doing in Arizona. I remember when GCC was started. I remember when the assembly began meeting at Prescott. Dan Stringer's father was my pastor when I was a little girl. One of the most joyous times of my life was attending the seventy-fifth anniversary of the Winslow FBC and seeing old friends again. That's where we first became a Christian family."

### Ash Fork FSBC

Pastor Dave Cox reported that much work has been done on the church building and grounds. In August 1994 a group of students from Mars Hill College, in North Carolina, spent a week doing volunteer work. They stained the front doors and painted the steps; refurbished the church sign and repainted the fellowship hall, kitchen, and children's classroom; added decorative borders in the fellowship hall and kitchen and papered the bathroom; put new flooring in the bathroom and stained the interior window trim; and began landscaping the front of the property. The leader plans to bring a group from another college to work in May 1996.

In January 1995 the church was recarpeted with a donation from a Flagstaff Baptist Church member. Ongoing projects include repainting the sanctuary and working on the two houses purchased in 1987. One now houses the clothes closet. A talented layman, Marty Yerian, has volunteered to upgrade the property. He has replaced the front walk, brought the flagstone walk out to the street, and added decorative cinders around the building.

A recent highlight for Ash Fork FSBC came when a local motel manager, a native of India, stopped by the church during one of the church workdays and began asking Spence Estus questions. The man had picked up a Gideon Bible at his motel and began reading it to improve his English. Starting to read at Genesis, he had become confused and moved on to the New Testament, where the concepts were also new to him. He had no religious background, no wrong teachings to unlearn, and was fascinated by ideas in the Gospels.

Spence, and sometimes Toney, Estus began spending Thursday evenings at the motel, going through the gospels with P. J. and "Mama," the aunt who raised him. Mama did not understand much English, but she loved to sit and listen; then P. J. would explain the discussion to her later. He started coming to SS regularly to expand his knowledge. He told Dave that his mornings were spent on motel work, but the afternoons belonged to God. He read the Bible for hours at a time and wrote down questions to ask and new insights to discuss, filling legal pads with notes.

The man's sister, who runs a motel in Flagstaff, took him to task for having so much contact with Americans. "Don't you know they'll pretend to be your friends, and then take you for everything they can?" she warned. He responded, "Yes, that is the way the world treats you, but not the people of God!"

Although P. J. was excited about all he was learning, he wanted to be sure he understood what was involved in making a commitment to Christ. For instance, he asked how much it cost to be baptized and join the church and was astonished to learn there was no charge. When Dave, Carol, Spence, and Toney visited him and Mama to go over some questions and eat a snack, they were served a four-course meal. Carol confessed, "Trying to do it justice was a challenge because we had just come from a potluck at the church."

After all his questions had been answered, P. J. declared his belief in Christ as his Savior. He was baptized in 1995. Since then he has been transferred to a motel in Willcox. The Coxes feel sure God has provided him a mission field among other East Indian motel owners.

**Grand Canyon FBC**

Pastor Steve Burke reported a busy summer in 1995. The first weekend in June, thirteen summer missionaries and Innovators arrived, and from then until September, he worked long hours. The summer program included teaching ESL classes, a melodrama at the campgrounds, tennis instruction for tourists, a coffeehouse for singles, a sports and recreation night for the youth, and BYBCs in various locations. Not long after the summer volunteers departed, the Burkes' fifth child, little Benjamin Robert, was born on August 31, two weeks early. He has red hair like Joshua, Christy, Julie, and Angel. Steve resigned as pastor, effective December 31, 1995, to move back to Oklahoma.

GCBA churches had already begun to rejoice in January 1996. With their property mortgage paid off, East Valley members saw their utilities connected and building plans drawn. New families began attending services. After a year of anticipation, hard work, and prayer, Williams FBC celebrated completion of their construction and renovation project with an open house and rededication ceremonies on February 25. Fredonia had thirteen new people start attending services. Sedona FBC reported the conversion of Jim Shirley, an eighty-five-year-old man with terminal cancer snatched as a brand from the burning. Grand Canyon FBC celebrated its twenty-fifth anniversary in February.

On January 7 Bethel began 9:00 A.M. Sunday worship services at Parks in the school library. Steve Martin preached to thirteen persons present, representing six families. Faith Baptist mission at Parks had ceased operation in 1985.

### 1996: Year of Jubilee for GCBA

The Old Testament Jubilee was a time of celebration, with debts cancelled and new beginnings projected. For GCBA, 1996 is a time for looking back to remember what God has done among us, and a time for looking ahead in faith to rejoice because of what he will yet accomplish through us.

It is fitting that the 1996 GCBA annual meeting be at Williams FBC, for it is the oldest church in our association. Although not one of the constituting churches of GCBA, it organized in 1941, before any of the six original GCBA churches. Even as a Northern Baptist church, Williams FBC from its beginning numbered many Southern Baptists in its membership who looked to SBC churches for fellowship and assistance to fill the pulpit and work in its VBSs. In 1948 GCBA seated its messengers as a participating church.

During 1996 GCBA churches will be inviting former missionaries and pastors to lead revivals or special heritage services and to speak in churches on Sunday, October 27, following the anniversary celebration.

Throughout the year pastors will be encouraging charter members and old-timers to share special memories of inspiring, humorous, or challenging events. Specially appointed Jubilee chairmen in the churches will be making up scrapbooks or picture albums to visually depict their history and will bring them to display at the annual meeting at Williams. To applaud the work among our Indian and Hispanic fellow Christians, we will invite singers to bring special music in Spanish and Navajo at the anniversary celebration.

Churches will be encouraging volunteers to help with building programs during this year of celebration. They will be enlisting youth teams from across the nation to a summer of all-out endeavor to reach, win, baptize, and disciple new people for Christ through VBSs, BYBCs, sports clinics, concerts, door-to-door visitation, tract and Scripture distribution, and innovative efforts in every community.

GCBA will be inviting all formerly affiliated churches to send a carload of people to the October 26 meeting and allow time on the program for introductions and greetings. Everyone attending will receive a free copy of the GCBA fifty-year history, REMEMBER THE WONDERS. Church members will help give out copies of REMEMBER THE WONDERS to as many former members and friends as possible, and invite them to share in the anniversary program at Williams.

The association will also provide copies of REMEMBER THE WONDERS to public libraries in cities where GCBA churches are now, or formerly were, located. GCBA will also send copies to the SBC Historical Commission, the Arizona Baptist Historical Society, the HMB, BSSB, seminaries, Baptist colleges, and Arizona state colleges.

Even after fifty years, GCBA still faces many problems of a pioneer mission field. Therefore, the missionary, pastors, associational officers, and laypersons should strive to develop partnership relationships with states, associations, churches, and persons across the nation who will be willing to help us in one or more of the following areas: revival crusades; special projects; telephone surveys; home Bible fellowships for mission points; assistance in purchasing property and getting buildings up; personal outreach ministries by every church member; motor-home summer vacations in beautiful northern Arizona spent in strengthening churches and missions; retirement in the GCBA area to help Baptist work; brochure preparation by artists and printers; mailouts; specific church needs such as RV park ministries; and literacy or ESL classes.